JOE BOB GOES BACK TO THE DRIVE-IN

Also by Joe Bob Briggs:

JOE BOB GOES TO THE DRIVE-IN
A GUIDE TO WESTERN CIVILIZATION OR, MY STORY

JOE BOB GOES BACK TO THE DRIVE-IN

Joe Bob Briggs

Delacorte Press

Published by
Delacorte Press
Bantam Doubleday Dell Publishing Group, Inc.
666 Fifth Avenue
New York, New York 10103

The columns included in this book were originally distributed by Universal Press Syndicate, with the following exceptions: "Joe Bob Goes to the Drive-In" first appeared in *Cineaste;* "Joe Bob Briggs' Guilty Pleasures" in *Film Comment;* "The Drive-In Guide to the Oscars" in *Us Magazine;* "Working on the Chain Gang" in *Rolling Stone;* and "Why I Love Wayne Newton" in *Interview.*

Library of Congress Cataloging in Publication Data

Briggs, Joe Bob.
    Joe Bob goes back to the drive-in / Joe Bob Briggs.
        p.   cm.
    ISBN 0-385-29770-X
    1. Drive-in theaters—Humor.   2. American wit and humor.
I. Title.
PN6231.D73B7   1990
791.43'75—dc20   89-38198   CIP

Manufactured in the United States of America

Published simultaneously in Canada

May 1990

10 9 8 7 6 5 4 3 2 1
BVG

Contents

INTRODUCTION

Joe Bob, a Vegas Kinda Guy

by Wayne Newton

If you've ever seen my show in Las Vegas, then you know I love to have a good time. But when people ask me what *I* consider a good time, I say "Joe Bob Briggs." I met Joe Bob a few years back, when I was going through a pretty low period in my life, and Joe Bob was the tonic I needed. He's a funny man and a funny writer, but he always tells the truth. That's rare in the media, not to mention life.

A lot of people come to my shows to feel better, and I always try to lift them up, give them the song that they need—"Danke Schoen," "Red Roses," "Bill Bailey," "MacArthur Park," or "The Battle Hymn of the Republic." Some people think it's corny to do the standards all the time, but I learned a long time ago that the audience is more important than I am. Joe Bob is the same way. He loves his audience. Editors may not understand the kind of needling he specializes in, but the people always do. Because it makes them feel better.

If Joe Bob Briggs were a song in my show, it would have to be "Dixie." Not the "Dixie" of rabble-rousers and Southern rednecks, but the "Dixie" sung by people who love their roots and the land they came out of. I'm from Virginia, so I understand Joe Bob. He makes me laugh and, although he wouldn't want anyone to know this, he is really not as snide as people think. He's simply Texan. I know many Texans through my interest in Arabian horses, and Texans are different. They're taller, for one thing.

Joe Bob's a solid six-foot-four. They tend to be talkative, for another. Joe Bob has had something to say about every subject except basket-weaving, and, for all I know, he's written a book about that, too. And Texans like Joe Bob are also great Americans.

This is what people don't understand about Joe Bob. Underneath that tough hide is a guy who cares about more than drive-in movies. He cares about his country. It's been said that "greatness is he that reminds you of no other," so surely Joe Bob is a great man and my life is a lot better because he's my friend. I'm proud of that.

ANOTHER
INTRODUCTION

Who Is Joe Bob Briggs?

by Gary Alan Crowdus, founder and editor, *Cineaste* magazine

Cineaste wasn't doing the job. *Film Quarterly* couldn't have cared less. Even *American Film* wasn't doing its patriotic duty. Let's face it, for years *nobody* was providing regular coverage of drive-in movies—the splatter films, kung fu movies, T&A flicks, creature features, and assorted other exploitation films that have for decades provided popular entertainment for motorized moviegoers throughout the nation.

That void in American film criticism was filled on January 15th, 1982, when the first "Joe Bob Goes to the Drive-In" column appeared in the *Dallas Times Herald*. As a film review, it didn't offer a lot in the way of critical analysis, but it did give readers the lowdown on *The Grim Reaper,* an Italian horror film about cannibalism which tells the story of a homicidal maniac "who likes to kill people and then chew on them for a while." In the following weeks, *Times Herald* readers were surprised to find comic, no-holds-barred writeups of such exploitation fare as *The Beast Within, Intimate Moments, Kill Squad,* and *Fury of the Succubus,* plus the occasional "art film" like *Mad Monkey Kung Fu* ("one of the best foreign films of 1982, direct from Hong Kong, with a stop in Burbank for dubbing").

Joe Bob Briggs, America's foremost drive-in movie expert, had arrived, and he was a man with a mission. He had come to spread the drive-in gospel, to preach the glories of this disreputable genre, and to warn his readers against the temptations of "indoor movies" which, as Joe Bob pointed out, were "just for poor people who can't afford their own cars." Each week, Joe Bob left his trailer home in Grapevine, Texas, to drive his blue '73 Oldsmobile Toronado to one of his favorite Dallas area drive-ins where, he estimated, he had seen, in *natural* darkness, "out under the stars like God intended, in the privacy of my personal automobile," over 6,800 movies. Joe Bob thus not only qualified as a true connoisseur of drive-in movies, but, coming from a West Texas, Southern Baptist, white-trash background, he was also a man of the people, a critic truly at one with his audience.

Joe Bob has been at the job for over eight years now and those who don't read the *Dallas Observer* or one of the fifty or so other newspapers around the U.S. in which Joe Bob is syndicated can discover what they've been missing in *Joe Bob Goes to the Drive-In* (Delacorte Press, 1987), a collection of some of Joe Bob's best reviews, the first-ever volume of laugh-out-loud film criticism. In addition to film reviews, the book includes Joe Bob's musings on issues of concern to us all, including the difference between B-B-Q and barbecue, the questions on the written test for the Dallas Cowboys Cheerleaders, a history of the drive-in, Joe Bob's Guide to Impeccable Drive-In Etiquette, announcements of the winners of the annual Hubbies (probably the only film awards engraved on Chevy hubcaps), an account of how he drove to the Cannes Film Festival, and an answer to the question, "Why do the contestants on *Family Feud* always

play instead of pass?" As Joe Bob would doubtless agree, we're talking your full $8.95's worth here.

The book's focus, however, is on drive-in movies, especially the kinds of movies shown *only* at drive-ins and sometimes only at drive-ins in the South and Southwest, with Joe Bob's three basic categories being "Blood," "Breasts," and "Beasts." The Joe Bob Briggs Theory of Film Criticism is also pretty straightforward—"A movie can be absolutely anything, except *boring.*" As a result, Joe Bob practices a kind of Bottom-Line Film Criticism, and the typical Joe Bob review—which is usually preceded by some outspoken social commentary or rambling accounts of encounters with one or more of his four ex-wives, current girlfriends, or oddball buddies—consists of a colorful plot synopsis and a concluding paragraph which rates the crucial ingredients, depending upon the category of film being reviewed, essential to any exploitation film worthy of the name. This typically involves the number of bare breasts, beheadings or other violent deaths, kung fu exhibitions, motor vehicle crashes, beasts, gallons of blood, and gross-out scenes. Particularly impressive directorial touches are also noted, such as "excellent rat attack," "superb cattle-prod effects" or "excellent midget performance in the Spanish-maid-costume scene."

Joe Bob is a man who knows and enjoys his drive-in movies, and although he tends to be a generous critic, he is stingy with his 4-star ratings and works hard to distinguish superior sleaze from average, run-of-the-mill sleaze. His highest praise is reserved for those few films that really deliver the goods, whether it's breast counts or body counts, the kind of film in which there's "absolutely no plot to get in the way of the movie." Joe Bob was beside himself, for example, with lavish praise for *Bolero,* starring Bo "Is it time to get nekkid again, John?" Derek, a film which heralded the birth of a drive-in star. Although Joe Bob is particularly fond of splatter flicks, the *Halloweens* and *Friday the 13ths* that feature "your basic Spam-in-a-Cabin" plot, a truly top-notch entry in this genre must pass his ultimate test as "a movie where *anybody* can die at *any time.*" One of Joe Bob's 4-star classics is *The Texas Chainsaw Massacre,* which he describes as a movie that "can scare the bejabbers out of you to the point where you think it was *made* by a cannibal."

While we're on the subject of films with roman numerals in their titles, Joe Bob has a no-nonsense attitude about sequels—"If you're gonna make a sequel, *make a sequel.* Bring the dead people back to life and *do it all over again* . . . If you know what you're doing, the sequel can be *exactly the same movie* as the first one." When Joe Bob criticizes *Halloween III* for being a "rip-off," for example, what he means is that it doesn't star Jamie Lee Curtis, Donald Pleasance, and the slasher, so he trashes the producers for having "Gone Hollywood. They obviously got stoked up on cocaine and forgot their roots." This all-important critical principle is also succinctly expressed in the headline of another Joe Bob review—"*Friday the 13th, Part 4,* Had Better Be Good—They've Made It Four Times."

Dealing, as he does, with popular entertainment that confronts the burning social issues of our day—sex, violence, and death—and being the opinionated, outspoken kind of guy he is, Joe Bob has frequently found himself in trouble with his editors and some of his readers. Occasionally, in the throes of his enthusiasm for a particularly gruesome splatter flick or one of those R-rated heavy breather movies, Joe Bob's language would tend to get just a little too *colorful* for a family newspaper, so the editorial watchdogs at the *Dallas Times Herald*—the "High Sheriffs," as Joe Bob called them—would remove offending words and phrases from his column. At first, Joe Bob responded by alerting his readers to this censorship with substitutions like "(there used to be a hysterically funny joke right here but the High Sheriffs didn't think you'd understand it)" or "(High Sheriffs took a bunch of stuff out here, so if you wanna know what it was, write in and I'll send it to you)." After a period of time during which Joe Bob ridiculed his editors or tried unsuccessfully to sneak the offending words into his column, he finally just invented some new words. Female breasts became "garbonzas" or "hooters," unmentionable male sex organs became "gazebos," farts (the source of much amusement in drive-in comedies) were referred to as "pooting," and a famous, all-purpose American expletive got decoded as "bullstuff."

These were just creative writing challenges for Joe Bob, however, compared to the real problems he encountered when some of the *Times Herald*'s readers began protesting his column. The feminists, for example, were outraged by Joe Bob's celebration of splatter films and the bimbos-behind-bars flicks which they felt were degrading to women, and his reviews of *Gas Pump Girls, Chained Heat, Pieces,* and *Ten Violent Women* were attacked as "demeaning and reactionary." Joe Bob responded by restating his ethical drive-in principles on these matters, such as "I do not believe in slapping women around, unless they beg for it," and "I am violently opposed to the random mutilation, torture, and head-drilling of women *unless it's necessary to the plot*." These ladies were in no mood for jokes, however, and the protest widened to a postcard writing campaign calling for the cancellation of Joe Bob's column. At that point, Joe Bob knew he had to take the challenge seriously, so he publicly challenged the president of the Dallas chapter of the National Organization for Women to a nude mud-wrestling match.

Despite his Baptist upbringing, Joe Bob also upset many of his brethren in the religious community, including assorted Baptist preachers, Pentecostal ministers, Catholics, and Donald Wildmon's Citizens for Decency, among others, with his reviews of horny teenager movies like *Senior Snatch, Beach Girls, Going All the Way,* and *The Last American Virgin.* Several Texas Sunday School classes, especially the young boys, were forbidden to read "Joe Bob Goes to the Drive-In."

And, alright, we won't try to hide the fact from *Cineaste* readers, Joe Bob also received protest mail from gays, blacks, Mexican-Americans, Mothers Against Drunk Drivers, animal rights activists, the Dallas Cowboys Cheerleaders, college professors, and the National Cancer Society. Even the Dallas County drive-in owners protested, claiming that Joe Bob's column was "disgusting, redneck, and violent," that drive-ins today are "family entertainment centers," and that Joe Bob was "not representative of the typical drive-in patron." By spring 1984, when the column had become nationally syndicated, protest letters demanding cancellation of Joe Bob's column were pouring in from San Francisco, Cleveland, Denver, and other cities. Luckily for Joe Bob, his fans and devoted readers always far

outnumbered his critics and he easily weathered the occasional storms of protest.

A protest with a difference, however, occurred in April 1985 when Joe Bob's spoof of the U.S.A. for Africa rock song and video "We Are the World" was criticized by some Dallas blacks as racist. Joe Bob's version of the song, "We Are the Weird," featured all the drive-in movie stars—Leatherface, Jason, Pia Zadora, Chuck Bronson, the Swamp Thing, Mamie Van Doren, the Mutant—in a parody of wealthy rock stars singing for famine relief. A local black politician organized a massive, boisterous protest at the *Times Herald* offices at which the paper's editors caved in to the pressure and agreed to cancel Joe Bob's column. The *Los Angeles Times* syndicate in turn cancelled the national syndication of the column, and Joe Bob Briggs appeared to be one dead drive-in movie critic. When the *Dallas Times Herald* refused to publish Joe Bob's resignation column, it was immediately published by *The Dallas Observer,* where the column continues to appear today.

One result of the controversy was to reveal Joe Bob's true identity, which had always remained something of a mystery. Speculation was that Joe Bob Briggs was actually John Bloom, who had initially claimed credit for "discovering" Joe Bob, although to many it seemed unlikely that the *Times Herald*'s bright young film critic who wrote appreciative reviews of foreign films could be confused with a tasteless lowbrow like Briggs. When Bloom resigned from the *Times Herald* immediately after Joe Bob's "firing," it became clear that Joe Bob Briggs, drive-in movie critic, *was,* in fact, John Bloom, a Dallas-born, 32-year-old honors graduate in English from Vanderbilt University (the "Harvard of the South"), and former prize-winning investigative journalist at *Texas Monthly* magazine.*

Partially in response to criticisms that he was "hiding behind a newspaper column," Joe Bob decided to go public by accepting some of the many invitations he had received for speaking engagements. Exaggerating his natural Texas accent, and outfitting himself in blue jeans, Western style shirts, loud sports coats, and cowboy hats, Joe Bob tried out a stand-up comedy act in places like Cleveland, San Francisco, Austin, and Raleigh. In it, he reprised some of the funniest material from his columns, recounted his firing by the "*Dallas Slimes Herald,*" performed his own country songs such as "You Said You Were a Virgin, But Your Baby Ain't Named Jesus," and led an audience sing-along of the notorious "We Are the Weird." In October 1986 Joe Bob premiered as the weekly host of "Drive-In Theater" on The Movie Channel cable TV network, where he continues to appear today, recently hosting a month's worth of programs from his trailer home in Grapevine, Texas. Joe Bob also published his autobiography, *A Guide to Western Civilization, or My Story* (Delacorte Press, 1988), and does thrice-weekly radio broadcasts of the "Joe Bob Briggs' Drive-In Movie and Video Tape Review."

As a humorist, Joe Bob has chosen an ideal subject to write about. Exploitation movies, which have long had the reputation of being so bad that they're good, are made to order for humor writing. Whether they're laughably inept, mediocre efforts, or commercially

*This is a lie perpetuated by the liberal eastern establishment pinko media.—Joe Bob

calculated projects designed to appeal to an audience's prurient or baser instincts, or perhaps the hipper, more stylish productions which have fun playing with genre conventions, exploitation movies revel in spectacular, frequently outrageous effects which invite an equally audacious critical style. In "Joe Bob Goes to the Drive-In," even the most preposterous exploitation movies have met their critical match.

One of the best things about the Joe Bob columns is that you don't have to enjoy—or even see, for that matter—the drive-in movies he reviews. The Joe Bob plot synopsis says it all, both in the sense of literally explaining what the movie is about as well as making an implicit statement about the truly ludicrous qualities of these films. The columns are written in a breezy, conversational style, blending farcical yarns with sharply satiric commentary, and are filled with inventive colloquialisms, hilarious metaphors and similes, and a little dialect thrown in for regional flavor. At their best, the reviews have a dual critical edge, combining an honest enthusiasm for exploitation movies with a witty acknowledgment of their inherently absurd nature, without betraying the sincerity of either sentiment. This is not corn pone humor. In fact, Joe Bob is one of the sharpest good ol' boys you'll ever meet, and, make no mistake about it, his "Joe Bob Goes to the Drive-In" reviews are some of the funniest, most original and inventive satirical humor being written in America today.

As a satirist, everything and everyone is fair game for Joe Bob who is, he has joked, an "equal opportunity offender." Joe Bob takes special delight in deflating self-righteousness wherever he finds it, especially among people or organizations promoting causes. Although he has poked fun at feminists, gays, blacks, Hispanics, leftists, animal rights activists, and fundamentalist preachers, among others, "the first target of Joe Bob's column," he has explained, "is always Joe Bob. That's the saving grace of it." Although Joe Bob does occasionally stray into Archie Bunker territory, he is no bigot. He may be highly opinionated and somewhat peevish, but he's not intolerant. He's a true American in the sense that he honors the national tradition of pluralism among his fellow citizens. On the other hand, just because Joe Bob practices a "different strokes for different folks" philosophy doesn't mean he's obligated to care much for you or your particular cause.

Many of Joe Bob's attitudes—such as his knee-jerk xenophobia, his obsession with female breasts, or his all-purpose anti-communist invective— are pushed to such comic extremes that they become self-critiques, exposing these attitudes for the idiocy that they are. (Uh, wait a minute, is it too late to reconsider that reference to female breasts?) Actually, the charges of racism and sexism against Joe Bob's column have been either unfounded or overstated, especially since most political or religious activists, whether of the left or the right, have never been noted for their healthy sense of humor. In this regard, more than a few *Cineaste* readers are likely to get all bent out of shape reading this defense of a much-maligned drive-in movie reviewer, and I'm tempted to cite just a little chapter and verse here in order to disprove the charges, but I'd only succeed in blowing Joe Bob's notorious reputation, because the man is actually a pussycat. Besides, I'd much rather encourage interested readers, especially fans of humor writing, to check out the books for themselves.

It's also important to note, in this regard, that Joe Bob Briggs was initially thrust into the public eye as a result of the "We Are the Weird" controversy and the cancellation of his column. When Joe Bob was interviewed by journalists and TV talk show hosts during his national book tour last year, it was understandable why they chose to focus on his reputation as a racist and a sexist—not only did it make for good copy and TV images, but it was also much easier than offering a carefully considered evaluation of the book or an informed appreciation of his style of humor writing. Ironically, Joe Bob's terrible reputation has to some extent been encouraged by Joe Bob himself, not only because he is a satirical humorist who likes to get a rise out of people, but also because he is an enterprising journalist who seems to understand, as George Bernard Shaw advised, that "The secret of success is to offend the greatest number of people." But if the protests helped to build Joe Bob's journalistic reputation, they were also useful in helping him to identify sacred cows. Explaining why hate mail always gets privileged placement in Joe Bob's Mailbag section of the column, Joe Bob has commented:

Hate mail gets first priority and always goes at the top of the mailbag column. Why? Cause it's more interesting. This made some of the fans mad, who couldn't understand why the fundamentalists and the gays and the Mothers Against Drunk Drivers and other special interest groups always got to say everything they wanted and the angry defenders of Joe Bob got stuck at the end or didn't get in at all. And it's cause I always thought any people that self-righteous would do it to theirselves. We didn't have to do nothin.

It's a matter of faith with Joe Bob that "The drive-in will never die," yet his weekly column includes a "Communist Alert!" section which reports on the demise of yet another drive-in somewhere in the U.S. If the drive-in is not dying, then, it's certainly endangered by the multiplexing of American indoor cinemas and the increasing popularity of home video cassettes. Exploitation movies, of course, will live on forever, so Joe Bob can take some comfort in the realization that even if one day, God forbid, the drive-in *were* to die, he need only retool and retitle his column, and all his loyal fans could read "Joe Bob Fast-Forwards the VCR." ■

BACK TO THE DRIVE-IN

Joe Bob Almost Checks Out

November 22, 1963.
April 16, 1985.

They said it couldn't happen again.

I guess I'll always remember where I was when they killed me on national TV, right after the Maybelline commercial. I guess we all will. Who couldn't remember the look on the High Sheriff's face when he said, "Joe Bob's dead!" I know a lot of people ran through the streets of downtown Dallas, screaming hysterically:

"The drive-in critic's dead!"

"Oh my God, Joe Bob is history!"

"He's outta here!"

"He owed me twenty bucks!"

Stuff like that. Even though the High Sheriff was arrested at the scene by TV reporters with bad hair, there were immediate rumors of an international Communist conspiracy, the "three-gun theory," the "act of God theory," the bizarre "one-garbonza theory," and the "What would happen if you dropped Joe Bob Briggs off a seven-story building and watched him splatter all over the pavement?" theory.

Course, I immediately called my personal lawyer, Bubba Barclay, and I said, "Bubba, how dead am I?"

And Bubba said, "I don't know, let's go over to Parkland Emergency and find out."

So me and Bubba fired up the Toronado and hauled it up Stemmons Freeway, topped out at a good 35, 40 miles an hour, and, course, when we got there it was pandemonium. The first thing I did, I jumped out of the car and grabbed this old crippled guy with IVs hanging out of his arms, and I blinked back tears, and I said to him, "How do you spell pandemonium?"

3

And he told me and I went on in-side and tried to revive me.

It was not a pretty sight. The whole right side of my face was ripped off and sewed on my stomach. My eyeballs were stuck on the back of my knees. All the interns were standin around saying "Hey! You! Want a hit of this stuff?" There were guys with walkie-talkies running all over the hospital, screaming *We have to find somebody that knows the Drive-In Oath! We have to find somebody before this gets to Moscow.*"

Course, it was already too late. I guess the saddest story, the kind of thing that just makes you sick, is when they announced the news to an ele-mentary school class in the little Com-munist Russia town of Vladi-tube-sock. Hearing that Joe Bob was dead, six- and seven-year-olds cheered.

All over eastern Mesquite, children were sent home from school. In Fort Worth, junior high school students were asked to write essays on the topic, "Joe Bob Briggs: Who Gets All His Money?"

Out here at the trailer park, we had candlelight vigils till 2 a.m., which is the time we burned down three mobile homes from letting drunks carry the candles.

Pope John Paul II was so grief-stricken that he refused to comment.

All over the world people were ask-ing the question, "Why? Why this senseless tragedy? Who's next? Wayne Newton?" Other people were asking the question, "Huh?"

How did it happen? people been asking me. What the heck, who the heck, and heck.

It was all for one simple reason: *I wanted to do something for poor little starving nekkid African kids.*

I know it's not a popular cause. I coulda picked something easy, like starting a cable-TV network for the

Ayatollah. But that's just the kinda guy I am. Yes, it's true. I wrote "We Are the Weird." I didn't even want credit for it. I'd be just as happy if I never saw a penny from it and all the money went straight to my four ex-wives. It was just something I wanted to do. Most of the money was gonna go to building a chain of Wyatt's Cafeterias in every na-tion of Africa. The rest was gonna be spent on buying basketball schol-arships to the University of Houston for every Ethiopian child that wanted one.

Hey, call me sentimental, call me hokey, call me a guy that sleeps in his underwear. You know, in this Easter season of ours, I like to reflect on the meaning of life, which is "43."

But the times we're living in, you can't try to help people anymore. First the National Organization of Bimbos tries to wipe Joe Bob off the face of the earth for saying I'm opposed to slap-ping women around like dead mack-erels, unless it's necessary to the plot. Then ever Pentacostal preacher in Mis-sissippi and all my fellow Babtists give me a "F" for writing the *Gospel Ac-cording to Joe Bob* ("Life is a fern bar, let's get outta here"). All my Meskin friends in Corpus Christi turn against me, even though I love the Meskin peo-ple, specially the ones that sneak in. The Catholics write in about how my head should be blown off in a Christian manner. Lester Dimskim writes in cause I called him "the stupidest Lester I ever met."

But I guess what hurts the most is when the Brothers turned against me. Me, the first guy to write about the Negro-dancing spin-on-your-head per-manent-brain-damage musical. Me, the guy who watched *Roots* three times and learned to pronounce the ancient African term "colored people." Me, the guy who wrote a song for poor starving helpless nekkid black kids.

When 250 individuals of the black persuasion came down to the *Dallas Crimes Herald* and said, "No, we don't wanna go to the Fairmont Hotel where we can all see, we wanna do it the stupid way and crowd everbody in a little room where they explain the *Crimes Herald* dental insurance plan," which by the way is a pretty decent plan, I knew I was probly gonna die. Here are the protester's demands:

Numero Uno: "We want for Joe Bob Briggs to become a black person."

Yeah, they got me on that one. I never have done that.

Numero Two-o: "Joe Bob Briggs wrote 'stupid Negroes' once and 'stupid white people' only TWICE in that column. We insist this inequality be corrected."

Hey, fair's fair.

Numero Three-o: "We are not satisfied with the Crimes Herald *putting a notice on Page One that said 'Joe Bob Briggs is the scum of the earth and we the High Sheriffs want him turned into a Sunkist Tuna.' The* Crimes Herald *needs to make him dead."*

You know, "dead" is one of those words that makes you stop and think. It made me stop and think, specially after I was dead.

Numero Four-o: "We resent Joe Bob Briggs dedicating the proceeds from 'We Are the Weird' to the United Negro College Fund."

Okay, but a Negro mind is a terrible thing to waste.

Numero Five-o: "Joe Bob Briggs has cooties."

Hey, I don't have to take that kind of remark.

In fact, there *is* something that makes me p.o.ed about all this. There's one thing the *Crimes Herald* did that is absolutely unforgivable. I'm sorry, I'm trying to forget it, but I just can't.

On that Tuesday and Wednesday, when the *Crimes Herald* put me on the Front Page as an official racist and bigot, they put Henry Lee Lucas at the top of the page and *me* at the bottom. All Henry Lee did is say he's a mass murderer, so *what the heck is the explanation?*

I'm sorry, it bothers me. Sure, I can find other papers to print "Joe Bob Goes to the Drive-In." They *love* me in Grambling, Louisiana. But it just won't be the same.

I wanna leave you now with a few "miracle" facts of world history:

1. Lincoln and Kennedy were both assassinated on a Friday. Joe Bob was assassinated on a Tuesday. Makes you think.

2. Lincoln and Kennedy were both succeeded by a man named "Johnson." Joe Bob was killed by a High Sheriff named Tom Johnson.

3. Lincoln and Kennedy put their pants on one leg at a time. Joe Bob puts his on two legs at a time.

4. Lincoln and Kennedy never could get a laugh either.

Lust in the Dust is another drive-in flick I *would* review except for I don't have no space left. So let's just put it this way:

Four breasts. Fifteen dead bodies. One riot. One brawl. One gang rape, with midget. Two quarts blood. One beast (Divine). Thigh crushing. Bullwhip fu. Nekkid bimbo-wrestling. Drive-In Academy Award nominations for Lainie Kazan, as a singing balloon, doing the hit song "Let Me Take You South of My Border"; Tab Hunter, for breathing; Paul Bartel, "Mr. *Eating Raoul*," who directed this baby; and, of course, Divine, the best 300-pound transvestite actor in Baltimore. Best nudie Western since *Linda and Abilene*. Three stars. Joe Bob says check it out. So there. ∎

Seeking That Special Fifth Ex-Wife

It's been three months now since I put my "Personal" ad in the newspaper, asking for female seeking true love to go find it somewhere else and come marry me instead. So far I got 34 proposals of marriage and enough Polaroid snapshots to open up a kennel. I think all the rest of my mail was swiped by Communist postal employees. There's probly thousands of sensitive, caring, airhead nymphos sitting out there right now, waiting on the mailman, hoping each day will bring a Joe Bob Briggs pre-nuptial contract into their all-Naugahyde living room.

I've decided to go pre-nuptial on this deal, due to the advice of my personal attorney, Bubba Barclay. Bubba says any guy with four ex-wives can't be too careful when he's searching for ex-wife number five, and so I need plenty of pre-nuptials. I told Bubba that's fine, so long as he don't pre-nuptial me into the hospital, so he drew up the following list of polite demands for any dynamic, intelligent slut desiring to be my wife:

Numero Uno: I, the wife of Joe Bob Briggs, agree to keep my own name in a feminist manner.

This is so I won't have to admit she's my wife if I don't feel like it. Like if I got married to somebody named Brenda Bodiddley, her name would *still* be Brenda Bodiddley, instead of Brenda Briggs or Brenda Bodiddley-Briggs, and there's nothing she could do about it. But if I wanted to change my own name to Joe Bob Bodiddley, in order to write checks, then I would have the right to do it.

Numero Two-o: I, the spouse of Joe Bob Briggs, agree to carry out my spousely duties in a spousal manner.

All this means is, I can say, "How bout spousing up this filthy house ever once in a while?" or "When you gonna spouse up some chicken-fried steak?" It guarantees my wife's legal rights under the law.

Numero Three-o: I, the future ex-wife of Joe Bob Briggs, agree not to weigh more than 185 pounds at any time during the aforesaid and aftersaid marriage.

We call this the Porker Clause, to protect against what happened to Clyde Sturgis that time he married a girl from Eureka Springs, Arkansas, and she ballooned up on him *all in the hips* and he had to build a room on the backside of the house to hold her thighs.

Numero Four-o: I, the personal meat of Joe Bob Briggs, agree to follow all financial advice offered by my devoted husband.

Also known as the Santa Clause. A lot of cynical people out there think this means I won't give the bimbo any jack when we break up. Nothing could be further from the truth. She'll get ten, twenty bucks, depending on her level of remorse.

Numero Five-o: I, the property of Joe Bob Briggs, agree to wear a bag over my head whenever requested.

You know, I could be cruel about this and say it's because she's ugly. But there's no way I could know this in advance. This is *merely* a preventive clause, *in case* she's ugly.

Numero Six-o: I, Joe Bob Briggs, agree to have and to hold.

I figured it was the least I could do. Some people just wanna *have* women and some people just wanna *hold* women, but I'm willing to do both at the same time, till death do us part or I get bored, whichever comes first.

Speaking of wives that need to be caged up and electrocuted by the Mafia, Big Steve just came out with another comedy called *Cat's Eye* that's probly gonna put him on the hit list of the National Organization of Bimbos. As you know, this is only the 17th book, movie, and history of the state of Maine that Stephen King's come up with this year, but Big Steve promises to try to turn em out faster from now on. (By the way, after I was assassinated, the K-Man was one of the first to call and offer to send the Maine National Guard down to Texas to rearrange some faces, but I told him, no, there wasn't a whole heck of a lot three guys could do.)

Anyhow, *Cat's Eye* is about this little obnoxious cat that runs all up and down the East Coast, looking into the camera and saying stuff like, "Hey, how else could Big Steve go take three of his old short stories and hook em together if I wasn't here to make it look like there's some deep reason for it?" Damned smart cat.

So first the cat runs into the story Steve wrote called "Quitters, Inc.," the one about the guy who goes to Marlboro School, but when he gets there, a Mafia guy is waiting. If you can't quit smoking, they turn your wife into a human cattle prod. James Woods can't quit smoking, so Alan King lights up the Juice Room with a little spouse meat, till Jimbo learns his lesson. I won't give away the ending, but fingers roll.

Then the cat runs off to Atlantic City and watches a fat-cat gambler bet

Robert Hays can't walk all the way around a high-rise on the ledge. First prize: the fat cat's heavy wife. Great Klaxon-horn impalement, but they wimped out and didn't do it onscreen, the disgusting way Big Steve wrote it.

Next the cat decides to lengthen Drew Barrymore's acting career by busting into her bedroom and fighting

JOE BOB'S MAILBAG

You Sir, have a severe mental problem or you have a Terminal case of Dumb A—, I suggest you see a psychiatrist as soon as possible, to protect the other citizens from yur feeble thinkings.
ANONYMOUS POSTCARD WITH KANGAROOS ON IT.
Wahroonga, N.S.W., Australia

DEAR ANONYMOUS:
I think you're wahroonga.

DEAR JOE BOB: So sorry to hear about your recent cancellation, some folks just don't have much of a sense of humor. It must be tough to go from the Dallas paper to oblivion in one short column. Sic transit gloria; if you don't speak latin, that means Gloria threw up on the bus.

I understand that you may have been rescued from limbo by another syndicate which will distribute your column elsewhere. Don't let the bluenoses get you down. I'm looking forward to your review of Ilsa, Shewolf of the SS Part II.
Regards,
PITT DICKEY, ATTY.
FAYETTEVILLE, N.C.

DEAR PITT: Say-la-vee. In case you don't speak French, that means "You can't get nookie on cable."

against a midget troll monster to prove it's not cats that steal children's breath, but ugly little rat-face trolls that jump out of the wall and slobber all over the Tinker toys. When the cat and the troll battle to the death, it's one of the finest special-effects sequences ever filmed in Wilmington, North Carolina.

What we got here is no breasts. (PG-13 on a Big Steve flick?) One pint blood. Three beasts, including Alan King. Barbecued cat. Barbecued wife. Cameo appearance by Cujo. Gratuitous double plug for the song "I'll Be Watching You." Head rolls. Finger rolls. Two dead bodies. One dead bird.

Cat fu. Troll fu. Reddy Kilowatt fu. Drive-In Academy Award nominations for Drew Barrymore, who said "Please, can I have another movie, please, can I?"; Candy Clark, evil wife of the year (she tries to kill the cat); Kenneth McMillan, as the fat cat; Lewis Teague, who said, "I know I screwed up *Cujo*, Steve, but I can direct, really I can";Dino De Laurentiis, the D-Man, who was the first to say "When monkey die, everybody cry"; and Big Steve, the one and only.

Call it three and a half stars. Joe Bob says check it out. ■

Buying First Amendments from Bubba

Last week I drove up to Tulsa to visit with Oral Roberts and see if he could bring me back from the grave. Oral wasn't in, so I had to talk to Oral's unsaved half brother, Anal Roberts, and all Anal could tell me was if I got somebody to lay hands on me I could probly keep on writing about the drive-in for all the newspapers in Salinas, Kansas, plus one dimwit in North Carolina that thinks I'm Tyrone Biggs, the champeen boxer.

I told Anal I wouldn't have no problem getting somebody to lay hands on me, specially if I could locate the Nookie Sisters of Boulder, Colorado, but then Anal told me they'd have to lay hands on my *head,* and I *recoiled in horror.* I told him that was the most disgusting thing I ever heard and I wasn't gonna have anything to do with it. I've heard of people gettin turned into vegetables from trying stuff like that.

Course, Anal was furious, cause it's illegal to recoil in public in Tulsa. So I fired up the Toronado and hauled it on up to Kansas City to talk to my new High Sheriffs and find out how many of my First Amendment rights been violated.

The reason I knew I had some First Amendments was Rhett Beavers showed up at the trailer to tell me about em. "Joe Bob," he told me, "it's against the Constitution to kill you unless you're a Communist."

I told Rhett I might be dead but I wasn't no Communist.

He said, "No, really, you got to talk to Bubba Barclay and see what you can do about getting yourself a First Amendment."

So I went over to Bubba Barclay's law office and make-believe photo ID service and I said to Bubba, "Goldurn it, I'm declaring the First Amendment."

And Bubba said, "What?"

And I said, "I want some First Amendment rights right now, before the '86 models come in."

And then Bubba and me had a big fight over Bubba's legal fees, cause Bubba said it'd take him a whole hour just to look up the First Amendment in the Krankaway County Law Journal and see what it was. But finally I gave in and agreed to fork over the full two bucks. It was the principal of the thing.

The way it turned out, Rhett Beavers was right. Bubba looked up the First Amendment, and it said I have the "right to bare arms." A lot of people don't understand the U.S. Constitution, and so they read that and they say, "Hey, all that means is you can wear muscle shirts to a Neil Diamond concert." These are what is known in America as stupid people.

The right to wear muscle shirts to a Neil Diamond concert is guaranteed by the 22nd Amendment. But the right to bare arms means I can own a .22 rifle if I want to.

Course, you know what happens ever time a drive-in movie critic gets assassinated. *Somebody* starts screaming for gun control. But I think the First Amendment's pretty clear on that matter, and I don't wanna see any more jacking around with our God-given constitutional rights to discriminate against ourselves. Is that clear? I thought so.

One other thing I found out from Bubba is the 94th Amendment: "the right to be obnoxious." Lots of people take this right for granted. They go around being obnoxious, not even thinkin about the people less fortunate than us, in countries where you have to get *permission* to be obnoxious. Like one thing I could do to be obnoxious would be to tell everybody to take their pickups down to the *Dallas Crimes Herald* and honk their horns till somebody came out, but I want it understood that I do *not* want any such display. That would be unfair to the descendants of Lee Harvey Oswald

that killed me last April. We don't need any *Jack Ruby*s going down there and depriving those people of their right to a long and embarrassing public humiliation.

Speaking of public humiliation, the star of *Barbarian Queen* is this Malibu beach bunny named Lana Clarkson that went down to Argentina and took sword lessons from somebody named José. Lana has arms like a couple of No. 2 Faber pencils, but that's cause all the beef is concentrated somewhere else, if you know what I mean and I think you do. Lana was discovered by the King of the Drive-In, Roger Corman, producer of more than 200 drive-in movies, who's been down in Argentina saying "Hey, gimme 10 pesos and I'll let you be a piece of furniture in my movie." The result, as we all know, is *Barbarian Queen*.

We start off, as usual, with some Invading Hordes. This time the Invading Hordes carry off a few virgins, rape some tribal mothers, fire a few slow-motion arrows through the head, burn some bamboo, and pretty much turn the jungle into suburban Newark. The Barbarian Queen escapes in a canoe with a couple other ancient bimbo tribeswomen that wear Mary Kay Cosmetics, but first she has to clobber six Meskin guys with a cardboard sword. Finally the B.Q. speaks: "I'll be no man's slave and no man's whore."

Next thing, we got the Journey (where one of the bimbos starts having rape-mares), then, of course, we got the Soothsayer (blind old lady), then another gratuitous gang rape that's necessary to the plot, then the Fortress City (which looks exactly like the Fortress City in *The Warrior and the Sorceress*), and then, finally the scene we're all waiting for: Torture City.

Pretty decent torturer in this one. "You know," he says, "pain is a won-

JOE BOB'S MAILBAG

DEAR JOE BOB: I am interested in submitting my entry into the Joe Bob Future Wife Sweepstakes. When I first read about your intentions I wasn't sure you were sincere. I also felt a little insecure. After *all,* a journalist who is practically the Pulitzer Prize winner of the Drive-In Movie Review would make anyone feel small in comparison. But I thought, what the hey? I'll just sign my initials & I have nothing to lose.

So here's the low-down: W/F, non-smoker, mostly white (but more Jewish), 27, petite, seeks young man of honorable intentions.

That's all I'm going to say. No ugly check, no measurements. If you wish to discuss The Meaning of Life & other meaningful subjects you can write back.
Sincerely,
R.O.
SAN JOSE, CALIF.

DEAR SKINNY WHITE GIRL: I respect your right to be ugly.

DEAR JOE BOB: I was terribly depressed all week, actually couldn't eat or go out on dates with men, but now I feel like I have a whole new chance at life—"Joe Bob Goes to the Drive-In" has been picked up by Universal Press Syndicate! Now if you could *please* let me know of a paper which will carry it so I can get copies . . . I miss you already, Joe Bob. I've only missed one issue and if that's life without you, I'll pass. *Please reply.* You're the greatest!!
Thanks,
KELLI STEVENS
ARLINGTON

DEAR KELLI: I was the same way. Couldn't go out on dates with men all week either.

SIR: We are dead, but we did not want to let that get in our way because this is a serious matter. We had hoped that perhaps we were wrong and that improvement of this odious little vermin that populate our earth was possible. We see that it is not. Censorship by voices sure that theirs is the only to "right-think" has forced the removal of one of ours who still lives. Joe Bob Briggs has, evidently, been placed in our ranks. He, too, may be villified by the small minds of his age, just as we were by those in ours.
We are, Sir,
your affectionate friends and servants,
JONATHAN SWIFT, FRANCOIS-MARIE AROUET DE VOLTAIRE, JEAN-BAPTISTE POQUELIN MOLIERE, MIGUEL DE CERVANTES, FRANCOIS RABELAIS, SAMUEL CLEMENS, ARISTOPHANES, ALEXANDER POPE, WILLIAM HOGRATH, HENRY FIELDING, EVELYN WAUGH, GEORGE GORDON, LORD BYRON

DEAR BOWLING TEAM: How bout them Lakers?

DEAR EDITOR: The Joe Bob debacle verifies the black community's claim of substandard education in thier schools. Even their best leaders never gained an understanding of parody and satire.
Sincerely yours,
LEE APPLEMAN
DALLAS

DEAR LEE: Hey, it's not their fault if there not educated as us are.

derful thing. You are much too beautiful a girl to let yourself be broken into food for the royal dogs. When I command you to strip your garment off, you do as I say!" But it's pretty soon after that that we get Mr. Body Grease, the gladiator, to come along and ruin everybody's fun.

It's no *Conan the Barbarian II,* but it's got what it takes, namely: forty-six breasts, including two on the male lead. Thirty-one dead bodies. Heads roll. Head spills. Three gang rapes. Women in chains. Orgy. Slave-girl sharing. One bird's-nest bra. The diabolical garbonza torture. Sword fu. Torch fu. Thigh fu (you have to see it to believe it). Drive-In Academy Award nominations for Lana Clarkson, for saying "I'll be no man's slave and no man's whore!" with feeling, and Hector Olivera, the best drive-in director in Argentina. Roger Corman, the King of the Drive-In, is back. Three stars.

Joe Bob says check it out. ■

"Peeved and Eaten Up" by *Tomboy*

Feeling kinda depressed lately, ever since they asked me to make a speech to the Optimist Club of Fort Worth and so I talked for 15 minutes on the meaninglessness of life before they kicked me out. Ever since I got killed in Dallas, I been making speeches on the First Amendment, specially the part about how women, minorities, and Communists can say any obnoxious thing they want to and we don't have the right to wrap a tetherball around their throat. This is one of our most precious rights.

Usually, in the question-and-answer session, they say stuff like "Do you think starving Ethiopian children are funny? What kind of sick person are you?"

And I'd like to say right here and now that I am *opposed* to starvation in Ethiopia. I refuse to vote for starvation. I refuse to give any money to organizations *promoting* starvation. And I will not have starvation in my own house at any time. Thanks for giving me a chance to set this record straight.

But, like I say, I been depressed ever since they killed me, and the only thing I been able to do for it is go over to the Dallas-Fort Worth Airport Holiday Inn North in Irving and sign up for "Peeved and Eaten Up" Seminar Training (PEST). The local franchise is owned by my good friend, the psycho-astrologist Dr. Moses Foot. Dr. Foot weighs about 230 and he has a big chunk of scrap iron where his right arm used to be before he stuck it in a vat of boiling acid to prove he was more macho than Dr. Heinrich "Still a Nazi and Proud of It" Kronstammer. Dr. Foot is the best there is.

The way PEST works is they teach you how to *never* go to the bathroom or wash your face again for the rest of your life. Let's face it, some people don't have any more self-control than they need to go to the bathroom two, three times a week. But when you sign up for PEST, you go into this big Holiday Inn meeting room with 40 other depressed people and you sit there while Dr. Foot encourages you to turn your life around.

First he says things like "You're nothing but a little scum weasel, aren't you? Your feet smell like you been wading around in lizard guts."

You can see how this makes you start feeling better right off.

Then pretty soon somebody asks if they can go to the bathroom, and Dr. Foot says, "Your bathroom days are behind you, Cream-of-Wheat face."

And you start to realize PEST is gonna change your life, forever. Some people take a long time to catch on. A lot of em sit there with their legs crossed for the first two days, but after that the veins start sticking out on their forehead and you can see their insides turning into Jell-O and it's about then that Dr. Foot brings on the Chinese snake torture (I won't spoil the surprise for those of you who haven't enrolled yet), and then he tells you how you can make a quick million in chinchilla farms if you just peel off one foot of your own skin per night before you go to bed, and then he pulls out a bullwhip and starts demonstrating the "permanent manicure" as a new PEST method of personal grooming. All the time he's doing this, Dr. Foot keeps yelling, "Are you p.o.ed yet? Are you eat up with hate?"

And then finally we all jump up out of our chairs, jerk the chains off our necks, and dogpile on Dr. Foot. After we beat him to a bloody pulp, we stand around his limp broken body, join hands, and all sing folk songs about love and brotherhood. Then we all go over to the restaurant and order the Mexican plate, charge it to Dr. Foot's room, and go home feeling like we can go to the bathroom any time we want. I'm feeling better already, just thinking about it.

Speaking of pests, Betsy Russell is back from her collision with a Max Factor truck in *Avenging Angel* with something called *Tomboy*. Betsy's been giving out interviews in El Lay about how from now on she is "no longer accepting exploitation roles" and will not expose her hooters for the rest of her life unless they're necessary to the plot. In other words, Betsy now has the most conceited garbonzas *per square inch* than any breasts in Hollywood.

Anyhow, *Tomboy* is Betsy's last drive-in flick, and it's about how all she wants to do in life is crawl around underneath cars spurting her axle grease and saying stuff like "Mind if I check your suspension?" and generally acting like Jennifer Beals sniffing 40-weight Uniflo. But then this wimp race-car driver named Randy Starr comes along and sweeps her off her back and takes her to an orgy and starts slapping her around in the weight room until they fall on the floor and make the sign of the epileptic sperm whale.

Next thing, Betsy decides she wants to drive race cars, only everybody tells her she's *just a girl* and so she can't but then she turns Bella Abzug on us and becomes so freaked out that they let her try it just to make her shut up for five minutes. Ever time she drives the car, though, she zips her suit up over her face so we won't mistake her for a stunt driver.

What we got here is 29 breasts, most of them C cups and above. No dead bodies. No blood. No beasts. Four motor vehicle chases. Gratuitous grease-monkey dancing. Drive-In Academy Award nomination for Kristi Somers, Betsy's airhead valley girl girlfriend, who does a donut commercial, wearing an all-flour bra, with the slogan "Eat it. Eat it all."

Betsy needs a couple more pounds of makeup to get this more than two stars.

Joe Bob says check it out anyway. ■

Back in Frogland

CANNES, which is in France—The reason they got so many nekkid beaches over here is cause this is the only country in the world with G-rated garbonzas. I rolled into town sniffin for lambchops, and I'm telling you, most of these girls oughta rent theirselves out as javelins.

Ever since France went Communist two, three years ago, I been boycotting the Cannes Film Festival, even though this is where I discovered *Basket Case, Hundra,* and *Evil Dead*. I figure the frog Commies would start forcing the women to let all their armpit hair grow out—I was right about that one, too—but I knew sooner or later the quiche capital of the world would run em all out for slobbering vodka all over the crapes, which get their name from being made out of crape paper.

Due to the devaluation of the dollar, I had to sell Cherry Dilday to 35 Turkish sailors in Houston to get enough jack for them to smuggle me on the container ship, and then they wanted *extra* for the Toronado, and then, of course, they wanted a refund for Cherry Dilday. Ever year this happens. Five minutes alone with her, and they start screaming, "Allah save us! No! We repent! We trade for pesos!"—anything to avoid delivering on what they owe. And I have to tell em, "Hey, what do you think she is, a piece of *meat*?" and then I make em give Cherry two quarters for the insult.

Some of your foreign cultures have no respect for women.

Anyhow, once I got over I started scoping the groceries. As you probly heard, France's only got three drive-ins left since the Commie frogs took over, and so you gotta watch 900 flicks here before you can find one decent drive-in classic.

First I watched a bunch of Japanese flicks with close-ups of grasshoppers having sex. Then I saw some German movies about fat guys with bad beards saying "I think I kill myself now." Then I saw some French flicks about nekkid people screaming at each other and ordering the wrong wine. Then I saw some Italian movies starring Marcello Mastroianni and 50 guys that look exactly like Marcello Mastroianni, trying to mash their noses up against the camera so they look like a school of large-mouth bass.

Then I went to a café and had a cup of mud.

Then I saw some Communist Russia flicks about tractor-trailer rigs that fall in love with International Harvester combines. Then I saw some Meskin movies about guys named Paolo that wanna go to New York and sell plastic burros.

In other words, same stuff they had three years ago.

And then I found *Pray for Death*.

I don't know how it happens, but even in Communist years over here, there's always one great drive-in classic that slips through. I don't wanna go too far, since it hasn't had its official world outdoor premiere yet, but *Pray for Death* is probly gonna be the greatest kung fu flick since Bruce kickboxed his way into eternity. I'll give you a hint: 17 dead bodies before the title of the movie even comes on.

What we got here is the first movie ever made about a Japanese Ninja who comes to Houston to fix up an old house and join a neighborhood improvement group. All Sho Kosugi wants to do is lay bathroom tiles, replace wood shingles, and play Frisbee with his little Yokohama younguns. But NOOOOOOOOOOOOOOO. This mush-face mobster gets his jollies out of pouring gasoline on people and saying "Hey, how about a Viking funeral?" and he decides to use Sho's family to take the blame for some missing California nose candy. So he kidnaps Sho's little kid, then he runs over the other one, then he sneaks into Sho's wife's hospital room and fiddles around with her life-support equipment, and pretty soon we got one p.o.ed Ninja in a business suit.

What we got here is *Enter the Dragon, Death Wish,* and *Halloween* all combined into one flick. It goes to Numero Uno on the JBB Best of '85 list as soon as it gets the official outdoor premiere.

In the meantime, you guys got to settle for *Exterminator 2,* which is finally sneaking around the country on the midnight double-feature circuit even though I been begging em to release it for months. It's been five years since Robert Ginty came back from Nam and started barbecuing New York City drug dealers with a U.S. Marine flamethrower, and since then all his best friends keep getting killed again. So this time big Bob buys himself a garbage truck, puts gun turrets and grenade launchers on it, and *literally* cleans up the streets. Or, as Bob says in the movie when he sees some junkies hanging around Central Park, "Looks like some *garbage* needs to be removed."

The real Bernhard Goetz story has Mario Van Peebles as the scum-of-the-earth gang leader, wearing shoulder pads and a Brylcreem flat-top when he's not organizing the electric crucifixions of white people down in the subway. Bob keeps trying to find him, making Post Toasties out of everybody in sight, until the last big Smokey-the-Bear finale in a waterfront warehouse.

What we got here is 39 dead bodies. Four breasts. Six people turned into human Bic lighters. Three exploding cars. One exploding copter. One exploding Mario Van Peebles. Gratuitous flashdancing. Negro dancing necessary to the plot. Three motor vehicle chases. Nunchucks and napalm. One crucifixion. Kung fu. Subway fu. Trash compactor fu. Hefty fu. Academy Award nominations for Big Bob, for turning New York into a Roman candle; Mario Van Peebles, for his haircut; and Mark Buntzman, the director, who got through this with only second-degree burns.

Four stars. Joe Bob says check it out. ∎

Communist Alert!

Joe Bob's new paper, the *Dallas Observer,* took out a big ad in the *Dallas Slimes Herald* that said, "Joe Bob Briggs is alive and well and living at the non-Communist *Dallas Observer.*" But the *Slimes Herald* ripped the word "non-Communist" out of the ad and left a big blank space in the paper. They said they thought we were implying they were Communists. They were right.

All Choked Up Over *Rambo*

Ever Memorial Day I like to go out to the graveyard and put a wreath out for Huey Studds and say a little prayer. Huey is one of the tragedies of Nam. Huey was there at Tet Ninh. He was knocked over by a heat-seeking missile at Kom Song. Huey was the first man to volunteer for Van Nuys. And, course, he saw the worst of it all at Loch Ness.

A Huey Studds don't come along ever day in this country. Huey was a hero. They don't make em like Huey anymore, cause they can't get spare parts. We got a name for what Huey was. That name is "Jerk." But we got another name for what Huey was, too. It's the four saddest words in the American language:

Missing In Action.

Fifteen years. Fifteen long, tough, horrible years. The Disco Years. The K-Tel Years. The years when America learned how to counterfeit VISA cards. Huey missed all those years. Ever since April 7, 1970, the day Huey dropped out of sight at Schlong Vat, while loading 980 unmarked crates of Marlboros onto an armored personnel carrier. They don't know what it was that happened. Maybe Huey slipped and fell into a box of broken glass disguised as discount jewelry. Maybe the Cong snuck up from behind and tried to steal some Jack Daniels and Huey had to shish-ka-bob hisself on an enemy bayonet. All they know is what the captain wrote down in the little "pink book" that day:

Studds, Huey Q., PFC, Amarillo Tex., Jerk, MIA

Course, the *real* tragedy of it is the Army don't know where he is, but we all know where Huey's been the last 15 years. He's been in Van Buren, Ark., workin for Lester Scraggs selling home video and satellite TV. But the Army don't know that. Ever year Huey goes down to the Federal Building in Fort Smith and says "Hey, I ain't missing," but they never do figure out how Huey was just put down wrong in the book. And so I guess for the rest of his life he'll be saddled with it.

Missing In Action.

Say a little prayer for Huey this year, if you think of it. Maybe you can use the one I wrote. It goes something like this. "Dear God, please tell the Army that Huey's walkin around rippin people off on their VCRs and tryin to get em to rent *Gandhi* so he won't have to eat the commission. The Cong didn't get him, even though they should have. He's still a jerk. Amen."

Course, things like this wouldn't even happen if we had Sly Stallone runnin the Army. I guess you know what's comin. I guess you've already seen it 24 times by now. I guess you only got one question left, and that question is: "Joe Bob, why can't Sylvester Stallone ever wear a clean shirt?"

We're talkin Rambo. We're talkin Rocky Goes to Nam. We're talking, of course, *Second Blood*.

A lot of you scoffed at the man. A lot of you said he couldn't do it again, specially since he wasted half of Colorado in *First Blood* to prove what a patriotic American he was. But now they decide to let Rambo out of jail so he can go over to Nam, parachute down to the bamboo prisons where they're keeping 47,000 American prisoners that weren't let out by Bronson or Norris or *Uncommon Valor,* fall in love with a Viet Bimbo, kung fu some Russians, suffer through the dreaded Oriental electric-bedspring torture, lose his shirt, and say stuff like "I always thought the best weapon was the mind."

Course, we already know that the future of Western democracy depends on Rocky's mind. But fortunately, Sylvester brought along *a few simple weapons.* Carefully concealed in his boots are eight AK-47 Kalashnikov assault rifles with laser scopes and hundred-round ammo clips. Behind his belt are hidden 943 daggers, throwing stars, exploding bronze-tipped arrows, and a knife the size of Mongolia. Rambo doesn't *need* any of this stuff, of course. All he *needs* is a bow and arrow, so he can turn the Cong into buffalo meat.

One more thing about the plot. The GIs tell him to bail out into Commie land, and then they *leave him hanging out there like a piece of limp sausage to die.* In other words, what we got here is Rambo against the Viet Commies, the Russian Commies, *and* the Washington Commies. Thank God he knows how to hot-wire a military chopper to get our boys out of there.

What we got here is the Exploding Bamboo Champion of all time. Body count: 77. No breasts. One beast (Rambo). Three quarts blood. Two exploding boats. Eighteen exploding bamboo huts. One exploding village. One exploding Russian gunship. One exploding Russian. Two motor vehicle chases. *Story of O* yucky mud torture. One exploding rice paddy. Kung fu. Snake fu. Bow-and-arrow fu. Chopper fu. Bazooka fu. Drive-In Academy Award nominations for Sly Rocky Rambo, the greatest mumbledy lips on the drive-in screen (you can understand at least *half* the man's lines this year, including religious stuff like "To survive war, you gotta *become* war"); Julia Nickson, trying to slant her eyes, make like a Viet Bimbo, and say stuff like "Maybe go America? Live quiet life?"; and Richard Crenna, back from *Rambo Uno,* hanging around going "Little Luke still believes in you, big guy."

No question about it. Four stars. Made me want to go out and kill a few Communists. Joe Bob says check it out. ∎

JOE BOB'S MAILBAG

DEAR JOE BOB: What do you think of this "Spousal Maintenance" bill (copy enclosed) that's pending in the Texas Legislature in Austin? Isn't this really spelled P-E-R-M-A-N-E-N-T A-L-I-M-O-N-Y?

The State Bar of Texas is sponsoring this law through a faction of women's libbers who seem to have taken over that organization. Under community property, the women already get at least half of everything when you divorce them. Now they want money for life. It's to where you can't afford to divorce one of them. (That's probably what they want anyway.)

The women pushing this law say it's real "limited." The wife can't get but $18,000 a year alimony. Next thing you know, Texas will be just like New York and California. What do you think?
A FAN
PORTLAND, TEX.

DEAR FAN: It says they get 1500 bucks a month or 20 percent of the guy's salary, whichever is less. This is outrageous.

I refuse to give any of my ex-wives the 35 bucks they'd get under this law, and I will go to jail for my principles.

DEAR JOE BOB: We been wondrin' how you tally breasts: F'r instance do two breasts attached to the same bimbo shown at the same time count as one or two? And how would you count the behemoth boob in Woody Allen's *Everything You Ever Wanted to Know About Sex*? (We know you don't review films from foreign countries like New York.) Also, would the aforementioned (look it up) scene from *Sex* count as "breast-foo"? These are important questions since we want to be sure to get our money's worth.
Breast wishes,
CHERYL & MARK
OAKLAND, CALIF.

DEAR CHERYL & MARK: Every single hooter, but only once per scene. Stunt breasts are a separate category.

DEAR MR. BRIGGS: Your fans in the Public Affairs Department of Shell Oil Company request a copy of "We Are the Weird."
THANKS,
BRUCE KLEINMAN
SHELL OIL COMPANY, HOUSTON

DEAR BRUCE: After your boss reads this and you get fired, come on up to Dallas and I'll give you one.

Rambo-izing the U.S. of A.

I been to see *Rambo* 43 times now and I been Rambo-in all over Texas. Just call me a Rambo fool. I went out and bought me a laser-guided bow and arrow just to shoot innocent little birds with. I'm lookin around for somebody to steal me a video so I can run the chopper explosion in slo-mo. I got so excited I got Sly Stallone on the horn this week and I said, "Sly, let's talk merchandising."

And Sly answered back like he always does. He said, "Whah?"

And I said, "I don't guess I have to tell *you*, big guy, but *Rambo*'s through the roof. You did it, fellow. They said nobody could make a movie about Nam cause America was *sick and tired* of thinking Nam Nam Nam all the time, and you said, 'I can do it.' Just like that. 'I can do it.' Actually, what you really said was more like 'Ahknit,' but we know *exactly* what you meant.

No Jane Fonda wheelchair weenie bullstuff. No Francis Coppola super slo-mo swamp fu. If you wanna talk Nam, you gotta *think* Nam. And if you wanna think Nam, you gotta *be* Nam. And if you wanna *be* Nam, you gotta pay Sylvester a flat two million to go jump in the mud and make his face look like a *map* of Nam. You know what I mean? You know where I'm coming from here?"

And Sly said, "Whah?"

And then I knew I had his attention. Sly needs me. This Rambo thing is too big for the guy to handle. America's got Rambo on the brain, and if we don't take advantage of it immediately, people might start committing suicide cause they can't buy Rambo beer coolers and Rambo hand-held heat-seeking missile launchers and, of course, the Rambo extra-support soldier-of-fortune jockstrap. You can have me for a half mill, Sly. Here's just a few of the things I can do for you:

Rambo Disco: Heard of the Mambo? Put on the Frank Stallone soundtrack to *Stayin' Alive* and try the Rambo. Train your lower lip to do the Reverse Frug, just like Sly taught it to Johnny Travolta. Learn to leave your shirt at home and act like you forgot.

Ramboterias: Chow down with Rambo's favorite jungle food, including chopped Spam, snake sushi, and a great big ole glass of raw eggs to wash it down with. The kids might wanna order the Rambo Plate: fresh chicken heads.

Rambowling: Watch the pins scatter when you let the lead fly with a U.S.-Marine-issue M-16 automatic combat assault rifle. But look out for Mr. Manager!

Rambocize: Highly trained Vietnamese immigrants will leap onto your shoulders, so that you can raise both arms and flip em headfirst into a pile of writhing human flesh. Tones up the deltoids, pecs, and lower-leg muscles. Ladies! Try oriental foot-binding and the special Piranha Sauna.

Not to mention **Rambo Wear, Rambo Hair, Rambo Sambo**'s (24-hour pancakes), and the Empty-V special, *Video-Rambo: The Making of Sly Stallone's Elevator Combat Boots.* Just send the check to P.O. Box 2002, Dallas, and we'll put in orders for about a hundred thou worth of **Rambo Cong Thongs.** Believe me, Sly, the bank is waiting.

Speaking of midgets with voices like Betty Boop, Kurt Thomas has this new flick called *Gymkata,* where he goes over to Yugoslavia and starts gymnasticking people to death. What happened was, Kurt just got back from winning his gold medal in El Lay, and the CIA came over to his house and said, "Hey, Kurt, we got a mission for you. We need you to go over to Hindu Land and fight 900 warriors to the death so we can stick a nuke missile base right in the middle of this Ayrab Country. If you win the fight, the king says we can do it."

So Kurt stands on a three-foot cardboard box, looks the guy right in the Adam's apple, and says, "Yeah, I'll do it." And then he starts training for the Big Game by walking on his hands and ridin around on a Clydesdale and throwin cardboard knives and letting big black guys beat him up. Next thing you know, there he is gettin off the tour boat in Hindu Ville, where this guy says, "Kurt, the reason these people are spitting in your face is there's just a *little* anti-American sentiment here," and then the guy gets an arrow through his stomach and Kurt has to run through the alleys of Zagreb until he finds one that happens to have a horizontal gymnastics bar set up between two buildings. So he grabs the bar and starts spinning around and kicking guys in the teeth cause they wear turbans and carry those big curved knives like Yul Brynner. The reason they had to go to Yugoslavia to make *Gymkata* is the whole country has gymnastics equipment hidden in the rocks and stickin out of buildings, and it gives Kurt a big advantage over the guys with machine guns trying to kill him.

Next thing, Kurt's girlfriend gets kidnapped in a terrorist training camp, and Kurt has to go in there and gymnastick his way out. Then the two of em decide to take a whitewater raft trip, only on the way down the river, eight Ninja warriors come out of the woods and carry everybody off to the Hindu Castle, where they put Kurt in a big bed so some transvestite maids can come mop his brow and get him ready to be killed in the big race. The way the race works is, they say "Run like hell," and all the warriors take off, and then the Ninjas chase em on horseback and shoot em through the back with arrows and spear em in the privates until nobody's left. But Kurt's been practicing his steak-knife twirling so much that he survives the flaming-rope torture, the Grand Canyon cleaver attack, the gymkata-fu struggle against a crazed 800-pound Norwegian Viking named Thor, and the final Race Through the Loony Bin, where everybody tries to make it through a prison full of zombies carrying farm implements.

Oh yeah, I forgot. Kurt falls in love with the king's daughter, and she likes him even though he kisses like a fish.

No breasts. Body count: 85. Twelve impalements. One gallon blood. One beast. Kung fu scenes: 10. Gymnastics fu. Machine-gun fu. Loonie fu. One motor vehicle chase. One pitchfork through throat. Hands roll. Sickle in stomach. Pig-licking. Drive-In Academy Award nomination for the nation of Yugoslavia. Three stars.

Joe Bob says check it out. ∎

JOE BOB'S MAILBAG

DEAR JOE BOB: We in New Zealand beg your forgiveness for being late in extending our sympathy on your demise. We rely on friends to forward your column to us and you had been dead several weeks before we got the word.

The last information we had about you was when we heard that you had recoiled in public in Tulsa—bloody Hell!!!

As we are starving for information about your death, could you please send us a copy of your "We Are the Weird" article. We here in New Zealand promise to go ahead and play rugby against South Africa no matter what you may have said.

For your information, it has happened here, can you believe it—there is not one drive-in in all of New Zealand. The way we overcome this disaster is to have your drive-in movie reviews mailed to us. Then the boys call up the local Tete-a-Tete Escort service and we act out each movie based on your descriptive appraisal. It is really quite something to see—except all those car headlights are beginning to hurt my eyes!!

Keep up the good work in Kansas City, Joe Bob. Don't let it happen there.
CAPT. MICHAEL A. THOMPSON
LINTON CAMP OFFICERS' MESS
PALMERSTON NORTH, NEW ZEALAND

DEAR CAPN: Put some American nukes in down there and we'll THINK about sending you a drive-in.

Babtist and Proud

In the beginning God created the Babtists. And the Babtists looked at their ownselves and said, "We good."

And God saw it was too late.

Not but a few days ago, Dallas was crawling with my fellow Babtists. They poured in on Greyhounds for a week, got off, scratched their pants and said, "Hey, where's that place where they killed Kennedy?" They filled up ever Motel Six between here and Lawton, Okla. We know this cause they stole all the Gideon Bibles out of the rooms.

Time for the Southern Babtist Convention.

If you're not a Babtist, you might not know what I'm getting at here, but we don't care cause you're going to hell anyhow. I wish I didn't have to tell you that. I wish I could put it in a nice way and that you would understand the love in my heart that goes out to you and surrounds you with peace and Christian love and convinces you in the depths of your own being that you're the scum of the earth. But I'm afraid God's getting ready to turn you into a Post Toastie and there's nothing I can personally do about it.

Myself, I already been saved and babtized, and what I love about being a Babtist is you only have to do it once. After that, all you got to do is go to the Southern Babtist Convention ever year and discuss the most important religious issues of the modern world and hide all the Coors in your trunk till the convention's over. This year we had 30,000 Big B's in town. You could see em hanging around the post office going "Excuse me, but I'm a worker for the Lord and could you direct me to the neighborhood where the prostitutes and smut merchants infect this great city?" Some of these Babtists were so lonely I'm thinking of setting up a Christian Dating Service, just for the next convention, but *absolutely no kinky stuff*. That'll have to wait till they get back home to the privacy of their own VCR.

We had major-league religious issues to talk over this year. The liberals are trying to take over Babtist churches all over this country and turn us into Hairy Krishnas. That's why I was down there at the Convention Center, roaming around like a water buffalo, trying to provide gavel-to-gavel coverage for the drive-in-going public. And make no mistake about it, with the good Lord's help we'll reach the final answers on the following questions of the hour.

Numero Uno: Did Elvis go to hell cause he turned hisself into a walking drug-store right before he died, and if so, can he get outta hell if his "Religious Hits" album goes back on the charts?

Numero Two-o: Did God create everything in six days or did He cheat?

Numero Three-o: How many times can you have sex out of wedlock before God goes Rambo on you and zaps you into Guam?

Numero Four-o: Did God say ever word in the Bible? If so, try this one from Song of Solomon 6:6, "Thy teeth are as a flock of sheep which go up from the washing." Is the Big Guy that disgusting—and where's He been hanging out anyhow?

Speaking of bad haircuts, there's this great Chuck Norris lookalike named Darby Hinton in *Malibu Express,* except of course Darby don't have near the same acting ability, and about all Darby does is hang around on his yacht and fight off nekkid girls until it's time to go get in his DeLorean and solve a murder case. He keeps solving the same murder case over and over again, discovering Russian spies and dead bodies and little girls that wanna flick his Bic. This is one of those flicks where there's so much plot you forget what it is, and so it's like having no plot at all, which is the way my good buddy Andy Sidaris likes to do it. Andy is a producer for ABC Sports who likes to go out with a movie camera and find some *Playboy* Playmates and take pictures of their garbonzas and embarrass the network. Andy wrote, directed, produced, and punched the little holes in the side of the film, and when he called up to demand a review of his flick, I said, "Andy, what was the message you were trying to evoke in this picture?"

And Andy said, "I get to make all the actresses take their clothes off while I watch."

The man's a cinema genius.

Anyhow, what we got here is four—that's right, *four*—official *Playboy* Playmates, including all the ones who put "Actress" on their Playmate Profile sheet and two of the ones that remembered to cross the "t." They take a lot of showers and giggle. We got the one and only Miss Overdrive. We got Mr. Universe. We got Mr. Arizona. And, of course, we got Sybil Danning, the drive-in ripaway-bra queen. She's in the movie for about five minutes, but with Syb, that's all it takes.

We got 72 breasts, including a couple on a girl named June Khnockers that oughta count double ever time she jumps out of her jumpsuit. Four dead bodies. Four shower scenes. Sybil in a red zoot suit. Two brawls. Four motor vehicle chases, including the first Winnebago-vs.-helicopter chase. Kung fu. *Dukes of Hazzard*–ripoff Hillbilly fu. Gratuitous aerobic weight training. Great transvestite bar scene ("The Screaming Cockatoo"). Phone sex, also known as Lip Service. Ear rolls. One exploding fat guy. Drive-In Academy Award nomination for Andy Sidaris, who screwed up the World Series coverage cause he was off writing lines like "Greed is an *awful* thing."

Three stars. Take a shower, Andy. Joe Bob says check it out. ■

Fraternity Vacation
Brims with Religious Groceries

We finally run all the liberal Babtists out of town so we could get down to the serious binness of choosing missionaries to send out all over the world to demonstrate the Missionary Position to unsaved savages that are going to hell at the present time cause they think they can have sex just any old way they please.

In other words, we saved this country at the Southern Babtist Convention. We decided that a Babtist is still a Babtist, so we should still do everthing the way we did it in the year

1850, which is when we discovered the first liberal coming around, trying to get us to sprinkle instead of Babtize, trying to get us to tongue-talkin so we couldn't tell what all we were saying to each other instead of letting us just talk all at the same time like we normally do.

We also decided on the following New Ten Commandments:

Commandment Numero Uno: Homosexuality is a sin, specially if you're a gay person.

Numero Two-o: God meant ever word he said, exactly like he said it in English, like "Thy teeth are as a flock of sheep." This is why all Babtists have bad breath.

Numero Three-o: Playboy, Penthouse, and *Hustler* are agents of Satan, but that didn't bother me cause the only one I have a subscription to is *Melons Monthly.* Okay okay, sometimes I pick up a *Hustler* on the newsstand, but I only read it for the articles.

Numero Four-o: We need more nukes so we can deal with Russia in a Christian manner.

Numero Five-o: The Babtists over in Russia served Coke and everything when Billy Graham went over there, so they're probly pretty nice people even though we're gonna turn em into fried potato skins.

Numero Six-o: Abortion is a terrible sin, but the Babtists would of made an exception for Garry Trudeau's mother.

Numero Seven-o: God wants us to be rich and live till we're 120, and the only reason we never do get there is the house takes a 5 percent rake, so the longer you play the worse you get behind.

Numero Eight-o: God loves America, which is why the typhoons wipe out 40,000 people in Bangladesh instead of in Cincinnati, even though Cincinnati could use a little Spray-n-Wash.

Numero Nine-o: People of the Jewish persuasion should move over to Israel and get it ready for when the J-Man comes back.

Numero Ten-o: Catholics are jerks.

Can you imagine what a better world we would live in today if ever one of us would simply follow these 10 simple rules of God? It's not that hard. Come on! Let's give it a try! Let's make this into a better America! Let's be Babtist!

Speaking of people that have to get it on the side, *Fraternity Vacation* is a pretty decent drive-in flick, even though I was expecting it to be a *Spring Break* ripoff with a bunch of guys hanging around the disco in Lauderdale drinking Miller Lite. This is a *lot* different. It's a bunch of guys hanging around the disco in *Palm Springs* drinking Miller Lite.

The object here, let's face it, is groceries. And, as we all know, nobody can get any cause their idea of getting a girl's attention is to walk up and say, "What do I do for a living? Besides flying the Space Shuttle, you mean?" But Wendell the goofball gets all the girls he wants *because* he can do a perfect Wayne Newton impression, including the complete lyrics to "Donka Shane." Course, what eventually happens is the most outstanding set of cantaloupes in the history of feed and grain stores checks into the apartment next door, and pretty soon everybody's taking thousand-buck bets on the first man to get squeezing rights.

We got eight breasts. No blood. One beast (John Vernon, as the police chief). Two motor vehicle chases. Kung fu. Mercedes fu. Three pool scenes. One herpes scene. Gratuitous aerobics. Gratuitous disco dancing. Grocery delivery. Academy Award nominations for Stephen Geoffreys, as Wendel the Walking Nuke, for Donka-Shaning all over the screen; Tim Robbins, as Larry "Mother" Tucker, a drive-in kind of guy; and Cameron Dye, another drive-in kind of guy. No nominations for Sheree J. Wilson, the Ta-Ta Goddess, cause she used stunt breasts.

Three stars. Joe Bob says check it out. ∎

JOE BOB'S MAILBAG

BRIGGS YOU SCUM: First you get cancelled then I have to find out from the rest of the fellows down at the Happy Tappy that my wife is slipping out behind my back with a fellow who drives a red Toronado and making the sign of the two-humped whale behind closed doors at the Notale Motel here in Tempe.

Of course, I've tried to discuss the matter with her and she says this fellow kept buying her Singapore Slings and talking about what a hot shot he was in the Big D. Claimed he was you. And as you know, and I'm sure you do, that all it takes to wake up with a smile on your face is to tell just about any woman that you are Joe Bob, the drive-in movie man. Hell, I've done it myself from time to time.

I'm warning you Briggs. Stay away from my woman or you'll be more than cancelled in my book. Next time you look in the rear-view mirror and see the chrome grill of a Ford pickup, it'll be me, and there won't be no smile on my face or on yours.

I've bet ol' Bruce down at the bar that you'll be cancelled within five weeks. Go ahead and make my day . . .
PAUL MORRIS
TEMPE, ARIZ.
P.S. By now you may have noticed that the little woman left you with more than just a smile on your face. Consider it my present to you.

DEAR PAUL: It wasn't me, and also she's a liar.

DEAR MR. BRIGGS: My son and husband are great fans of yours. Since we do not receive a paper that carries your column, my brother-in-law cuts them out of the Dallas paper for us. When they arrive (in a bundle), my son and husband read them to anyone who happens to be around.

My daughter is a fledgling writer. She "publishes" a monthly (or bi-monthly depending on her free time) magazine. I thought you might enjoy this article from her December issue. Anastasia is 10 years old:

"Dear Joe Bob Briggs: Sometimes I think you're a total queer. I even think you should do it with E.T. But sometimes I think you are 'T-totally awesome.' How much is a shirt that says 'Joe Bob Briggs' on it? I've heard that they are something like twenty-dollars. If they are, they are too much for me and I won't buy one so if they are, bite mine. Sincerely, Sam the Ham."
FONDA HENSON WORKMAN
GREAT FALLS, MONT.

DEAR FONDA: I can't wait till little Anastasia is eleven.

Peeking at Pelvises and Pecs

A little while ago the High Sheriff at Columbia Pictures said, "Hey, you, get me Travolta on the horn."

And so his secretary brushed some petrified maroon El Lay hair-do out of her eyes, ripped off her black surgical gloves, and called up the man with the trick britches and told him to get his million-dollar caboose down to the back lot. And when he got there, the High Sheriff was ready to drive his foot through the linoleum.

"Johnbaby, it's not workin, what can I say?"

And John hiked up his pants and got this painful expression on his face and said, "That really hurts me."

And the High Sheriff said, "Johnbaby, the critics are *animals.*"

And the Fever-Man said, "No, these pants hurt me. When I take em off at night, I have stitches all over my famous lower torso where the seams were."

And the High Sheriff said, "All right, that's *just* the kind of thing I'm talkin about. A few World War I trenches on your thighs, and all of a sudden you start *whining,* and listen to me, Johnbaby, I'm serious on this deal, I'm *not* gonna put up with it anymore."

"Okay, just tell me what to do."

"Okay, now listen to me, John. Remember this and never forget it. *The pelvis is the franchise.* Do you under-stand me?"

"The pelvis is the franchise?"

"The pelvis is the franchise, and what we're talkin about is image. Remember when we did the Tony Manero thing, the Fever thing?"

"Was that the one where Sissy Spacek gets possessed by the devil?"

"No, John, think Bee Gees. Brooklyn. You know, the pilot for *Dance Fever.*"

"Oh yeah."

"Okay, and do you know *why* the Fever thing worked? Do you?"

"Why?"

"*For God's sake, think, Johnny.* It starts with a P."

"Don't tell me. P . . . Starts with a P . . ."

"*Pelvis,* John."

"Oh yeah, right, pelvis."

"*Your pelvis,* Johnny. We *used* it in the Fever thing. We didn't do the talk thing. We didn't do the plot thing. We did the pelvis thing. Okay, and then what came next?"

"The thigh bone?"

"The *Urban Cowboy* thing came next, John. And what happened there? We didn't use the pelvis. And what happens when we don't do the pelvis thing? El bombolo Manero. Okay, and what was after that?"

"We go get some ice cream?"

"No, after that was the *Grease* thing. Olivia Newton-John, who used to be a big deal just like you used to be a big deal. And what'd we do there, John? Let me spell it out for you. P.E.L.V.I.S. Remember the check we wrote you for 30 mill, the one you spent on gold neck chains? Remember? Okay, and *then* what happens? You go make a TV movie on us, you go do the *Bubble Boy,* and listen to me, John, look at me, it hurts me to have to tell you this, but think about it. You're a kid living inside a germ-free plastic bubble. Are you thinkin pelvis? You're *not* thinkin pelvis. You're thinkin bubble. That's why *Bubble Boy* went down the toilet, John. I tried to tell you, but you wouldn't listen. Bubble boys don't dance, John. So we had to come back with *Two of a Kind* and let you diddle around with Olivia some more, just to *assure people your pelvis was still working.*"

"Oh."

"It is, isn't it?"

"What?"

"It *is* in working condition, isn't it?"

"Oh yeah, I think so. I don't know. I'll check."

"So listen to me, Johnbaby. Here's the bottom line. They don't want bubble, they don't want cowboy, they don't want dialogue. Look at me, John. Quit doing that and look at me. And, John, they don't want *conceited.* That thing in *Staying Alive,* the strut thing. John, you had everything. You had the pelvis. You had the Fever. You had the Manero. You had Sly behind the camera. You had it all, and what did you do? You blew the pelvis thing with the strut thing. You did conceited. That's why I got somethin for you, John, somethin that's got it all. They're gonna love you in this, Johnny. They'll forget conceited when they see this."

"What is it?"

"A little thing called *Perfect.*"

"I'll do it."

And ever since then we been waitin to see if the rumors are true—if it's *really* true that Jamie Lee Curtis, the former scream queen of the drive-in, went indoor bullstuff on us and made two hours of gratuitous aerobic dancing. I have to admit I had a hard time chokin it up to get over to the drive-in and check this one out. I heard what they were sayin about her. I knew she was gonna do it with the Pelvis Man. I heard all the rumors. So here's what I found out.

Travolta-Man is the Mick Jagger Editor of *Rolling Stone,* and he goes around investigating corruption in America so much that Carly Simon throws a Bloody Mary in his face. His dream is to write up a big story on a guy that looks like John DeLorean, or else to hang around the aerobics dance class and watch women's breasts bounce up and down. So anyhow, while he's investigating Slimnasticize University, he falls in love with Jamie Lee Curtis's body-length leotard and jumps her battery. Then he says a bunch of stuff about "Emersonian America" and "the great physical awakening of the baby-boomer generation," and then he jumps on the airplane and goes to New York and says the f-word to some lawyers. John does that for the rest of the movie. He keeps jumping on airplanes and saying the f-word, and then going back to El Lay and watching Jamie Lee's pelvis (great three-minute *dueling pelvis* scene) and trying to get her to talk about the time she didn't win the Olympic gold medal for swimming cause she was makin the sign of the two-humped whale with her coach. But she keeps getting mad at Travolta-Man for being a reporter, and so he goes to Morocco for no reason and then he goes to a male strip club with Larraine Newman, who looks like she's strung out on Pepto Bismol, and then he gets beat up by a black guy and goes to prison cause he won't turn over his tapes. But I know what you're thinkin. And the answer to the big questions are:

Yes, Travolta-Man sticks a sack of potatoes inside his jogging suit and does the pelvis thing . . . And no, Jamie Lee hasn't sold out. This is the best horror film of 1985.

Six breasts. One pint blood. Dueling pelvises. Forty beasts (all aerobics instructors). Gratuitous Boy George demonstration. Gratuitous Moroccan belly dancing. Gratuitous Carly Simon. Leotard fu. Drive-In Academy Award nominations for Jamie Lee, for giving her theory of physics on screen; and the T-Man, for saying things like "Popular culture is to society what dreams are to an individual." *The movie that refuses to end*.

Two and a half stars. Joe Bob says check it out. ■

Go Ahead, Crush Me with Your Thighs

Thought I'd check up on this Co-Cola deal, find out if it was true about some wimps in Atlanta polluting the national drink, and so I invited some perverts over for the Joe Bob Briggs Taste Test while I was writing up this column.

First we took a half a Co-Cola, poured three quarts of cherry juice in there, packed in some crushed ice from the 7-Eleven, and scarfed it up like hamsters rootin around in a Jell-O vat. And I have to tell you, it tasted like plain ole ordinary Co-Cola to me.

The second test was, we mixed in about three fingers of Bacardi, stirred it up with Co-Cola poured in a glass that said "World's Greatest Bowler" on the outside, and tossed it down our throats like apple juice. I had four, five of these before I could tell that the new Bacardi-and-Coke tastes *exactly* the same as the old one.

Next thing, we tried some Black-and-Coke, which is Jack Daniel's stoked up with a few droplets of Co-Cola, and then we tried Black-and-Decker-and-Coke, which is my own personal recipe and must *always* be consumed through a straw or else you get this sound between your ears like Madonna getting mangled in a blender.

Results: tasted exactly like Old Coke.

Finally, we went for it—Tequila and Coke, better known out in Grapevine as Coca-tila, where it's also used as an industrial cleaning solvent. And for the ladies: Cutty-and-Coke. Back in the fifties, when people were superstitious out in West Texas, they said Coca-tila would get in your bloodstream and harden up and you'd do a complete zombie blackout and forget your mother's name. But, with the *new* Co-Cola, I did about eight shooters and it had no effect on me whatsoever.

I did about eight shooters and it had no effect on me whatsoever.

Another thing they used to say about Coca-tila is I forgot.

So you see, people start these *rumors* all the time about how they're gonna ruin Co-Cola and put punk-rocker drugs in it and poison us, but I don't believe it except for the people that've been planning to kill my dog for eight years, and the other thing they say about Co-Cola is how it tastes like Pepsi now, but it really tastes more like peppermint Schnapps if you ask me, or else my name ain't Boe Rob Jiggs.

Speaking of people that take care of their bodies, the drive-in flick *Pumping Iron II: The Women* asks the question, "Are women just a piece of meat or what?" This is the best movie about people that wear their muscles on the outside of their bodies since *Pumping Iron Numero Uno,* the 1977 classic where drive-in superstar Arnold Schwarzenegger and Lou Ferrigno popped their deltoids for the first time. If they ever make *Karen the Barbarian,* we got four contenders for the part:

Rachel, this El Lay valley girl with a designer hairdo and little Indian frilly dealies on her ankles and a European guy named Christian hanging around, playin with her triceps, givin her Flashdance leotard advice, till Rachel says, "I'd marry Christian in a second, but I don't feel I know him well enough." Rachel has quite a few bulges in her tiger-skin jumpsuit and she's the favorite to win the World Bodybuilding Champeenship at Caesars Palace.

Lori, this little moon-eyed gal from San Antone that wants to win the big prize so her boyfriend, The Hunk, can stop being a male dancer.

Carla, this girl from Newark who's into synchronized swimming and says the word "perameter" a lot. Carla has fairly enormous perameters.

Bev, the world's strongest woman, who chows down in Australia till she's ready to come to Vegas and imitate the Roman Legion. We're talkin muscles. We're talkin so much muscle that Bev's legs look like a map of the Mexico City subway system. The only person alive with more muscle than Bev is her trainer, Mr. America, Steve Michalak. Steve's idea of a good time is to hang around a gym in New York City goin, "If we add five more pounds to Bev's weights, how much will that be? Got a calculator?"

Anyhow, all these walking beef cookies show up in Vegas and puff up their pecs and walk up to the judges and put their bikinis in a little pile for inspection. Rachel gets her bra disqualified three times and you could gag her with a spoon and so she goes and lays down in a cancer-light-ray suntan machine until she feels better. "I love the Lord," she says. And then somebody says, *"Okay, oil em up!"* And they take Wayne Newton's name off the marquee and pretty soon we got Muscle Dancing all over the stage. I don't wanna give the ending away, but the judges got to decide the question, "What the heck is a woman *supposed* to look like anyhow?" which I don't know about you, but I been trying to decide that all my life.

Four breasts (but a lot of see-through nipple tops). No blood. Seven beasts (boyfriends and trainers). One male stripper. Gratuitous Flashdancing. Gratuitous Wayne Newton. Jiggle fu. One hot-tub scene. One pool scene. Two shower scenes. Academy Award nominations for Bev Francis, for saying "Some men just can't handle muscles"; Lori Bowen, for saying "Someday, honey, we'll have enough money so you won't have to strip anymore"; and Rachel McLish, for saying "You're really dealing with human beings. You can't depend on them. It even says so in the Bible."

Four stars. Joe Bob says check it out. ■

Tough Talk About Terrorists

Last week I read up on all the hostage gossip to try to figure out what we, the drive-in-going public, can do to stop this senseless tragedy. It just makes you sick the way TWA treated those people. Some of em didn't even get their luggage back. Let's face it, today it's only a Jumbo 747 aircraft or two. Tomorrow it might be '49 Mercurys. It's too easy to say "Hey, Muskrat-Face Camel Jockey! I fly Ford!" Cause if you said that, they'd just yell somethin back at you like "Allah el Dollah" and try to trade you for some Levi's. No, there's a lot of serious questions left unanswered in the wake of the crisis, and here's some of the stupider ones:

Uno: If you were goin from Athens to Rome, but they flew you to Beirut instead, would you get extra miles added on your Frequent Flyer card? Also, do you get complimentary cocktails the *whole 18 days* or just *one* complimentary cocktail for each day you're sittin there in Beirut? Do they carry enough Bloody Mary mix for the whole time?

Two-o: If the movie they're showin is something like Kristy McNichol in *Just the Way You Are,* is there any way to force the armed terrorists to watch it so you can just let em puke their guts out and die right there in the aisle?

Three-o: The next time I go through the metal detector, is it okay if I bring along a couple AR-15 9-millimeter semi-automatic shoulder-mount chopped blowback 20-shot carbines and about 80 clips full of Frontier 124-grain hardball ammo and a few hand-loaded semi-wadcutters? This is some material I keep around the house for sporting purposes only, but what the hey, who knows what we could do with it if a slime-spewing Islamic goat-herder jumped on the plane and said, "Take off silk shirts, gold chains, and geev to us!"

Okay, so let's put it to a democratic drive-in vote about what we should do now that the little Middle East Beard-Off is over. All votes will be kept strictly confidential.

A. Should we have Beirut or not? Couldn't we just say, "Sorry, your time is up" and Handi-Wipe it into the ocean? If you favor this option in peacetime, mark the "H" box on your ballot, for Housecleaning.

B. What would God do to us if we told Israel to take a hike? Okay, okay, so they're the chosen people, but HE chose em, not us. Did you choose em? I didn't choose em. Maybe what we need here is a clarification from The Big Guy, somebody like Billy Graham to sit down and have a heart-to-heart and say, "Okay, now, are You sure it's *these guys* You want? Have You seen the *shvetzahs* on some of these Israeli bimbos? Have You noticed the ones that sit out in the desert all day going 'kvilla himmel Clairol,' which translates into 'my hair used to look like I washed it once a week'?" If you think God made a big mistake, mark the "B" box on your ballot, for "The Bible says we don't have to do this."

C. Ted Koppel wouldn't have a career if it wasn't for hostages. If you favor trading Ted Koppel to the terrorists in exchange for any future hostages, mark the "N" box on your ballot, for Alfred E. Neuman Negotiating Tactics. It's time we started taking these things cereal.

Speaking of human beans that look like comic strips, Arnold the Barbarian was hanging around Rome on the set of *Red Sonja* when Dino started filming it, and Dino kept staring at the toothpick arms of his new star, Brigitte Nielsen, and finally Dino said "Where's-a the beef-a?" and ordered Arnold into the movie even though he wasn't supposed to be there. That's how come Arnold is in this Conan flick that's not really a Conan flick cause it's about a tribe of Danish Amazons, which are the scariest kind cause they all wear their hair like Anne Murray. And what happens is they all get wiped out in the first scene, except for Brigitte, who survives to witness the terrifying six-minute-long death of her twin sister, the Whining Dane, who got speared cause she witnessed the evil queen Gedren throwing 20 virgins into a pit of boiling grease. So Brigitte and Arnold put on about 80 pounds worth of face jewelry, buy two or three plastic swords, and ride off in search of Gedren's city so they can shishkebob her.

Only trouble is, Gedren has the greatest power in the world, The Talisman, which is a giant green lava lamp. As long as she keeps light pouring into the lava lamp, she can perform ever single part in *A Chorus Line* BY HERSELF and get perfect worldwide cable reception without an earth dish. Obviously, if this goes on very long, the world will be destroyed.

Fortunately, Brigitte and Arnold have a midget and a fatman to help em Benihana all the Vikings they run into, including a sword-happy hippie that tries to rip the midget apart by tying his hands to a horse, his feet to a tree, and making a wish, and another one wearing a chest protector who gets killed for saying "I will tell the future in your entrails, Red Woman!" None of this ever bothers Red Sonja, for whenever she grows angry, she simply shouts "Oh keep QUIET!"

Pretty soon, though, after they wrestle a few plastic alligators and have a cardboard swordfight to see if Arnold has "the stuff" to go for Red Sonja's groceries, it's time to go blow up the City of Eternal Night and make some Gedren Gumbo. You probly think you saw all this already at the end of *Conan the Destroyer,* and you probly did, but here it is again.

Two breasts. Seven quarts blood. Seventy dead bodies. One Viking funeral. One plastic mechanical alligator attack. Three beasts. One giant pet tarantula. Gratuitous belly dancing. Kung fu. Midget fu. Lava lamp fu. One head rolls. Two heads fly. One head squishes. Academy Award nominations for Arnold saying "Your thither's dying" and "I know you're brave girl but danger is my trade" and three other words; and Brigitte Nielsen, who can almost speak English, for saying "You slaughtered my parents! Like cattle! My brother! My sister!" and, of course, for Dino the De Laurentiis Man, the one and only Italian drive-in king, for saying "Arnold, you go-a fix-a movie. Okay?"

Three stars. Joe Bob says check it out. ∎

Intergalactic Love Pouches
Discovered in *Lifeforce*

Before I tell you about the android zombie breath-sucking space cadets in *Lifeforce,* I thought I'd mention the android zombie space cadets in the 1985 Miss Texas Pageant, which was one of our finest ever, even though we didn't have a single ventriloquist this year, unless you count the defending champeen, Tamara Hext, who lip-sinked all her songs like a kung fu movie. Nice job, Tam, but watch those Mary Kay products, how bout it? I had to put a sunscreen on my TV to cut down on the glare.

I don't know if you noticed, but Yankees are starting to sneak into the Miss Texas Pageant, which used to be one of the finest meat markets in the country for unemployed flute players and the Future Lounge Lizards of America. One year 76 *percent* of the Miss Texas losers immediately got jobs singing "Happy Days Are Here Again" at the Marriott-Ramada level on down to the Motel Five. (A Motel Five is a Motel Six without showers.) Another 15 percent were able to buy parts in neighborhood musicals like *Oklahoma!* and force their families to listen. Most contestants go on to long careers on the space shuttle, but even the losers normally find a rich guy to buy em an apartment where they can hide from his wife. In other words, these girls work hard, they do it all for you, and in the end it pays off in endorsements for used automotive products.

But now we got some Yankees coming down here from Boise or wherever they grow em, and the Yankees are getting up on stage and saying stuff like "My ambition is to be a computer analyst in the medical services field."

This will not do.

I'm sorry, I don't like to lay down rules like this, but let's get back to the basics here. Whatever happened to "I believe we can *be what we want to be, and I'm gonna reach out and grab me that star and hang on tight.*"

You see what I'm talkin about here? That's a Miss Texas ambition.

Or how bout this one (one of my personal favorites):

"Like the song says, Whoops! there goes another rubber tree plant!"

This year it was easy to tell the *real* Texans from the fakers. Like the Argentina bolo trick-roper—definitely Miss Texas material. Like Miss Plano, the one that sang opera while she was dressed up like a mechanical toy doll—great stuff. Like the girl who started doing deaf-mute hand language in the middle of her routine. And, of course, Miss Greenville, the winner after about 27 previous tries, who finally got her fiddle tuned up and did classical music *and* mountain music without mussing her bouffant.

The rest of you girls go on back to Chicago and try out your punk-rock medleys on somebody else.

Speaking of mummified people that look like aliens, *Lifeforce* is a drive-in classic. But the best thing about it is— TOBE IS BACK!

Tobe Hooper, the man who made drive-in history in 1974 with *Texas Chainsaw Massacre.* Tobe, the man who went on to *Sell Out* to teensy-weensy screen indoor bullstuff, even though *Salem's Lot* was one of the best versions of Stephen King ever made. Then Tobe goes *totally* wimparooney on us and makes *Poltergeist* where all he does is hang around the set and go "Steve! Hey, Steve! Somebody tell Spielberg I need him! Steve! Stevie boy! Is it okay to move the camera six inches?" After that humiliation, I was sure the guy was finished. But what does the man do?

Electric-lip space vampires. Some of the best ones I ever seen.

What happens here is Steve Railsback and some astronauts go up in outer space to look at Halley's Comet, but when they get up there they find three nekkid fashion models floating in frozen-dinner trays, and there's one named Mathilda May that's got intergalactic love pouches hanging off her. So Steve goes totally berserk and starts making the sign of the two-humped antelope inside Mathilda's see-through space coffin, and pretty soon everbody on the spaceship starts dying of outer-space lung cancer and turning into pieces of dried-up beef jerky. Everbody except Steve, who bails out and lands in Texas.

Next thing you know, some dimwits in London go up there and bring the spaceship back home with the three nekkid space vampires in body bags, only once they get down to Earth Mathilda starts flashing her hooters and kissing old men with her electrified mouth and deep-throating em to death. When she gets finished with you, you generally look like a half-smoked Tiparillo for exactly two hours, then you come back to life and look for somebody to suck the breath out of and turn *them* into a Tiparillo, and that lasts for two more hours, and then you do some more sucking, and well, you can see the implications here. This goes on for a half dozen exploding

bodies, with the British guys standing around going "Collect the pieces of those bodies and *watch them*!" Then the space vampires go prancing off into London and communicating with Steve Railsback in ESP and turning the whole world into rioting throat-sucking vampires. Fortunately, about the only place where they consider "sterilization by thermonuclear device" is London, and by then Mathilda's possessing the bodies of insane-asylum doctors and making all the pictures spin around in their frames and starting indoor hurricanes like in *Poltergeist*. Then somebody figures out there's only one way to kill these guys, and that's by takin a five-foot-long sword coated in lead and plunging it into their body—*not* in the heart, which is the way they kill vampires *in*

Communist Alert!

"Texas prison officials seized the artificial leg of Ronald Danford, serving 10 years for car theft, after allegedly finding he used it to hide marijuana. The leg was dismantled and confiscated when the prisoner, returning from a furlough, tried to sneak an ounce of marijuana into the Ramsey Unit. The bag was tucked inside a hollow part of the artificial leg at the knee joint. The leg will remain in custody as evidence." I ask you, how many more times does this have to happen before we pass the Artificial Limb Privacy Law? Remember, without eternal vigilance, it can happen here.

the movies, but two inches *below* the heart, in the "energy center." That thing about directly in the heart is just a myth.

Too bad, though, cause by now Steve Railsback is falling in love with Mathilda, and they're threatening to suck each other to death. But meanwhile a giant outer-space umbrella comes down from another galaxy and parks over London and starts sucking up dead souls from Westminster Abbey, destroying the British tourism in-dustry. The only guy who can save the world is Peter Firth. (All together now: "WHO?") Cause Peter has a sword and he knows what to do with it.

Sixteen breasts. Twenty-four dead bodies. Seventeen quarts blood. Fifty-seven beasts. Three gratuitous vampire attacks. Kung fu. Lip fu. Great scene where all London is full of frothing zombies. Instant beef-jerky manufac-turing. Electro-lips. Arm rolls. Hand rolls. Exploding actors. Four stars.

Joe Bob says check it out. ■

Wondering Where the Stuckey's Have Gone

Why is it you can't ever find a Stuckey's when you need one? I think some of the states been puttin in laws, you can't have a Stuckey's inside the city limits or else all the local de-partment stores would get run out of binness. But think about it. How many times has it happened to you? It's three in the a.m. You can't get to sleep. You're sitting up in bed, thinkin to yourself, "You know what I need right now? I need a Backseat Driver's Li-cense."

Sorry. You're out of luck. You'd have to drive 40 miles down the inter-state before you found a Stuckey's, and that's the ONLY place you can get Backseat Driver's Licenses.

I was thinking about this just last week when I took the Toronado down off blocks, fired it up, started out for Cleveland, and then had to stop and put out the fire. The first Stuckey's I stopped at, I spent 40 bucks just load-ing up on stuff I'll need for the rest of the year, and I still didn't find every-thing. They were already out of Texas Flyswatters, and they wouldn't let me order one from the plant. I asked em if they'd wrap up about 40 or 50 of their Heart Attack Burgers and freeze em so I'd have enough to last the winter, but they said they weren't set up for that kind of service and, besides, I could get the recipe at any industrial grease pit.

But I did manage to do a little early Christmas shopping, pick up a few gifts for my close personal friends up in Cleveburg. (I'm not counting the snow scenes with little alligators playing rugby inside. I always get a couple dozen of those for the kids.)

Like this year they had a new item called Fudge Smudge, which comes in a tin can and is *so soft* you can smear it all over a Ritz Cracker and still have some left over for breakfast. If you're going for the brittle, though, I would highly recommend the Mr. Peanut Vac-uum Gumbo Pack, which includes six different flavors that will stick to your teeth for at least 45 days and actually *fight decay* while wrapped around your molars like wax Halloween fangs.

They also had some new non-smoker ashtrays in the shape of Rhode Island, a shirt that said "Kiss Me, I'm Stupid" (what will they think of next?), quite a few icebox magnets with little poodles on em, and an official "Road Hog" coloring book. The only thing I couldn't find was a *Police Woman* highway litter bag, the one where Angie goes undercover as a hooker, so if anybody out there finds one (I hear they have em up on the Interstate 40 Stuckey's), get one for me and bill me the full 60 cents. I preciate it.

Speaking of fuzz busters, *Police Academy II* came out a long time ago and I didn't review it, but that's cause I've sorta been one lazy jerk this summer and I figured what the hey, ever week I get fired somewhere anyhow. But I decided I'm gonna be a lot more responsible from now on, except when I forget.

Basically what we got here is a bunch of fruitcakes running around saying "What would Baretta do in a case like this?" No plot to get in the way of the story. Steve Guttenberg is back from *Police Academy Numero Uno,* but he don't do much except go around arresting elementary school students and trying to find the evil gang painting the town brown and stealing all the paint they need to do it.

Four breasts. Tear-gas attack. Pooting. Gratuitous Buffy from *Family Affair.* Three motor vehicle chases (with beach buggy). Emergency tracheotomy. Exploding car. Nookie. Kung fu. Graffiti fu. Body-cavity search. Boiling goldfish. Drive-In Academy Award nominations for Bobcat Goldthwait, the bad guy, for saying "Don't make me flare my nostrils!"; Howard Hesseman, the captain, for saying "They are SCUM out there"; Peter Van Norden, as Vinnie, Chubb Fricke Lookalike of the Year, for consuming a side of beef on-camera; Colleen Camp, for disguising her chest as a Buckminster Fuller science project; and Bubba Smith, for going into a gay leather bar and making a fruit salad, if you know what I mean and I think you do.

It's no *Police Academy I,* but, oh, I guess two and a half. Check it out. ∎

Nyuk-nyuk-nyuk

Last week, when I was reading *Not Just a Stooge* by Joe Besser for the 14th time, I finally realized one of the facts of life: We can't *all* grow up to be one of the Three Stooges. Specially since there aren't any Three Stooges left except for Joe Besser and Joe De Rita, and they were both *fake* Three Stooges. Joe Besser, he *wanted* to be a Three Stooge, he *tried* to be a Three Stooge, but he couldn't nyuk-nyuk worth diddly. Joe De Rita, he had a "woo-woo" that was worse than Shemp trying to do a sideways arm-twist can-opener spastic attack. No, Curly Howard died in '52, and people wonder what's wrong with this country today.

But then I had another thought. Just because the young people of

America can't grow up to be one of the Three Stooges anymore, that don't mean we can't all be *like* the Three Stooges. Maybe we can't do everything at once. Maybe we can't snap our fingers on our fist like Moe did. Maybe we can't deliver the roundhouse haymaker sledgehammer fist to the skull on the very first try. Maybe we can't poke our best friend's eyes out with our fingers. But there's some things we all *can* do.

We can all grab our little brother around his neck and grab our little sister around her neck and ram the tops of their skulls together like cymbals in the marching bands. Anybody can do that.

We can all pour airplane glue on dad's chair before he sits down at the table, and then *die laughing* when he stands up and rams the back of the chair through his lower back.

We can all pull each other's teeth out for fun.

When you think about all the Three Stooges antics you can do in the privacy of your own home, you have to stop a minute and say, *"Hey! Moe! Try this on for size!"*

Just think what a happy country this would be if people got up every morning and said, "How would the Stooges do it if they were alive today?" Then every time you saw a fat lady on the street, you'd probably go right up to her, step on the hemline of her dress, unravel it, hose her down, and then stick her finger in an electrical socket. *Look at that hair!* Just like Larry's. Ha! Ha!

Or maybe, just maybe, you'd get up in the morning, grab your Bulgarian turban, put on some Coke-bottle glasses that make you blind, have your best friend frizz out his hair and stand up against the wall, throw some knives at him, and scream out "Maha!" 40

times before breakfast. People just don't have *fun* anymore.

Speaking of humane mental-health treatment, *Hellhole* came out this summer and nobody noticed. This one is by the same people that made *Concrete Jungle,* best bimbos-in-chains of '83, and *Chained Heat,* best bimbos-in-chains of '84. Those other flicks were about women being thrown into prison, where they were tortured, abused, mutilated, forced to take off their clothes ever five minutes, and stoked up with cheap drugs. *Hellhole* is nothing like that. This time it's about women being thrown into an *insane asylum* where they're tortured, abused, mutilated, forced to take off their clothes ever five minutes, and stoked up with *expensive* drugs.

It starts out with Judy Landers running through the streets with Ray Sharkey chasing her and almost catching her before the credits are over, but she gets away by falling off a girder, cracking her skull open on the pavement, and acting like she's dead. I've tried this several times myself down on Commerce Street on Friday night and I can verify that it usually works. Only problem is, they bandage her up and stick her in the loony-bimbo bin and have a bunch of whitecoats come see her and tell her how she's a schizophrenic paranoid amnesiac—either that or else she cracked her skull open on the pavement.

Then Ray Sharkey finds out Judy's alive, and so he dresses up like an orderly and sneaks in and starts helping out Nazi warden Mary Woronov, star of *Eating Raoul,* with a little chemical lobotomy experiment. At first it don't work, though; all it does is make Judy's hair look like used lettuce. So they have to call up Marjoe Gortner and ask him to come into the movie and start talking about how he used to be famous. Pretty soon Judy gets afraid Mary Woronov might start lobotomizing her some more and afraid Marjoe might start evangelizing her, and she jumps up and starts running through the basement like Mannix. Pretty soon we got lobotomized zombified loonies busting out of their cells all over the lot, like a casting call for *Love Boat*.

Sixteen breasts. Fourteen dead bodies. Two pints blood. Two beasts (orderlies with lambchop sideburns, saying stuff like "Hey, let's make a sandwich"). Nekkid lesbo wrestling.

One lesbo mudbath. One zombie attack. Glad Bag sniffing. Gratuitous hot-tub scene necessary to the plot. Two lobotomies. Ax in back. Glass in neck. Kung fu. Marjoe fu. Loony fu. Hypodermic fu. Drive-In Academy Award nominations for Judy Landers, for getting strapped down a lot; Mary Woronov, for saying "Listen! The loonies are singing!" Marjoe Gortner, for breathing; and Pierre de Moro, the director, for asking the question "How many times can I get away with this?"

Three stars. Joe Bob says check it out. ■

Fright Night: Cleveland

I guess it was about three months ago when my life changed forever. The big boys at the *Hee-Haw* network come out to the trailer house and they said, "Joe Bob, you could have a career. Joe Bob, you're funny. Joe Bob, you're an entertainer. Joe Bob, it smells terrible in here." And I guess that's the day the magic started.

I really didn't have anything to do with it myself. I said, "Well, okay, *maybe* if about 17 million of my fans demand that I take my show on the road, I *might* agree to take their money, but I don't want anything out of it personally."

So I guess it was maybe two, three weeks after that, the big boys come back to me and they laid it on the line. They said there was only three places in America where I could hold the world premiere of *An Evening With Joe Bob Briggs:*

Radio City Music Hall
The Rose Bowl

Or the High School Auditorium in Berea, Ohio.

Tell me honestly now, what would you of done? There was no doubt in my mind. I cranked up the Toronado, drove 1,500 miles through the heart of hostile Yankeeland, and rolled into suburban Cleveland at 3 in the a.m. It was something I waited all my life for. Cleveburg. The city where it all started. The city that invented the word "sleaze." The city where I left my heart and two of my toes. The city where everybody practices unemployment as a way of life. And, you know, the song is so true:

I wanna WAKE UP in the city that never works . . .

Where I'll be A Number One—king of the JERKS.

Like Chubb Fricke said to me one time, "Joe Bob, if your mind was a city, it'd be Cleveland." I'll never forget it.

Anyhow, the whole experience reminds me of the time Jackie Vernon was getting his start in show business, and everbody said, "The man'll never make it; he only knows five jokes." But you can see what Jackie is today, and he did it his way. He *still* only knows five jokes. Or Jan Murray. Same deal. They said he'd never make it *just because four or five of his audiences went to sleep.* But all the big comedians started out that way. Bill Dana, he *invented* "My name José Jimenez" years before he ever got credit for it. He had to say it 93,000 times before he got his *first* laugh. Not many people know that.

Anyhow, the audience was great. We laughed together, we cried together, we sang together. We all exchanged home phone numbers. I performed "We Are the Weird" for the first time since my assassination. I did "The Dirt Mine Blues" with all the fine musicians of the Joe Bob Briggs Orchestra. Both of them. And in the second hour of my act, I reminisced about the first hour of my act, the time when I had to pay my dues in this dog-eat-dog world of ours called show binness.

I thought the audience would never stop calling for encores. I had to do my drive-in hit song, "You Said You Were a Virgin, But Your Baby Ain't Named Jesus." I performed the entire talent competition from the 1985 Miss Texas Pageant, *including* the bolo-tie twirling. I did my impression of Madonna gettin mangled in a blender. The audience shouted "Joe Bob! Joe Bob! Joe Bob!" The audience yelled "Bravo!" The audience clapped its little heart out. And then, all too soon, the show was over. The guy had to leave.

Course, later on that night, I was the taste of the town. Several of my biggest fans took me down to the Cuyahoga River and showed me Cleveland at night. Someday we'll probly find their bodies.

It was something I'll always remember, the night when the whole world sat up, took notice, and said, "What?"

On the way back home, I stopped off in Tennessee at Twitty City, where Conway Twitty lives with his lovely wife and seven beautiful hair transplants, and Conway wanted to go to the drive-in and so I said, "Okay, but only if you take all the born-again Babtist cassette tapes out of your El Dorado," and Conway said okay and so we hauled it out I-65 to see *Fright Night,* which I thought Conway would like cause Roddy McDowall used to be a big star, too.

Fright Night has some of the best face-eating flying vulture-bat special effects I've seen. It's about a recent escapee from the Richard Gere Charm School who moves to the suburbs, sucks the blood out of prostitutes ever night, and starts sleeping all day long in a coffin in his basement. If the guy had just moved to Marin County, he could of got away with this, but instead he goes to this little town where a kid named Charley lives next door. When Charley notices people are getting their heads chopped off and their bodies stuffed in Hefty bags ever night, he starts to suspect something. But then, when he sees that the guy in the house wears sweaters exactly like George Hamilton, he *knows* he's a vampire. Then we get a lot of plot about how his friends don't believe him, the cops don't believe him, and his dingbat girlfriend Amy says, "Charley, is this some kind of trick to get me back?" And then one night the vampire comes over to visit at Charley's house, and while he's there he goes upstairs and starts bustin up the furniture, but before he can kill Charley, he gets a No. 3 Faber pencil through the hand and that makes him turn into a werewolf on-camera. (How many times do I have to tell you people? Always use a No. 2. I will no longer accept or grade vampires that are executed with No. 3s.)

Next thing, Charley goes and gets the nerd star of *Fraternity Vacation* to help him kill the vampire, only they can't do it without Roddy McDowall, who's a retired drive-in horror star that knows about wooden stakes and holy water and gold crosses and all the other garbage you need to turn Kendoll vampires into Alpo. And I guess that's about when the slime starts to fly.

Two breasts. Eight dead bodies. Eight gallons blood. Five slime-spewing vampires. Four transformation scenes, including wolf-dog, gooberhead melting-man, flying-lizard, and flaming-bat. Two heads roll (off camera). Hearts roll. Electric fingernails. Hefty fu. Pencil fu. Gratuitous Stu-debaker. Vampire flashdancing. Disco riot. Drive-In Academy Award nominations for Chris Sarandon, the Vidal Sassoon vampire, doing his best creature since he was Al Pacino's boyfriend in *Dog Day Afternoon;* Roddy, the original planet-of-the-apeman, for excellent stake-driving; William Ragsdale, the kid vampire-killer, the finest actor in El Dorado, Ark.; Amanda Bearse, for the scene where she frugs with the vampire and turns into a frothing bimbo with fangs; Stephen Geoffreys, for agreeing to take a supporting-vampire role after starring in *Fraternity Vacation;* and Tom Holland, the drive-in genius who wrote *The Beast Within, Class of 1984,* and *Psycho II,* who scores again.

This flick is in a league with *Nightmare on Elm Street* and goes straight to No. 2 on the Best of '85 List. Four stars. Joe Bob says check it out twice. ∎

Tina Turner in *Mad Max:* Almost as Scary as Aunt Bovina

Ever year my Great Aunt Bovina Briggs in Meridian, Miss., sends out a humongous Christmas letter to all 794 members of the Briggs family to tell us what ailments, deadly diseases, and divorces we all had during the past 12 months. Unfortunately, Aunt Bovina slipped last October and broke up most of her lower body into microscopic pieces, so she's just now gettin out the Christmas letter for 1984. Mine showed up in the mail last week, and I thought yall would wanna hear some of it, cause you're nosy.

Dear Briggsians,

Well, isn't Life Wonderful?!?! I'm off the old Artificial Life-Support Equipment, which was costing me $50 a day because my insurance company Refused to pay for a spare Battery Pack and so I'll have to sue them later, and the doctor says it'll be no time until I can sit up permanently and move around on a skateboard device. It's Wonderful what modern medicine can do these days.

Many of you remember my nephew, little Randy Kerbow, who lost his Face in Vietnam, and you'll be happy to know that little Randy was at my same hospital over in Jackson. I stopped by his room on my way out and said, "Hello, Randy, I'm already leaving but you're still here. Isn't it Wonderful how much more they know about Medicine since the time when they stuck You in here?" Randy didn't say anything, but I'm sure he sends everybody his Love.

Mavis Fetlock, who never should of married Jimmy Fetlock in 1942 cause he was just after her money, got a lovely new trailer home in Riverside Calif., where she still bottles her marvelous farkleberry preserves. Don't need any this year, Mavis!

Sarina Briggs' unmarried son, Purvis, decided not to get his Master's Degree at Columbia after all and so he's in Kentucky putting on a lecture and musical show about an Indian fellow named Sant Kraskavedis who can do all sorts of tricks! Purvis wrote me a letter in Indian about World Peace. He always was a Talented boy!

As most of you know by now, Arthur and Velda Scruggs bought some lakefront property up in north Arkansas, and so far they're not telling anybody how much it Cost!

Speaking of lovebirds, Stu Wilks and his second wife, Nadine, celebrated their fifth anniversary at their beautiful home in Mobile and decided to let Stu's boy out of military school if he'll stop playing that silly game with his stepmother's car. Boys will be Boys!

Of course, our big news this year was my favorite cousin Joe Bob Briggs, the Writer in the family, who is doing so well at the Dallas newspaper that the Editor went on network TV and talked about him! Joe Bob moved from Rockwall to Grapevine, Texas, this year because he was getting so famous, but he'll always just be little ole Joe Bob to us. Joe Bob says when he goes on Johnny Carson he'll say hi to Ed

and Doc for all of us! He said we should send him $20 each if we want him to say something. Ha Ha! That boy sure is funny! You can see why Joe Bob is living so high on the Hog! Don't get the big head, you rascal you! Really, Joe Bob, I want Doc's autograph.

I just wanted the world to know that there's still *some people* that know how to put out a newspaper.

Speaking of nuclear mutant families, *Mad Max Beyond Thunderdome* hit the drive-ins last week, and I gotta admit, I wasn't expecting much. Mel Gibson's been off making so much indoor bullstuff I didn't know if he could come back and get low-down dirty and do another *Road Warrior* and start kickboxing with the punk-rock mohawk army again. But sometimes people'll surprise you, and after just ten minutes of the flick, Mel Gibson is *already* swimming around in pig manure, trying to pick a fight with this Championship Wrestling reject that has greased deltoids like Arnold the Barbarian but took a few too many iron claws without wearing proper headgear, and so now he has to wear a midget on his back so he'll know what he's killing. Anyhow, Tina Turner is the mean dragon-lady queen of the world, and she's so evil she looks like she's going into a property-settlement meeting with Ike, and she tells Mad Max he either fights this trained Rhinoceros Man or else. And he says "Or else what?" And she says or else I sing "Rollin on the River" at 78 rpm. Max says he'll fight.

So then Mad Max and the Rhino Man go into a giant birdcage and put on clown suspenders and try to pole each other in the privates and ram lances through each other's throats to show who's more macho, and Mad Max pretty much gets the royal bejabbers beat out of him, except he has a secret dog whistle that he can blow and turn the Rhino Man into a blither-ing Jimmy Carter speechwriter. But Tina is hacked cause Mad Max *refuses* to kill the Rhino Man, and so what ends up happening is they go play *Wheel of Fortune* and the wheel says Mel Gibson has to put on a paper Mickey Mouse head and sit backwards on a camel until the camel dies and dumps him in a sand dune in the Sa-hara Desert.

But Mad Max's life is saved by a pig-manure shoveler who sends out some homing monkeys to take water to him, and then some mud-face kids and their whining bimbo mamas come find his worthless body and say, "Hey, you need a haircut," and clean him up and work some Bugs Bunny voodoo on him until he wakes up and then they do a punk-rock musical comedy show for him, and it ends up where Max has to slap a few of the women around cause they won't stay home where they be-long. But after a while Max says, okay, I'll follow everbody out into the Sahara Desert again and go back to the pig-manure town and bust some heads and

maybe they'll give us their midget to keep as a pet. So all those mud-face little jerks follow him back to Tina's place, and pretty soon we got a motor vehicle chase that's basically between a Mack Truck on railroad tracks, Mad Max in his zebra Camaro, and about 70 jillion Harley dune buggies with rocket thrusters on the back. We're talkin some Choo Choo fu.

Two breasts. Forty-five beasts, au-ditioning for Empty-V. Two gallons blood. Fourteen dead bodies. Gra-tuitous malfunctioning chain saw. Gra-tuitous game-show host. Midget dipping. Pig stampede. Three motor vehicle chases. Drive-In Academy Award nominations for Tina Turner, for doing it *rough;* Frank Thring, the Chubb Fricke Memorial Award for having a 78-inch neck and sitting around like a Buddha, saying stuff like "He can kill most people with his breath"; Angelo Rossitoo, best per-formance by a midget this year; and, of course, Mel Gibson, the Max-Man, for getting back to his roots.

To the Max. Four stars. Joe Bob says check it out. ∎

Zombies in Spam Cannisters

Return of the Living Dead is the greatest face-eating gut-spewer since *Basket Case* and deserves se-rious consideration as one of the finest zombie exploding-head comedies of all time. What we got here is a bunch of corpses that the U.S. Army decides to stick in pressurized Spam cannisters, perfectly preserving them like giant Starkist Tunas on Quaaludes. But a bunch of guys in the mailroom get the cadavers confused with some C-Ra-

tions and ship the human Spam spec-imens off to a medical supply warehouse in Louisville, Kentucky. Before you know it, the cannisters spring a leak, and what've we got? If you've ever been to Louisville, Ken-tucky, on a Saturday night, you *know* what we got—brain-eating zombies walking around downtown going "You got 20 cents for a blood transfusion?"

Course, soon as one of these zom-bies gets out of the can, it's all over for the two Rhodes scholars that found him. Here's the best part of it, though. First they try to kill the zombie with a pickax through the head—don't bother him. Then they *saw off* his head. No way, José Feliciano. He just keeps on talkin and twitchin. Then they start choppin him up into little pieces and sticking parts of him in Hefty bags, but what they end up with is a bunch of Hefty bags that hop around like Meskin jumpin beans. Pretty soon they go across the street and talk the funeral parlor into burning the Hefty bags in the crematory, but all that does is shoot a bunch of zombie gas out the top of the building and turn some punk rockers into nekkid heavy-metal foaming-at-the-mouth contestants on *Star Search*.

The bottom line here is: Everybody gets *real* sick, specially when the zombies start eating their brains.. Zombie-Rama.

Ten breasts. Two zombie breasts. One hundred twenty-five zombies. Body count 19 (plus fragments). Mummy dogs. One-half zombie dog. Ten gallons blood. Brain-eating. Gratuitous embalming. Nekkid punk-rocker fondue. Gratuitous midget zombie. Torso S&M. One motor vehicle chase (totaled by zombies). Heads roll. Brains roll. Arms roll. Hands roll. Drive-In Academy Award nominations for Linnea Quigley, for takin off all her clothes in the graveyard, flashdancing like Jennifer Beals on crystal, and saying "Do you ever fantasize about *horrible* ways of dying?" Don Calfa, as Ernie the mortician, for getting attacked by an arm; and Dan O'Bannon, the writer and director, the same guy that wrote *Alien*.

We're talking four stars. Joe Bob says check it out. ■

A Yuppie *Godzilla* for the '80s

Football just won't be the same this year, ever since the NC double-A came down here and arrested the entire team at SMU and said they can't have no more scholarships until 1997 and they have to give back all the money contributed to their daily Malt-O-Meal allowances. They claim we had those boys on salary, but all in the world we were doin was given em a little spare change for chores. Like Cleophus Starling, our split end—they made such a *big deal* out of him getting 280 bucks a day for being in charge of the pledge of allegiance, but I happen to know Cleophus worked all summer long just *learning* the pledge of alle-

giance and so he earned ever penny.

Or how about that "unnamed alumnus" who contributed $27,000 in unmarked bills to the Mustang Booster Club? I happen to know what that money was for; it's right there in the official budget: 747 tackling sleds, purchased 4/27/85 from David McDavid Pontiac, $27,000.

Then there was all the unfounded allegations they made about the Mulettes. The Mulettes are members of the "elite drill squad" who get up early in the morning and sometimes stay up all night long practicing their elite drills for recruiting purposes. And now that's all gone. The Mulettes got banned by the NC double-A, after they spent the whole year drilling their little hearts out. It's the kind of thing that makes you wonder where the *priorities* are. Whatever happened to getting an education in college?

But, of course, the biggest allegation was the one they made about Immanual "Goatman" Jones. That's the one that hurts the most, because the Goatman is such a sensitive guy, he can't handle all the publicity. All Goatman ever wanted to do was play football. For the past two years he's been our defensive line. And now this happens and who knows what it'll do to the rest of little Immanuel's life?

I know what they said. They said the Goatman's been takin 800 bucks a month under the table for the last three years. They said he's been taking it down to the 7-Eleven ever month and turning it into money orders and concealing said money orders in his worn-out athletic supporters. (A lot of people thought this part of the story was a little farfetched, but actually Goatman *does* go through two, three athletic supporters a day.)

But you know what didn't come out in the newspapers? You know what those know-it-alls didn't find out? You know what the Goatman was *doing* with all that money?

He was saving it up so his 62-year-old arthritic mama in Charleston, West Virginia, could buy a new face.

Okay, okay, so maybe Manny bent the rules a little bit. Maybe he squirreled away a few tamales in his jock-strap. But I think this world is a pretty sorry place if we can't understand a beautiful human action when one comes along. We might as well pack it in if we can't accept, one time in our life, a touching story of incredible human stupidity. I'm sorry, that's the way I feel.

* * *

Speaking of people that look like giant Mexican lizards, they just brought out a new *Godzilla* and, I'm telling you, the G-Man never looked better. What happens is Zilla's been out in the ocean ever since '74, when he splashed out to make *Godzilla vs. the Bionic Monster,* and he's finally runnin out of nuclear Kool-Aid, so he raises up and breathes on a ship and turns four Japanese guys into Gumby skeletons and forces the radio man to wrestle with a giant rubber crab. So pretty quick, Prime Minister Toenail figures out Godzilla's back, and he decides to keep it a secret for a while so they won't have mass panic in the streets of Tokyo and have to hire a bunch of extras at two bucks a day. But then that doesn't work cause Godzilla eats a Russian nuclear submarine and gets high on the juice and starts shooting his breath at people.

That Godzilla! What a guy! Pretty soon he's about to start World War III cause the Commonist Russians decide to nuke Tokyo, but Toenail calls the Pentagon and tells them to nuke the Russian nuke before everbody gets nuked, and so what happens is, while they're up in the sky playing nukie with each other, Godzilla eats a nuclear reactor and now he's like a junkie with 400 bucks in his pocket. He starts giving it these grins, and his eyes start to roll around like Milton Berle, and pretty soon you know what's coming—it's time to do the Tokyo Stomp.

While the G-Man is out there turning little Japanese guys into sushi, we got time for plot. So the Pentagon sends out for Raymond Burr and has him come down to the office and stand around staring at the camera, going "Godzilla—he's looking for something—he's confused—he's searching." In other words, Ray identifies with the guy. This is all Ray does the rest of the movie.

JOE BOB'S MAILBAG

DEAR MR. BRIGGS: We read your article today, "New Commandments for a Better America," in the Oakland Press. It leaves some questions in our minds. Why is it acceptable for a journalist such as yourself to malign Christians. To do so to other peoples (blacks, feminists, homosexuals, humanists, etc.) would be unacceptable, and considered chauvinistic, prejudiced, unenlightened, and unpluralistic. What is it about Christianity that you feel the need to attack it, even in the name of humor? Are you trying to convince yourself that there is no truth in it?

As you have probably suspected, we are Christians. And without knowing anything about you except your article today, we suspect that you are missing the forest for the trees—you are rejecting the Christ of the Bible based on the few things you know about Christians today. Please take the time to find out first hand about Jesus Christ from the Bible. And please have patience with we Christians. The reason we became Christians is because we admitted that we aren't perfect. But we're trying to reach our goal of perfection—to be like Christ.
JON AND KAREN WIANT
ROCHESTER HILLS, MICH.

DEAR FELLOW BAPTISTS: I don't have nothing against the J-Man. In fact, if you reach your goal of being like him, we won't need Christians anymore. We can have Wiantians.

One thing I figured out is, the Big Guy can take care of His Ownself.

DEAR JOE BOB: I want to marry u. I am 14, have red hair, blue eyes, and weigh 108. I'm into heavy metal, an I like your style. Love always.
YOUR TRUE LOVE, JENNY
OAKLAND, CALIF.

DEAR JENNY: Sorry, you're two pounds overweight. They have laws about that kind of thing, you know.

DEAR JOE BOB: I got this friend, "Houston" John McWaid, and he says they still shoot off 10,000 bottle rockets over La Porte, Texas, every 4th of July.

A couple of summers ago, "Houston" John, "Thumper" Thornton, and Ole Winescott did there righteous deed in the name of Texas and Miss Lily. Word has it that the townspeople got up in arms, and began putting on their anti-Rusky protection suits and arming themselves with Lone Star beer and bibles.

Does this still go on in La Porte? Are you going to be grand marshall at next year's Rose Parade in Pasadena . . . (that's Pasadena, Texas) Are you going up in space? Where's Amarillo Ed?
J. LAMBRIGHT
SAN FRANCISCO

DEAR J: Yes.

Next thing, they put Godzilla's brain on computer and figure out he likes bird whistles, and so they set up a satellite earth station that beams these mockingbird sounds to his brain so they can do the humane thing and lure him into a volcano. In case that don't work, they have a Super-X nuclear jet missile-launcher ready to blow his brains out. Meanwhile, Godzilla is disrupting rush hour, breathing on traffic copters, pukin up cruise missiles, and getting drunk all over again when the two missiles explode over Tokyo, turning the sky into a Leroy Neiman painting.

Two breasts (both Godzilla's). Two beasts (including Raymond Burr). Two quarts blood. Forty-eight dead bodies.

One motor vehicle crash. Kung fu. Lizard fu. Gratuitous power-drill mutilation. Four nuclear explosions. Helicopter-eating. Giant rubber-crab wrestling. Drive-In Academy Award nomination for Raymond Burr, for saying "You know, Nature has a way of reminding man just how puny we are, whether it tells us in the form of a tornado, an earthquake, or a Godzilla."

It's no *Godzilla on Monster Island,* but it's worth three stars. Joe Bob says check it out. ■

On Jerry Lewis & Frankenstein

I don't normally talk about it, but the last four years I been involved in a very special fund-raising effort with a bunch of very special people in a very special place. I don't even take any personal credit for it. It's very special to me. It's hundreds, even thousands of people just like me, who come together every Labor Day for one very special purpose. Together we believe we can create a miracle.

By now you know what I'm talkin about. I'm talking about a special show. I'm talkin about the annual Joe Bob Briggs Drive-In-Thon, the place where thousands of children bring their nickels and their dimes, their toys and their crutches and their Big Wheels, and we put em all in a big pile and auction em off so that one day, somehow, with enough research and dedication, and if God is willing, Jerry Lewis's career will walk again.

Sometimes it would be easy to get discouraged—like four years ago when Jerry had a relapse and made *Hardly Working.* Thank God the fund had enough money to send Jerry to France for a year, so all the critics could tell him what a comedy genius he was. By the time he got back, he was our nutty nutty guy again, but sadly, the rehabilitation process had taken away his ability to dance with a broom, to talk with his upper teeth biting into his lower chin, or to do the Spastic Stomp. He's been in more or less constant therapy ever since, and even *that* has side effects. One day the doctor went into Jerry's room—this story just breaks my heart—and he said, "Sing me a song, Jer, you know, a ballad," and so Jerry started in on "What the World Needs Now," snappin his fingers like Mel Torme on heroin, and Jerry actually started *carrying the melody.*

The doctor was terrified. We all were. We changed his medication, put Jerry back on life support, and gave him some funny glasses to wear. That helped a little bit, at least till we could get Stella Stevens to run into the room wearing a cashmere sweater two sizes too small, pin Jerry against the wall, and plant 30 lipstick marks all over his face. It was touch-and-go there for a while, but finally Jerry looked up at us and said, "Gee, you guys, Kamurmurmerdlewinny." Then we gave Jerry a 300-pound dumbbell to carry up and down the hallway, balancing it on his chest, and pretty soon he was happy again.

You know, our biggest enemy in a fight like this is sometimes the mind itself. Ever once in a while Jerry will try to give up on us completely and start saying things that make sense, and we'll have to remind him that he's one of the greatest comedians, actors, directors, and humanitarians the world has ever known, and so if he doesn't straighten up we're gonna force him to have *another* reunion with Dean Martin. As soon as we say that, Jerry jumps, raises his legs, and *leaps* into the arms of the nearest available six-foot-six supporting character. That's why we teach all our staff how to perform DPR—Dino Paralysis Resuscitation. Because, remember—a Jerry is a terrible thing to waste.

Speaking of having your brain fried, there's this new flick called *The Bride* based on *The Bride of Frankenstein,* with Sting as Dr. Frankenstein, only don't worry because they made him promise not to wear those diapers he had on in *Dune* and to keep his chest covered at all times. Anyhow, Sting is messing around in his haunted mansion with some gauze bandages, dead bodies, and giant electric microwaves, and this huge lightning storm comes along and shorts out his laboratory and produces something so hideous, so frightening, so utterly beyond what the mind can imagine that you can hardly bear to watch him unwrap it from its mummy cocoon. It stirs to life, it begins to move, it blinks—

It's Jennifer Beals, threatening to flashdance again.

I know what you're probly thinking. You're thinking everbody takes one look at her and runs away screamin in terror. Nope. Sting's been to enough punk-rock concerts, he knows what to expect. But the Frankenstein *monster* goes runnin away in terror, knocking over chemicals, setting everthing on fire, burning up the soundstage, and pretty soon he's off in Budapest, lost in a subplot with David Rappaport, who we all know is the finest midget actor working today. (Dave is a past winner of the "Best Midget" Drive-In Academy Award for his performance in *Time Bandits.*)

While the midget and the monster are off doing a circus act, Sting is trying to teach Jennifer Beals how to eat, drink, ride a horse, talk, and flashdance without a stunt double. She keeps saying "Who am I?" "What am I?" "Where am I?" and "Is my career starting yet?" And then, pretty soon, it's time for the biggie—monster sex. But Jennifer can't handle it, cause Viktor, the monster she was made for, is off in Budapest learning about life from a midget and so she has to wait another hour or so till the plot can get him all the way back into the movie. By that time she's almost lost her virginity twice, the midget's been murdered, and Viktor wants to burn down the set again.

Excellent monster fu. Four breasts, but I'm gonna count em as eight, cause they're these humongous fat-lady circus breasts that are the biggest breasts in the history of breasts. One gallon blood. Two beasts. One head rolls. Midget trapeze. Gratuitous Geraldine Page. Monster hangover. Crypt. Boneyard. Haunted mansion. Stake through heart. Four dead bodies. Drive-In Academy Award nominations for Sting, Jennifer, Dave, and Clancy Brown, who might be my favorite Frankenstein monster ever. Four stars.

Joe Bob says check it out. ∎

Those Nutty Ninjas Are Back

Normally the Dallas High Sheriffs don't allow protesters inside the city limits, cause after the demonstration instead of leavin town they go over to the Dobbs House and pick fights with the waitresses and somebody ends up havin to go in there and clean all the Patty Melts up off the styrene seat covers. But last week they made an exception, and we had *four* demonstrations in one day:

Numero Uno: My two Babtist buddies, Jerry Falwell and Donnie Wildmon, brought about 10,000 born-again wimps to town to march on the world headquarters of 7-Eleven and try to get em to stop sellin *Playboy* and *Penthouse.*

Numero Two-o: A bunch of liberal atheists showed up at the same protest to tell Jerry Falwell he was the scum of the earth for going to South Africa and havin barbeque with white people. There were about 2,000 of these foreign-affairs experts walkin around with cards that said "STOP VIOLENCE! KILL FALWELL!" They also wanted to get out of their apartments and buy a house, so everbody called em the "anti-apartment" people.

Numero Three-o: Members of the homosexual persuasion showed up and started complaining about the judges in Norleans that said the Texas "sodomy" law is legal. For those of you that don't know what sodomy is, it means making a left turn without a car.

Numero Four-o: Me and Rhett Beavers went down there to try to get 7-Eleven to start carrying *Hustler, Oui,* and *Melons Monthly.*

I wanna tell you, I *tried* to do all I could. We had all these perverts screamin at one another, using up valuable TV videotape while all the reporters' haircuts were withering in the heat, and so I suggested a compromise. What we needed was a negotiator acceptable to all sides. We needed to go find us a born-again black lesbian Playmate of the Month to come in and sort things out, and I volunteered to go recruit one.

Unfortunately, it turned out there's only one born-again black lesbian Playmate of the Month in history, Ms. Zelda Swanson, and she was tied up at a tent meeting in Withers, Georgia. She would of been happy to do it, but the owners of the tent refused to untie her.

So I stepped in instead and tried to restore order. The first thing I did, I tried to get Jerry Falwell to kiss and make up with the gay guys, by saying "Hey, Jerry, try it, you might like it, this is the '80s, man," and Jerry basically said that I should take my eternal soul and stock it in Dr. Gene Scott's saxophone and ask him to play "Rock of Ages," the jazz version. So I went over to one of the anti-apartment people and I said, "You know, nobody ever has anything *good* to say about repressive murdering dictatorships. If you people would just lighten up a little bit and try to see that the world is made up of all kinds of people and . . ." And that's about all I said before seven big guys started air-conditioning my wardrobe for me. And so I looked at all these sodomy guys standing there, and I thought what the heck, and so I said, "Okay, listen, you guys *gotta* listen to me. What do you guys want in life, after all? A few Judy Garland records, some sushi bars, a few of those cocktails with little umbrellas on top. But you're always making such a *big deal* out of these Sodom and Gomorrah laws we got here. Couldn't you just take *some* of that poodle-stitching off your shirts?"

It's too bad you can't say in a fambly newspaper what those guys did to me, but all I got to say is, "It's a pretty sick country we got here when nobody is willing to compromise anymore."

Speaking of people that like to put on pajamas and bend their bodies into pretzels, *American Ninja* is the best kung fu face-ripper since *Revenge of the Ninja,* mainly because it was made by the masters. You know, a lot of times people from *non*oriental cultures try to work in kung fu and, course, they always fall flat on their schnozzolas. But this one was written and directed by those three Japanese geniuses: Avi Kleinberger, Gideon Amir, and Sam Firstenberg. And, of course, it was produced, as usual, by those two avid students of oriental martial arts, Menahem Golan and Yoram Globus. These are the five guys who *originated* the ancient Chinese battle cry, "Next year in Hong Kong!"

What we got here is an Army private named Joe who gets amnesia and so he can't remember how he got to be the greatest kung fu Ninja master in the world. All he knows is, every time his supply-truck convoy is attacked by 30 or 40 black Ninja masters, he just goes berserk and turns into the Mr. Goodwrench of martial arts and starts throwing deadly tire tools. But it gets Joe into trouble, cause who likes *such a showoff*? Also, there's a mean French guy named Mr. Ortega who wears pink ties and mumbles a lot about Joe, but nobody can understand him cause the soundman put the mike in his navel, but Mr. Ortega owns his own super-Ninja master, and he tells the super-Ninja master to kill Joe so they can sell a laser-missile to the Mafia. Basically that's your plot, but I want you to check these numbers:

Body count 121, a new modern record. Eight kung fu scenes, four in pajamas. One gallon blood. Four motor vehicle chases. Exploding car. Exploding motorcycle. Two exploding trucks. Four exploding jeeps. Exploding ship. Exploding copter. Exploding Ninja. Trash-can fu. Watermelon fu. Mr. Goodwrench fu. Drive-In Academy Award nominations for Michael Dudikoff, as G.I. Joe, for saying "There's so much I remember, but there's also so much I don't"; Guich Koock, the former owner of Luckenbach, Texas, as the evil Colonel, nominated for being named Guich Koock; Judie Aronson, as the gratuitous bimbo, for saying "What do you think I am, a jungle baby?"; Tadashi Yamashita, as the evil Ninja, for correctly pronouncing all four words of his dialogue; and, of course, Sam Firstenberg, the world's greatest martial arts director, for saying "Excuse me! Excuse me! Could we have a little more dynamite over there, please?"

Four stars. Joe Bob says check it out. ■

Chainsaw Collectors' Column

Today's lesson is on *Saw*. And I'm tellin you scumheads, I'm doing this for the *last* time. Ever year the same thing happens. They re-release *The Texas Chainsaw Massacre,* and you guys expect me to take time out from serious drive-in reviewing to go *rehash* all the *Saw* trivia. So I'm gonna put all your questions in one place, and I want you to *clip this sucker out* and save it for next year. I don't wanna have to tell you again.

Okay, here goes.

Numero uno: Did the story of Chainsaw *really happen?*

Whenever I get asked this, I don't even hardly wanna dignify it with a response. *Of course* it happened. There's two movies based on the same real-life event—*Psycho* and *Saw*—but *Psycho* gets all the publicity. Actually, *Saw* is a whole lot closer to the true story of Edward Gein, a handyman in Plainfield, Wisconsin, that liked to dig up fresh graves, cut the skin off corpses, wear it on various parts of his own body, and dance in the moonlight. When the guys in white suits finally got him in 1957, they said he'd been collecting body parts for years—had skulls on the bedposts, a human heart in a saucepan, and a lady out in his barn dressed like a deer. Eddie died last year in the Central State Hospital for the Criminally Insane, where he was making rock jewelry.

Numero Two-o: When Tobe Hooper made Saw, *why did he locate it in Texas?*

Tobe was livin in Austin, but he really didn't care where it was located. They only made it Texas when somebody come up with the title, which,

you got to admit, is one of the all-time greatest titles in the history of the universe. It was shot in Round Rock, Texas, for about 40 cents.

Numero Three-o: Where was Saw *first shown to the public?*

Empire Theatre, San Francisco, fall of '74. They sneaked it on the back end of a Walter Matthau picture, and the audience barfed, stormed the lobby, demanded their money back, and started throwin punches. A legend was born.

Numero Four-o: Is it true Saw *has been banned more than any other movie in history?*

Naw, not really. *Deep Throat* has been sued a lot more times. But the difference with *Saw* is, it's the first *R-rated* flick ever to get 11 continuous years of flack. When the National Organization of Bimbos or the Babtist Church wants to get on my case, they always say, *"This guy is so sick he LIKES movies like* Texas Chainsaw Massacre.*"* They use it like some kind of put-down, like they never saw it. Or maybe I should say, they never got sawed by it.

Numero Five-o: Is it true Leatherface—"Mr. Chainsaw"—never worked again?

That's right. Gunnar Hansen, the actor that played Leatherface, moved up to Maine to write poetry and build rock houses. I'm not makin this up.

Numero Six-o: Is it true that the director had trouble gettin work after Saw?

Sort of. Tobe Hopper was just a boy from Austin that liked movies, and *Saw* was his first crack at it. After that he made *Eaten Alive,* also known as

Horror Hotel Massacre, where Neville Brand runs a little swamp motel where he feeds the overnight guests to the alligators. Then Tobe made *Salem's Lot* for TV, and that was pretty decent. Then Spielberg let him make *Poltergeist,* but nobody could figure out whether Tobe was doing it or the Spielman. And then this year Tobe got back on track with his new masterpiece, *Lifeforce,* about nekkid outer-space bloodsuckers.

Numero Seven-o: Where did Sally, the only survivor in the movie, learn to scream like that?

Marilyn Burns, "The Screamer," is truly acknowledged to be the finest motion-picture screamer known to mankind—far better than Jamie Lee Curtis and other imitators. But it might be because she had so much to scream about. When they were makin this picture, it was 110 degrees inside the Cannibal House, and all the meat on the

table was dead rotting animals filled with formaldehyde. The smell, plus all the sticky blood they poured on Marilyn, plus she got dragged around through the underbrush for a couple weeks and busted up both knees, and you start figurin those were real screams.

Numero Eight-o: Is it true Saw *is one of the most successful films in history?*

Yep. Nobody knows exactly how much, but it's probly made $100 million at the box office. The reason we don't know is that the sleazoid distributors ran off with all the money for the first 10 years. The actors just started getting checks last year, and they were puny.

Numero Nine-o: Is it true there's gonna be a Texas Chainsaw Massacre II?

Unfortunately, yes. What happened was, Tobe Hooper sold himself for about the next five years to the Cannon Film Co., which you probly remember as the guys that do all the *Death Wishes* and the Chuck Bronsons and the Ninja flicks. And part of the deal is, if Tobe wants to make his other two flicks, he's got to make *Chainsaw II.* So it's gonna happen. Probly won't have the original actors, though. Leatherface already carved em up. I'm sendin a letter off to Marilyn Burns, though, to see if she'd agree to scream a little bit more for us.

Numero Ten-o: A lot of slasher movies are based on Saw, *like* Friday the 13th *and* Halloween, *and don't you think they're gettin a lot more scary with all the special blood effects they have now?*

Nope. No way, José. You take somebody to see *Saw* that hasn't ever seen it before, and you'll know what I mean when I say:

Saw is still the king. Joe Bob says, *at least* once a year, check it out. ∎

Communist Alert!

The cops went out to the Trail Drive-In in Alvarado, Texas, and hauled off the manager, Pat Auler, and made her pay 200 bucks for "explicit sexual display." But they said they couldn't remember what flick was showing that night, and so I guess they're accusing Pat her ownself of publicly displaying her explicits. I'm getting sick and tired of these lies about the drive-in that used to be the Chisholm Trail D.I., but when they put in X-rated, they decided to call it just "The Trail." I can identify with a name like that. Remember, without eternal vigilance, it can happen here.

Frisky in 'Frisco

I got real suspicious when everbody in San Francisco started being *nice* to me. The National Organization of Bimbos didn't show up for the nude mud-wrestling match. Nobody came over from Berkeley to forcibly adjust my values. Things picked up a little bit when I went on a radio show and this guy called in to say I was a sick slimeball racist, but then I scored a 62 percent in the 800-number popularity poll. About the only time I really got scared was when this bimbo with 11 rolls of nickels stuffed down her bra ran up on the stage and threatened to unleash her atomic duffel bags on me. It only took two black-belt nightclub bodyguards to wrestle her to the ground. We bagged her up and sold her to a guy that wanted to do some medical experiments. In other words, I couldn't get arrested in San Francisco. But let me tell you just how *weird* that city's got lately:

I sang four of my country-western songs and nobody puked.

I don't know what I expected. Maybe I wanted somebody to threaten to sing some Peter, Paul, and Mary medleys in public. Maybe I wanted somebody to force me to look at the comb Tony Bennett uses ever morning. Maybe I wanted some guy to come up to me wearing a dress and say, "Hey, grope my grapes." I don't know what I expected, but I knew it would be Weird.

Instead, all I got was tours.

"Joe Bob, come take a tour of Midgettown." That was pretty interesting, had some great wet noodle dinners down there.

"Joe Bob, come ride on a cable car." It probly saved the city a million dollars when they asked me to do that, cause I informed several city officials that they invented the *bus* now and so they don't have to run those streetcars any more.

"Joe Bob, put on a funny hat and come be on TV and say 'fu' a lot." I guess I had to give out 35, 40 interviews while I was there, but the worst one was this *Entertainment Tonight* deal where they attacked me with one of those *P.M. Magazine* hostess ladies and her idea of a question was "Do you like making people mad at you?" Evidently they didn't use my answer, which was "Only airheads on TV."

"Joe Bob, come out to my drive-in." But the drive-in scene was pretty miserable in San Fran. Total Communist victory inside the city limits: zero drive-ins. But I did find this fairly decent one called the Island Auto Drive, built on a landfill next door to the Navy base in Alameda. Some *really* nasty girls hanging out there, and would the one with the tattoo please send her phone number again, cause when the mustard dried up I couldn't read it.

"Joe Bob, come look at Carol Doda." Now *that* was somethin I could preciate. This is the lady that *claims* to be the first topless dancer in the Newnited States, startin in 1960, and she's definitely the one with the most durable breasts in history, cause she's still up there wiggling her Pop Tarts after 25 years. Carol Doda has the only breasts listed on the National Register of Historic Places. I personally interviewed both of them while I was in town, and I can verify that they are beautifully restored. You know, in this day and age, when so many breasts are being torn down and destroyed in the name of "progress," it's great to see a city that protects its "golden gates" like that.

I'm sorry, I hate to break the news to San Francisco, but you people only registered a measly six on the Maniac Meter. I might give you another chance next year, but frankly, I've met more lunatics in Baton Rouge, Louisiana.

Speaking of stuff that don't make sense, they made a sequel to *Hercules* starring Big Lou Ferrigno again, but Sybil Danning's not in this one cause she gave Lou a hard time on the first flick. In case you haven't noticed *Hercules II* yet, it's cause so far they only got four drive-ins in America to agree to put it up on the screen. It's one of those "special" pictures, and they don't wanna spring it on us all at once.

It's a pretty decent sequel, mainly cause the first 15 minutes is footage from the first flick. Remember the scene where Lou wrestles the rubber alligator and the sequence where he slays the giant electric katydid? They look *exactly* the same when you see em in Part 2. It's pretty incredible. But here's the new twist in this one:

They dubbed Lou's voice!

Are you believing it? We don't get to listen to Lou anymore when he says "My dethtiny ith writhen in the sthars." Now Lou goes around talkin like the Queen of England, saying "thou" and "whither" and even "thither." It's really confusing, if you think about it, cause all through the flick you think Lou's got a sister and all it is, he's going *thither*. Course, we've got all the usual Herc-man action: manacle-whirling, stuffed-animal wrestling, gratuitous laser-beam zapping. But I don't know, it's just not the same without Lou's *voice*.

Absolutely no plot to get in the way

JOE BOB'S MAILBAG

DEAR JOE-BOB: Do you really read these or does some girl you have to pay do it for you and then gives you the ones that might interest you a bit? If so, I hope you see this, but I wish the girl wouldn't see it before you, because it is personal.

Are you married? Are you an Aquarian? If so, I would love to have your dog, I mean baby, perhaps a puppy. I am a Leo. So I could boss you around and keep up to date on more movies than you with my hands tied behind my neck, and my legs handcuffed to the doorknobs. Get the picture? Good luck with your wife. My divorce is final the 23rd of October. Yours in lust,
KIMBERLY DAVIS
SAN FRANCISCO

DEAR KIMBERLY: Do you really expect me to let Joe Bob himself see this letter?

DEAR MR. BOB: I wanted to thank you for filling me in on the film *Fright Night*—it makes such a nice change from reading dull bishop's registers, which is what I do. But I want to ask you, what is a Drive-Inn? We went all the way past Suchtermuchty, into Edinburgh and couldn't find anyone to tell us (if indeed they knew) so we're still a wee bit confused.

My wife wants to know if you are married. There are some nice lasses over here who would make you a fine wife. Keep in touch,
MR. SEYMOUR
ST. JOHN'S HOUSE
UNIVERSITY OF ST. ANDREWS
CENTRE FOR ADVANCED HISTORICAL
    STUDIES
FIFE, SCOTLAND

DEAR MR. S: A drive-in is this secret place we go to in America to make fun of Scottish people.

of the story. Four breasts. Seventeen dead bodies. One gallon blood. Four beasts. Virgin sacrifice. Maybe-a-virgin sacrifice. Giant shag rug attack. Attack of the Slime People. Amazons dressed up like Al Jolson. Lou transformed into underwater sperm cell. Giant crawdaddy. Darth Vader lookalike. Head rolls. Kung fu. Thunderbolt fu. Abdominal Snowman fu. Lou fu.

Drive-In Academy Award nominations for Pamela Pratt, Queen of the Amazons, for sleeping with a guy named Garth, zapping him into outer space, then hangin him up by his ankles to dry; and Big Lou, for saying "I kill now."

Two stars. Joe Bob says check it out if you can. ■

Real Men Eat Egg Fu Yung

Me and Rhett Beavers and Wanda Bodine all jumped in the Toronado and went to Texarkana last week to check out the "Gateway to Texas" Rest Stop where the Texas Legislature is trying to kick out all the sissy boys. In case you hadn't heard about it, what happened is this place got a four-star rating in a national travel guide for homosexuals, and ever since then the horse manure's been hittin the fan up there.

"We just don't want that activity around here," said Alex Short Jr., the legislature guy up there in Texarkana. "Some of them out there are holding hands, and it's something foreign to East Texas. Now what they're doing as far as holding hands and hugging is not illegal activity. But it just makes sense if that sucker got four stars that there's more going on out there than just holding hands." Alex is getting the state to spend thousands of dollars building fences and clearing away underbrush so the little homos won't have anywhere to hold more than each other's hands.

So we decided to check it out. One precaution I did take is I made Wanda Bodine put on some Mary Kay Cosmetics and a dress and then I handcuffed her to me so it'd be obvious we have a normal hetero-nookie relationship, as the Lord intended.

So anyhow we got there about 4:30 in the afternoon, and the first thing we did is we sent Rhett to get a picnic table and I went on inside the Tourist Bureau and went up to the state trooper and said, real casual, "I'd like to know where I can go around here to sniff some bluebonnets and do some crocheting in the nude."

I figured the guy would take me for a sissyboy and eject me from the premises right off, but instead he said, "I just *love* the flamingos on your blouse."

Right then I knew we were in trouble. No telling how many individuals of the homosexual persuasion walk into the "Gateway to Texas" Rest Stop ever day and request *illegal* tourist information. I want you to know I stayed there until I got the full story, and I was *shocked* and *appalled*. Here's just a *few* of the things I found out:

1. You can get a tourist brochure called "Sheep Do It: A Guide to the 'Special' Dude Ranches of Southwest Texas."

2. They have something at the rest stop called a "Pet Path." I'm sorry, this is too disgusting for me.

3. You can go in the back room and see a six-minute audio-visual presentation about the State Fair of Texas, called "Big Tex: How He Got To Be So Big."

4. They have a naturalist on call, who will give group lectures about the mating habits of the mule.

5. If you know what to ask for, the state trooper will reach down behind the counter and sell you some bubblegum cards that have pictures of all the members of the Texas Legislature wearing bolo ties and penny loafers. Phone numbers are extra. And you know what it said on one of em? "Meet me behind the rose bush and I'll show you my gladiola."

These politicians got to be *stopped*.

Ever since *Year of the Dragon* came out, the Chinamen up in New York been rioting and hittin each other over the head with wet noodles and markin up the prices on pu-pu trays. I have no idea why they're so p.o.ed. Probly has something to do with them being short and wearing stupid hats all their lives. But anyhow, the flick is a pretty decent documentary on what happens when you let the Orientals run hogwild selling heroin to each other. Sooner or later, the inevitable is gonna happen: *Innocent tourists will be killed*.

What we got here is a bunch of 16-year-old kids with machine guns running around Chinatown, shootin up restaurants, until Mickey Rourke gets so sick of it that he starts sleeping with a Chinese fashion model TV reporter. This makes the Chinese Mafia so mad that they stuff two Chinese gang members in a soybean vat, kill Mickey's wife, rape his fashion model, shoot his

partner, wreck some cars, and go to Thailand to cut the head off of a sensitive, caring individual named White Powder Ma. But when they're not busy with all that stuff, they just sit around and mumble stuff in Chinese subtitles, like "We brought the orange to this country, we brought the grape, we built

---

Communist Alert!

"KUNG FU FAN KILLED IN MOVIE THEATRE KARATE ATTACK" according to the *New York Post*. "A Manhattan man used karate chops in a deadly attack on an elderly man while the two were watching a Kung Fu movie in a Times Square theater. Robert Smalls, 45, was seized by theater security guards minutes after he bloodied the unidentified victim with a barrage of karate chops and punches. The bizarre incident created an uproar in the Apollo Theater at 233 W. 42d St., where dozens of moviegoers were watching *The Last Dragon,* a film about violent Chinatown gangs. 'It's entirely possible that the sheer ferocity of the attack scared him to death,' one investigator said. Witnesses told police the dispute between Smalls and the other man erupted after Smalls put his feet up on the seat in front of him, blocking the way to the aisle." I don't know how many times I have to remind you people—either go to the drive-in where it's safe or else *carry your nunchucks with you to the movie.* Otherwise, when will all this senseless slaughter stop? Remember, without eternal vigilance, it can happen here.

your irrigation systems, but most of our ancestors were sent back home because we were *coolies.*" You know, gangster talk.

Then ever once in a while Mickey Rourke busts into the police commissioner's office and starts yelling "It's just like Nam! It's just like Nam!" and grabs his head and tells him what an honest cop should do—buy a machine gun and go huntin for Chinese. Eventually he does this, but not before he freaks out three or four times with Vietnam flashbacks, screams at his Chinese fashion model TV reporter about how TV is a "vampire," and tells Michael Cimino he needs another closeup.

Oh yeah, I almost forgot, this is Big Mike Cimino's first movie since *Heaven's Gate.* Mike is the only guy makin drive-in movies that cost $40 million. But he proved he still has the stuff. He can make a movie *almost* as good as *Heaven's Gate* for only 14 mill. He's also responsible for *discovering* Ariane, the Chinese fashion model TV reporter who changes her expression two, three times in the movie, specially when Mickey is slapping her around and talking about his Polish heritage.

Six breasts. Four gallons blood. Twenty-five dead bodies. Bullet in forehead. Knife in heart. Miniskirted bimbos with automatic weapons. Head rolls. Restaurant brawl. Gambling den brawl. Three motor vehicle chases, with three crash-and-burns. Soybean fu. Egg Fu Yung. Drive-In Academy Award nominations for Mickey Rourke, for saying "F—- civil rights!"; Ariane, for opening her eyes long enough to scream "The press is independent! Not just another undercover cop!"; Dino DeLaurentiis, for saying "No, no, my little Cimino, okay, I geev money"; and Big Mike, for saying "Please, Dino, can I just build *one* full-scale replica of Chinatown? It won't cost much, and I promise I'll never ask for anything ever again."

Two and a half stars. Joe Bob says check it out. ■

Joebobneesh Briggs Will Save You All

You know, it's been two, three weeks now since that magic night in San Francisco, when so many people came to the Lord, dedicated their lives to the drive-in, marched down to the stage and prayed with me, and since that night many of them have enrolled in the "Jingle-Bob Jesus Christmas Fund," where you gradually gain enough casino chips for the remission of sins. Pretty soon we'll have enough money to buy me a saxophone, and then the actual Cable TV Self-Salvation Course can begin.

Course, most of you that dedicated your lives that night are just at the very first level of awareness right now, but pretty soon you'll be mailin in those nickels and dimes and frequent-flyer coupons and, before you know it, I'll be healin you. Then, and only then, can you move your permanent residence to the Joebobneesh trailer park and retirement community in Grapevine,

Texas, and start having sex with anything that moves.

Today I wanna go over a few of the things we learned that night, just to see if you're still following The Path or if you ran off and hid in the concession stand behind the artificial butter machine. Here are the Three First Principles:

1. Always open an Oreo cookie by pulling gently *with both hands* on the chocolate crust.

2. Never go home with anybody that knows the punk-rock request line number by heart.

3. Eat red meat.

I know many of you have already incorporated these principles into your daily lives and are ready for Pyramid Training. This is where we uncover the ancient mysteries of the Egyptian tombs by wrappin you up in mummy rags and letting you play pin-the-tail-on-the-donkey with a two-by-four with nails in it and a live donkey. The disciples that survive this part of the training will be ready to go on to Marlboro Aerobics, where you are trained to consume two packs of nonfilter 100s in one single daily *20-minute* workout. I know you may be thinking, "I would *never* have the breath for that." But you'd be surprised how quickly we can get you up to Liquid Lung Level.

Most of our spiritual novices have one question on their minds: "When do we get nekkid and slither around on our stomachs like homosexual gophers?"

This is a good question. I'm glad it came up at this point. The answer is that you can't participate in the Joebobneesh sexual cookies unless you have first answered the following Middle Eastern riddle:

"A kangaroo goes into a bar, sits down next to a drunk with a weasel on his head, bartender comes over and asks the kangaroo what he's drinking.

Kangaroo looks at the drunk again, says double daiquiri with a weasel twist. Bartender says we're out of weasel, kangaroo says how'd that drunk get one on his head. *And the drunk says . . .*"

If you know what the drunk says, you may qualify for Level 3 of Joebobneesh Self-Salvation Training, which requires enrollment at Raleigh Hills Hospital for the Very Drunk. Please send in your answers to Bhagwan Briggs, P.O. Box 2002, Dallas 75221, and I'll let you know whether you're accepted into the program. In the meantime, remember: Don't touch a toilet seat unless you're qualified.

* * *

JOE BOB'S MAILBAG

DEAR JOE BOB: I saw your show at Wolfgang's in S.F. on Sept 19 (11 PM) and it was truly *superb* except for the single-celled moron in the audience who kept yelling "I Love You Joe Bob" and who also tried to yell *his* phone number at you. Didn't see any garbonzas though.

I was also surprised at the number of minorities at the show, they must be confused about their respective persuasions. Lose the guy who opened your act for you, (the cracker from New Orleans) your audience deserves nothing less than the genuine article. When are you cutting your first album?

But did you see the *S.F. Chronicle*'s reviewer Steve Rubinstein? ["Joe Bob 'Live' Is a Pussycat"] Are you going to respond to this scandal? Have no fear, he'll be whistling a new tune out of a different orifice after the "posse" takes care of his wanton "editorializing." Thanks,
S.P. FERGUSON
SUNNYVALE, CALIF.

DEAR S.P.: You're probly talkin about the paragraph where Steve said my singin voice is like a castrated bullfrog. Actually, it was the best review I ever got. I'm usin it in all my ads now.

DEAR JOE BOB: I was tremendously flattered to be invited to spend an evening with you—too bad you had to go and invite 199 others—I don't go for that kinky menage-a-many stuff.

I got to tell you this, Joe Bob. Your singing is BAD! Man, you really aught to watch more Empty-V. You poor-white trash ain't got no soul. You got to get DOWN! Well, at least you hit the notes. Jill Bell says: stay home, don't go to the drive-in this weekend, and listen to Bessie Smith, Prince, or Benny Hill. I'm SURE you could come up with some really raunchy, excitable lyrics!

But Joe Bob Briggs a vegetarian? [She's talkin about my tribute to Johnny Cash, "The Ballad of the Death Row Vegetarian."] Come on now! Of course an ex-hippy, ex-California Girl like me is a vegie. But Joe Bob? He should be lamenting the loss of his steak for breakfast, lunch, and dinner, or Bar-B-Q and beer. And besides, Joe Bob needs them calories and cholesterol or how's he ever going to get one of those 9th-month-and-ready-to-deliver guts? Loved the duds—real sharp dresser. Always great and in form is your movie review *(Rambo)*. I loved your Baptist revelations—Joe Bob was definitely born to the ministry. And I was especially glad to hear you got initiated into feminism. If you ever need any further instruction, I've spent alot of time studying all about it.
With love,
Your poison-pen pal
JILL BELL
DALLAS

DEAR JILL: Wait'll you hear me sing "Feelins" at my next show. Really. It's great. You can't tell the difference between me and the original 1975 Morris Albert version.

This week's flick is based on actual Russian secret documents showing exactly how the Communists expect to take us over. I'm talking, of course, about *Invasion U.S.A.*, the one where the Ruskies land thousands of troops on Miami Beach, fan out through the Florida suburbs, leveling snake farms and flamingo ashtray shops ever which way you look, and eventually invade downtown Atlanta. If you've *seen* downtown Atlanta lately, you know why the Russians want it. It looks exactly like downtown Vladivostok.

Anyhow, the only thing out there that can stop the Russians is Chuck Norris and about 14 million rounds of wadcutter semi-automatic sawed-off machine-gun fire. Big Chuck don't just *star* in this baby. He *wrote* it. Of course, it takes a while for Chuck to get mad enough to strap on his supersonic "Gator Aid" burp guns. First the Russians dress up like the Coast Guard and machine-gun about 35 Cuban boat people so they can steal their cocaine. Then Rostov, a Russian agent that looks like Klaus Kinski after a three-day drunk, kung fus a drug smuggler, sticks a gun down the guy's pants, and pulls the trigger four times. Ouch! Those crazy Russians! You see the beauty here? These are *smart* Russians. They make the drug smugglers p.o.ed, the Cubans p.o.ed, the blacks p.o.ed. They blow up a few churches, a few elementary schools, a few handicapped kids' buses. Pretty soon you don't have to do nothing, you got Americans killing each other left and right. You got your riots. You got your civil unrest. You got your National Guard on the streets.

But Chuck, he don't wanna fight. The CIA keeps going out to his shack in the Everglades, saying, "Chuck, come on, man, you got to save the country," but Chuck, he's too busy catching alligators with his bare hands and playing with his pet armadillo and chainsawing logs and riding around on an airboat with his shirt off. But what finally does it is the Russians form an Airboat Armada, burn down his house, kill his buddy, and they *don't even pay for the airboats*. Finally Chuck can't take it anymore and it's Range Rover Fu.

Chuck will stop at nothing to get these Ruskies in their cheap Chevy vans and Mack truck cabs. One thing he has to do is bust his four-wheel-drive vehicle into a shopping mall and wreck fourteen department stores in one of the greatest car-chase, crash-and-burn, death-and-destruction, exploding-glass sequences ever filmed. The Russians all jump into a Nissan wimp-truck (of course), and grab a bimbo hostage in a pink jogging suit and hang her out the window by her hair, so Chuck has to steal a Mustang convertible, chase em down the highway, and *avoid* the dangling jogger when he tosses a grenade into the cab and waits for the Russian agents to turn into Caviar Helper.

Pretty soon Chuck is chasing Rostov all up and down Interstate 95, blowing up 20 guys here, 30 there, till finally he lures the Russians to downtown Atlanta by telling em "Hey, you guys ever heard of Underground Atlanta? It's great—saloons, discos, video arcades. No, *don't worry* about the crime thing. It's all cleaned up now.

Really. It's safe. There's ten, fifteen people down there ever night. You're gonna *love it*." The Russians can't resist a party, so pretty soon they steal ever Brink's Truck in the South and what we got is Revolving Restaurant Fu.

One hundred eighty-five bodies, a new modern record. No breasts. Four gallons blood. Alligator wrassling. Three motor vehicle chases, with eleven crashes. Nine exploding houses. Eight exploding cars, Three exploding trucks. One exploding chopper. One exploding Cuban dancehall (nice music). Seven exploding Russians. Finest invasion of Miami Beach ever filmed. Gratuitous bimbo reporter. Gratuitous Phyllis Diller. One dead Sony Trinitron. One dead Magnavox 21-inch console. (The Russians have no respect for TV.) Gazebos roll twice. Bimbo through window. Russian talk. Kung fu. Mall fu. Airboat fu. Bazooka fu. Knife through the hand three times fu. The Russians shoot up a modular office building and don't clean up their mess. Drive-In Academy Award nominations for Big Chuck, for saying "It's time to die"; for Richard Lynch, as Rostov the Ruskie; and Joseph Zito, the master, the drive-in director who did both *Friday the 13th Part 4, The Final Chapter* and *Missing in Action Numero Uno* and *Two-o*. Four stars.

Joe Bob says check it out. ■

Mellowing Out After Texas-OU

Excuse me if this don't make sense, but last week was the time of year when the entire state of Oklahoma comes down to Dallas to throw up on Neiman-Marcus and paint their teeth red and say stuff like, "I'll have one of them Vaseline cocktails." I went out to the Cotton Bowl and sat in the Oklahoma section, and when they won the dang football game 14–7 and started slapping each other upside the head to celebrate, I had to hire a chiropractor to pop my eyeballs back in their sockets. These people don't say "Let's party." They say "Let's go make like scrawny polar bears that just won a Publishers Clearing House trip to Acapulco." That night we had to bring out the Texas National Guard just to tell this one guy that you can't carry 47 rum-and-Cokes on the front seat of your car unless they're for personal use. Then we had to call out the U.S. National Guard when he proved they were for personal use.

I don't know, maybe I'm getting old, maybe I can't party like a jungle animal anymore, but there was something about Texas-Oklahoma Weekend that got to me this year. Maybe it was wakin up and finding out I was missing part of my left elbow. Maybe it was the nine bullet holes I found on the right rear fender of my Toronado. Maybe it's just my imagination, but it seems like there weren't as many armored personnel carriers on the streets this year.

Anyhow, when I woke on Sunday morning I was missing three years of my life. I remember up to about age nine, when my virginity was forcibly taken from me, and then it starts up again at age 12 when I got my first

parole. But in between there—nothing. It was probly some terrible trauma in my childhood that was triggered out of my memory last week when I was attacked by a Ponca City elementary school teacher who was performing the multiplication tables with her legs down on Commerce Street. It wasn't really her fault, I don't blame her, but when she did nine times twelve a lot of the guys at Sol's Turf Bar had to go change their shirts.

What I'm trying to say is, I'm checking it in on Texas-OU Weekend. A man has his limits. It gets to where you have to draw the line. I don't mind the usual stuff, like a little harmless live-rat swallowing or the traditional Sewage Run. But these folks from Oklahoma are a little too wild for me. I had my doubts the year they started celebrating Sadie Hawkins' "Transvestite-Choice" Day, but now these people are getting downright kinky.

I knew Arnold had it in him. I knew, after he made *Terminator,* it was only a matter of time till he made the ultimate *Rambo* ripoff. Arnold the Barbarian has the kind of deltoids Sly Stallone can only drool over and then say, "Oh, sorry, would you like me to wipe that wad of spit off your extremely muscular self, your Sirship?" We're talking *Commando,* where Arnold gets a burr haircut, rubs some dirt on his face, steals a shoulder-mounted rocket-launcher, 18 machine guns and 34,000 rounds of ammo, and kills a Meskin Army.

First we have a bunch of plot about how Arnold used to be a commando spy, only now the evil President

Poncho is killing all Arnold's men by posing as garbagemen and then waiting for em to haul their Hefty Bags out to the street, or by running em down with Cadillacs *on the showroom floor.* Meanwhile, Arnold is just minding his own binness, living out in the woods, chopping down sequoias with a Black-and-Decker and carrying the trees on his shoulder back to the house, so his 11-year-old simp daughter can play horsey with him.

Pretty soon, though, President Poncho grabs the daughter, machine-guns a few Marines, and tells Arnold if he don't go down to Guateragua and kill President José for him, then "I will mail your daughter to you in pieces." Arnold tells him this is a violation of U.S. postal laws, jumps off the plane that's flying him to Nicamala, and figures he's got 11 hours before they find out and turn his daughter into ballerina salad.

So what does Arnold do? He picks up a stewardess and steals her Porsche and tells her she has to help him. Pretty soon they're zipping into the Galleria, where Arnold kung-fus 37 security guards, and they go to a motel and ram a coffee-table leg through a Green Beret, and then Arnold gets bored and so they have to go down to the Army surplus store and ram a bull-dozer through the front of it and steal some assault rifles and foot flippers. Finally, they jump in a seaplane to fly out to a secret island and kill six or seven hundred people so Arnold can settle his differences in a civilized manner with a gay heavy-metal soldier of fortune that likes to wear bracelets and say things like "I will just love to kill you."

We're talking serious body count: 92. (Okay, okay, it's not *Invasion U.S.A.,* but they're *quality* agonizing deaths.) Two breasts. Two gallons blood. Three motor vehicle chases. Six car crashes, including four crash-and-burns. Fifteen exploding buildings. Two exploding jeeps. Exploding boat. Five gratuitous farm-implement deaths. Knives thrown into 17 different body parts. Arm rolls. Kung fu. Ca-dillac fu. Shopping mall fu. Bulldozer fu. Coffee table fu. Drive-In Academy Award nominations for Arnold the Bar-barian, for the scene where he picks up a phone booth, gives the occupant some directory assistance, chases him up a mountain, dangles him over a cliff by one leg, and goes "Whoops!"; Rae Dawn Chong, as the gratuitous stewar-dess; Vernon Wells, as a gay-leather-bar Marine; and Mark Lester, Mr. *Class of 1984* himself, for directing this sucker.

Four stars. Joe Bob says check it out. ■

JOE BOB'S
MAILBAG

JOE BOB: Thought you might like to know that, despite heavy flak from feminists and Communist censors, *you* are being taught at one of the nation's leading universities. (Mostly we just lead our students around by the nose):

"Comparative Literature IB, Section 10 (TTH 2–2:30), From Obsession to Art (Joe Bob Goes to College); The pen is mightier than the sword, but has it succumbed to the chainsaw? Are Tobe Hooper, John Carpenter, and Brian de Palma the legitimate offspring of Seneca, Ovid, and Shakespeare? If Shakespeare were alive today, would he be writing scripts for America's only indigenous theater—the Drive-In? These questions, though facetious, contain a challenge: can we define the difference between *Medea, Titus Andronicus,* and the latest slasher flick?"

Keep up the good work.
ERIC RUTLEDGE
DEPARTMENT OF COMPARATIVE
  LITERATURE
UNIVERSITY OF CALIFORNIA, BERKELEY

DEAR PROFESSOR ERIC: Harken! Methinks yonder breast ripens into plenty. Thither runs a bloody river, ebbing from his dangling head. Behold! Midterm Fu.

DEAR JOE BOB: After months of whispers in the Hollywood rumor mill, the sad truth was brutally exposed last Thursday night in, wouldn't you know, San Francisco: Joe Bob has AIDS. After Rock, we could only wonder, "Who's next." Joe Bob wandered out on the stage, wobbly and emaciated, a mere shadow of his former macho self. Pandering to an audience recruited from a KQED pledge night, the first hint of Joe Bob's true persuasion surfaced when he sidestepped audience requests for AIDS jokes. No doubt remained after Joe Bobbie was approached on stage by an offering of two enormous garbonzos, at which point he paled and recoiled in horror and distaste. We can only speculate on the origins of your affliction: Were the sisters transvestites? Have you had too many close encounters of the fourth kind with the high sheriffs? We've noticed that you haven't been seeing the movies in your reviews lately, perhaps due to a clandestine trip to Paris (not Texas). We can only pray for a miracle cure.
SLOAT BILL
PACIFICA, CALIF.

P.S. I haven't given my return address, as I've heard AIDS can be transmitted through the mail.

P.P.S. Will this letter get printed? No way, José!

DEAR SLOAT: If you'd seen them garbonzas, you'd realize they were evidently stuffed with explosive devices. They had more dents in em than a fat man's lawn chair. I didn't want another Three Mile Island. And as far as the AIDS jokes go—you wouldn't of been able to hear em through my gas mask.

The Biggest Chuck: Durning

Ever since Charles Durning played the Governor of Texas in *Best Little Whorehouse* and danced around the rotunda in a tu-tu, I've thought he might be my kinda guy. But now he's proved it in *Stand Alone,* or *Death Wish for Grandpas,* the best movie ever made about Medicare patients that decide to bayonet all the South American cocaine dealers in town. What I'm saying here is, we got three Chucks now—Bronson, Norris, and the man they call "Moby II." Actually, Chuck D. had to take a little time out from TV until the Japanese can build some bigger screens.

We start out with Chuck, back in '43, rippin the guts out of some Japaheeno soldiers in order to make the world safe for normal people. But now that's all just one big flashback in his head, and all he wants to do is play with his grandkid's toy tank and hang around Bert Remsen's diner like an old coot. Too bad, though, cause three Meskins come in there and machine-gun a punkola junkie and eat several Honey Buns without paying for em. All Chuck's friends say, "Hey, forget it, don't get involved, don't talk to the police, you're too fat." But Chuck won't listen to em. He goes downtown, looks at the snapshots, tried to I.D. the guys, and starts riding around in Pam Grier's sports car.

Next thing, the cops pick up the Meskins on a stolen-car rap, and they get Pam Grier for a lawyer, but then they don't need her cause the owner of the car won't press charges because he doesn't want his head turned into a vegetarian plate. Then one of the Meskins spots Charles Durning out driving around in the neighborhoods, and so they chase him through the streets and he ends up running down alleys like a Ringling Brothers elephant act. So now everybody says, "Hey, C.D., man, forget it, or these guys are gonna stick a needle in your navel and turn you into a custom floormat." But Chuck is *so honest* that he goes down and files a report and nails one of em, and pretty soon we got the Meskin Mafia blowing 9,000 holes in Bert Remsen's café and making him tell where Chuck lives.

This is okay with Chuck, though. All he does is drive down to the pool hall, pick up one of these Cocaine Cowboys by the shirt collar, and say, "I am Death! Come with Me!" Which, you may remember, is what Michael Cimino said to his boss right before *Heaven's Gate* and it all came true. Pretty soon Chuck is putting charcoal all over his face, greasing up his gun, and—here's the best part—ramming some big old crooked nails through a two-by-four. By the time the Meskins get to his house, he's ready to party.

Excellent scum removal. No breasts. Ten dead bodies. Three quarts blood. Three beasts. Four shootouts. One motor vehicle chase. Kung fu. Electrical outlet fu. Fat fu. Gratuitous Pam Grier. Drive-In Academy Award nominations for Charles Durning, the finest 400-pound actor alive; and Bert Remsen, still looking drunk after all these years.

Three stars. Joe Bob says check it out. ∎

JOE BOB'S MAILBAG

DEAR JOE BOB: WITH LOVE ALL THINGS ARE POSSIBLE. This paper has been sent to you for good luck. The original copy is in New England. It has been around the world nine times. The luck has now been sent to you. You will receive good luck within four days of receiving this letter. Providing you, in turn, send it on. This is no joke. You will receive it in the mail. Send copies to people you think need good luck. Do not send money as fate has no price. Do not keep this letter. It must leave your hands within 96 hours. An RAF officer received $70,000. Joe Elliot received $10,000 and lost it because he broke the chain. While in the Philippines, Gene Welch lost his wife six days after receiving the letter. He failed to circulate the letter. However, before her death he received $7,750,000. Please send twenty copies of this letter and see what happens in four days. The chain comes from Venezuela and was written by Saul Anthony De Croup, a missionary from South America. Since the copy must take a tour of the world you must make twenty copies and send them to friends and associates. After a few days you will get a surprise. This is true even if you are not superstitious. Do note the following: Constantine Dias received the chain in 1953.

He asked his secretary to make 20 copies and send them out. A few days later he won a lottery of two million dollars. Carla Donlitt, an office employee, received the letter and forgot that it had to leave her hands within 96 hours; she lost her job. Later after finding the letter again, she mailed out 20 copies. A few days later she got a better job. Dalan Fairchild received the letter and not believing, threw the letter away. Nine days later he died. Remember, send no money. Please do not ignore this. It works!!!!!!!

DEAR CHAIN: It's been 13 days now and I han't done nothin with this letter and so far nothing's ahppened which just goes to prove that xrtyuovghoqoughdljheyfdodf-jhldjeljheljflekjaaaaargh.

DEAR JOE BOB: I just saw *Rambo*, and the body count came out to 211, including estimations of villages at 60 people per village. I think that beats out your "modern record of 121 in *American Ninja.*"
APRIL JANOW
LOS ANGELES

DEAR AP: Are you trying to tell me that OFFSCREEN YING-YANGS are the same as BLOODIED-UP ON-SCREEN AMERICANS? I think you need to do a little homework before you start trying to talk body counts with "Mr. Body Count" himself.

DEAR JOE BOB: I am the bimbo waiting outside in the cold with the sign reading "BIMBO NEEDS TICKET." Do you know why I need a ticket, Joe Bob? In the first place, whoops, numero un-o, I would like to get into the bar. Numero two-o, I would like to get picked up by a *real* man. Numero three-o, I guess I'd like to see you. Joe Bob, I spent several hours standing on street corners selling . . . Avon, but (and this is the tear-jerker) by the time I had got enough quarters to buy a ticket they were all sold out!

My mama says you're a real giving type of guy, and I sure would be grateful for a ticket (ask my friend Larry, who got me a ticket for the Springsteen concert). (Oops, sorry, I heard that he's been booking shows same nights as you have and you're not thrilled, still *I* don't have a ticket.)

Well, anyway, I hope you like your flowers, and remember, there's an extremely unhappy bimbo out there since she doesn't have a ticket to see you.

Love,
"BOBBY SUE" FRANCESCO

P.S. I've reached the age of consent, almost.

P.S. I just got a ticket, so I guess it has all worked out . . . You're brilliant!

DEAR BOBBY SUE: I might of married you if I'd known you was there, but now you're ineligible, cause I refuse to marry anybody that would pay money to see my show.

JOE BOB: Keep up the OK work.
JEFF OR PHIL
SAN FRANCISCO
P.S. Consider this a piece of letter fu.

DEAR JEFF OR PHIL: Consider this a piece of form letter fu.

Headless Man Found in Topless Lab

Congratulations! If you're still reading this column after the first 12 words, then you have ALREADY WON one of three fabulous prizes. All you have to do to claim your prize—and remember, you ALREADY WON it—is to make an appointment to come by the Joe Bob Briggs Prize Notification Center at Lake Grapevine and say the following secret passwords:

"Gimme one a them prizes."

As soon as you say those words and leave your driver's license at the front desk, you will be eligible to draw for one of these great prizes:

• Seven weeks in fabulous Tahiti! (Airfare and hotel not included.)

• The world's largest microwave oven! This is the one you've read about. Recently approved by the Kansas legislature as the "safest" form of execution invented in recent years.

• An autographed photo of Ralph the Diving Pig.

Remember, one of these gifts is ALREADY yours. You don't have to do anything to get it, except come by Lake Grapevine and let us present a brief audio-visual demonstration on "Joe Bob Shores."

Maybe your friends have already told you about it. Maybe you were sayin to your wife last night, "Honey, I'm tired of this rat race. I'm ready for Joe Bob Shores." Maybe your wife said, "Yeah, but who has a hundred dollars for the lot?"

Ha ha ha. I always laugh when I hear stories like that. You might not believe this, but this month only, when you come down to claim your prizes, we're offering 7,500 lakeview lots (telescope not included) for only—you aren't gonna believe this—for just 40 bucks down. Think of it! Forty cold American gets you a little plot of dirt where you can start throwin away old inner tubes and beat-up lawn furniture. Forty on the table means you can go back home and say, *"We have a little chunk of the Shores!"*

Now I know what you're thinkin. You're remembering last year, when several unsavory individuals down in Mabank complained their lots were more than 37 miles *as a crow flies* from the actual lake. As you know, I proved those lots *were* inside the 37-mile limit, but this year I'm gonna make it even easier. For a limited time only, I'm offerin property on the lake at the same price as the "Thirty-Seven Mile Paradise" property. I would urge you to read the contracts, though, when they are presented to you by the former offensive line of the Dallas Cowboys, right after the "Human Animal" martial arts demonstration. The reason I'm pointin this out is a lot of people buy property on the lake and then it turns out they can't swim and I don't wanna be responsible. This property is *on the lake*.

For a map of Joe Bob Shores, or a copy of the pamphlet "True Stories of People That Got Electrocuted Trying to Hook Up Their Recreational Vehicles," write Joe Bob Briggs Prize Notification Center, P.O. Box 2002, Dallas, TX 75221.

We have a new Numero Uno. We have the best zombie-mutant medical-experiment flick since *Basket Case.* We have blood, we have breasts, we have beasts. We have instant drive-in classic. I'm talkin, of course, about *Re-Animator,* the only movie ever made where an actor gets his head cut off halfway through the movie but *finishes the movie*. David Gale, the actor that accomplished this for the first time in motion picture history, is a Drive-In Method Actor. What this means is, he actually *lives out* his parts before he does em for the camera. So Gale had to master the difficult trick of playing half the movie with his head *on* and half with his head *off.* You can imagine what a wise guy he was around the set! You never knew whether he'd have his old noodle on straight or be haulin it around like carry-on luggage.

What we got here is a story about Herbert West, this nerd-face space-cadet med student who starts messing around with secret-formula juice the color of urine—and finds out he has the power to bring somebody's brain back to life after it gets smushed under an 18-wheeler. So he goes up to Massachusetts, where they have an oversupply of dead brains, and moves in with a med student who's sleepin with the dean's daughter, and the first thing he does is pump so much juice into a dead cat that he almost gets his face clawed off.

So then Herbert cons the roommate into going down to the med-school dean and trying to get some more help on cat-brain research. "I've conquered brain death," he says. "We can defeat death!" And the dean basically says to get his hiney out of the office and also they're both kicked out of school and stop sleepin with his daughter.

Next thing, these two guys sneak into the morgue and start juicing up stiffs, until one guy gets out of hand and they have to ram a bone-saw through his back to make him stop breakin down doors and—*whoops!*—killing the dean. They look at the dead dean, look at each other, and then *no problema*. They juice him up and pretty soon he's standin up, waving his arms and slobbering all over everybody. They do have to put him in a rubber room and watch Dr. Carl Hill do a laser lobotomy on him, but other than that he's fine.

But now the evil Dr. Carl Hill knows he's got these guys, and so he goes over to the secret brain-juice laboratory and tells Herbert West that he wants all the records so he can win the Nobel Prize. Herbert West's answer is a shovel through the neck. Then he thinks, "What the hey, nobody's ever juiced *separate* body parts before," and from there on out Dr. Carl Hill tries to get himself back together, carryin his head around in a slime tray, doin laser lobotomies on all the other corpses, and pretty soon gettin up his own private army of walking mutant corpses. There's this one scene where he straps the dean's daughter down to the autopsy table, holds his head in his hands, and starts making love to her with it. That's about as far as I can go here, without getting the plug pulled by the high sheriffs.

A classic. Twenty-five gallons blood, the modern-day champion. Eight breasts. Twenty-seven dead bodies. Ten dead born-again bodies. One dead attack cat (three lives). Twenty-two zombies. Head smashing. Cat smashing. Flesh-ripping. Brain-fondling. Heads roll. Arms roll. Bone-saw fu. Lobotomy fu. Intestine fu. Drive-In Academy Award nominations for Jeffrey Combes as Herbert West, for wielding the green needle and saying "Come on, why not, this is the freshest body we have"; David Gale, as Dr. Carl Hill, for performing without his head and saying "I *will* be famous!"; Bruce Abbott, the med student, for saying "I'm sorry, honey, but your dead father's been lobotomized"; and Stuart Gordon, the director, for painting the room red.

Four stars. Joe Bob says check it out. ■

Communist Alert!

The Portales Drive-In in Portales, New Mexico, just got bought up for "investment purposes." I think we all know what that means. Pretty soon it's gonna be a Richard Simmons Anatomy Asylum if those people don't act immediately. Remember, without eternal vigilance, it can happen here.

JOE BOB'S MAILBAG

DEAR MANAGING EDITOR *(The Arizona Republic)*: On page 34 of this week's City Life was a UPS column by Joe Bob Briggs. This column was titled "It's About Salvation."

The author's satire not only did not amuse me but provoked me to speak out.

This article does not belong in your paper. This column is saying okey to the spaced-out drug mentality infecting our youth. Your Newspaper, and all media, are going to be held accountable, in the near future, for influencing people in an Anti-Christ and immoral way. Our society is a product of the Media and you should assume great responsibility.

Salvation cannot be mocked. "Jingle-Bob Jesus Christmas Fund."

This is an abomination. The Bible says in John 3:3, "Unless a man be Born again he cannot see the kingdom of God." Romans 10:9 tells us how to get "Born again." "If thou shall confess with thy mouth the Lord Jesus and believe in thine heart that God has raised him from the dead, thou shalt be saved."

That is the true Salvation according to God's word.

In the second paragraph of Brigg's article he makes lewd, horrifying sexual references.

This has no relationship to Jesus's death on a cross! This is Satan's mockery!

Your paper cannot prosper if you continue to sanction UPS trash.

My feelings are that you send reporters around to the real body of Christ and find out about the miracles Jesus is doing right now. I am not talking about your Religion Column, I am talking about what is really happening in these last days. What about equal time. Where are my rights to be represented.

Thank you for considering this matter.
Regards,
KATHLEEN BRANDT, TEMPE, ARIZ.; MARILYN ROVERS, PHOENIX; WALLY BRANDT, TEMPE; LANA ELDRIDGE, PHOENIX; BILL COMSTOCK, PHOENIX; TANDELLA A. EBSTER, PHOENIX; CONRAD C. MURPHY, SCOTTSDALE; JEFF M. HARRBIUS, MESA;

RENA M. LINN, PHOENIX; PATRICIA A. LINN, PHOENIX; ALLEN COOK, MESA; BRADY C. LINN, PHOENIX; COLLUM COMSTOCK, PHOENIX; WILLIAM COMSTOCK, PHOENIX; CAROLE MURPHY, SCOTTSDALE; RON ECKERSLEY, PHOENIX; WILLIAM D. GURNEY, MESA; TOM HOWARD, TEMPE.

DEAR FELLOW BABTISTS: I didn't mean any disrespect to the J-man.

DEAR JOE BOB: I know you aint Dear Abby or nothin like that but I think maybe your the guy that can help me with this situation I got. Like every real red blooded American kid I learned all about sex at the Drive-In movies and thats where this problem comes in. The wife is gettin real P.O.ed about havin to sleep in the car every night. What should I do?
Your friend,
BUZZ STALEY
SAN FRANCISCO
ps. The car is in her name.

DEAR BUZZ: Many a drab sex life can be improved simply by trying new and "daring" things. In your case, have you ever thought about doing "it" in some totally unexpected place, like a bed? Spring it on your wife some night when she's unprepared. If you've never tried it on a bed, you may even get a few jollies yourself.

A Guide to Halley's Big-Deal Comet

When the Halley's Big-Deal Comet comes to Texas this year, I've already got my seats reserved down at the Broke Spoke Dude Ranch in Bandera. I had to pay extra to get a room in the Claude Pomfret Cabin, but I know it'll be worth it cause they say you can't see the sucker unless you're in a place with absolutely no light and no noise and nothing going on. Claude Pomfret lives there, but he's been brain-dead for 10 years.

It was Chubb Fricke that come up with the idea and leased all the condos at the Broke Spoke. He said, speaking as an ex-professional bowler, that seeing the Big-Deal Comet was the one thing he had to do before he died. Either that or shake hands with Ed McMahon.

We're all pretty excited about it, and so I been giving weekly classes on the comet so we'll all know what we're seeing when it comes. Like here's a few things we learned about it this week:

Numero Uno: The last time the comet came through Texas, back in 1910, 12 towns and a guy named Phil disappeared. This time we're trying to head off this kind of disaster by sacrificing a guy named Phil to the heavens *before* the comet gets here. I'm not a superstitious kind of guy, but just for safety's sake I do believe we need to arrange 12 punji sticks in a circle and pour Kraft salad dressing in the middle and say "Hit the Pavement, Satan! Hit the Pavement, Satan!" four times. If this doesn't work, we should nuke Houston.

Numero Two-o: Don't be disappointed if the first thing you see is a little smudge in the sky like somebody's smeared Bosco syrup on the icebox door. Here's what you do. Check first to see whether you are looking through the wrong end of your telescope *or* whether your telescope is pointed at an icebox door with Bosco on it. If neither is the case, then *con-*

gratulations! You just sighted Halley's Comet. It always looks like a funny little smudge.

Numero Three-o: The law of gravity says that if you stand in South Texas and you stare out at the horizon at a 25-degree angle and you consider the elliptical orbit of all comets and you take the brightness of this particular comet into consideration, then you will *not* fall off the Earth.

Numero Four-o: Drink eight beers while you're waitin and you'll see it before anybody else does.

I'll be happy to answer any other astronomical questions about the comet yall might have who have not been schooled in scientific principles and breath vapor.

How long has it been? Three years? Four? How long should we have to wait before the number one drive-in star in the world, the man that makes Bernhard Goetz look like a wimp encyclopedia salesman from Sausalito, the Chucker, Mr. B.—*Bronson*—starts skimming scum again?

I'm sorry, but I was getting a *little* impatient. Normally I'm not a violent kind of guy. I like to play pinochle and sit around and watch geeks with orange hair molest 75-year-old women for their Medicaid money and say, "Oh, gee, gosh, where are the nice policemen?" But you know, you can *push me over the edge,* and then I have to do what Bronson does in *Death Wish 3*— get out my Browning automatic machine gun and start squeezing the trigger on homosexual biker gangs.

You'll be happy to know that Chuck is back in New York City where he belongs, out where the apartment buildings look like they got spray-painted with Agent Orange. And the first thing that happens, as soon as Chuck gets off the Greyhound, is a bunch of punkola gang members beat

this old man to a mushy pulp with a tire tool cause he won't fork over twenty bucks for old-people protection money. But get this—the cops think *Chuck did it.* So they book him and he has to spend the next ten minutes kung-fuing fat guys in his cell. Then this Swedish pervert gang leader gets real p.o.ed and tells Bronson, "Tell you what—I'm gonna kill a little old lady just for you." Anyhow, Bronson enjoys his stay in jail, cause they refuse to file charges, deny bail, and when he says "I want a lawyer," the police chief says "No you don't." This is what Chuck has been saying they should do all these years.

Anyhow, as long as Chuck is in the Crossbar Hotel, the Norwegian Animal gang is free to roam around sticking switchblades through each other's necks and swiping old ladies' purses— but pretty soon the police chief *recognizes* Chuck and he says "You're gonna work for me now," and so pretty soon Chuck is out on the streets, crowbarring creeps and making friends with Meskins and Jews. All Chuck's friends in the movie are Meskins and Jews. I don't know why this is, except it helps the plot when the thugs start seeping in through the windows and knocking off the little Jewish hat that the guy wears all the time while he's eating his gefiltafish.

But nothing seems to help. Even though Chuck *lives* in the neighborhood, people keep getting axes through their heads cause the Swede thinks they smell bad. So what does Chuck do? He buys an elephant gun.

We're talking a .475 Wildey Magnum with exploding big-game cartridges. Chuck spends one afternoon planting charges in the bullets, loads up, then gets that little grin on his face, and says, "Think I'll go down the street and get myself some ice cream."

Pretty soon you know what's gonna

happen. All Chuck's friends are gonna die grisly deaths so he can get *mad* enough to clean up the scum again.

Four breasts. Eighty-nine dead bodies. Five burning cars. Four exploding buildings. Three burning citizens. Switchblades through the neck. Old man set on fire like a Bic lighter. Three motor vehicle chases, with two crash-and-burns. Nail through head. Three creeps falling off buildings. Kung fu. Tire tool fu. Crowbar fu. Ax fu. Anti-tank missile launcher fu. Miranda-warning fu. Two-by-four with a nail on the end of it rigged to a spring trap fu. Gratuitous Martin Balsam. Drive-In Academy Award nominations for Chuck's new girlfriend, Deborah Raffin, for saying "Dammit, people have got to fight back and hard"; Big Chuck, for saying "It's like killing roaches—you have to kill em all, otherwise what's the point?"; and Michael Winner, the director, Mr. *Death Wish 2* himself, who does it again.

Four stars. Joe Bob says check it out.

JOE BOB'S MAILBAG

DEAR MR. BRIGGS: Are you a smoker . . . or an ex-smoker? If you've ever tried to quit cigarettes you know that giving up the habit can often be as funny as it is difficult.

Millions of cigarette smokers will try and quit for at least 24 hours on Thursday, November 21, the 9th annual nationwide celebration of the Great American Smokeout. Perhaps if I remind you of this event far enough in advance, you might consider doing a good-humored column about the smoking and quitting problem for publication on or shortly before Smokeout Day.

The Smokeout is the perfect time for story-telling, kidding, spoofing, and parody . . . the sorts of things, I hope, that especially appeal to you.
Sincerely,
JOANN SCHELLENBACH
DIRECTOR OF PRESS RELATIONS
AMERICAN CANCER SOCIETY
NEW YORK, N.Y.

DEAR JOAN: I support the God-given American right to put any disgusting thing in our mouth that we want to.

DEAR JOE BOB: Several months ago I told you the meaning of life & you asked me whether or not you existed. Despite some people denying it, I can assure you that you exist. If you are ever in doubt, remember: "I think, therefore I am."
Sincerely,
THE WRAITH
COLLEGE STATION, TEX.
P.S. You must use a fortune in stamps.

DEAR WRAITH: You don't exist, therefore I feel better.

It's a *Nightmare* Without Heather

It's been a whole 10 months now since *A Nightmare on Elm Street* came out, and so I can tell you, I been pretty sick of waitin on the dang sequel. It finally rolled into town a couple weeks ago, though, and I got to admit, Freddy Krueger, the best child molester in drive-in history, is still pretty impressive using those knife-fingers to turn teenagers into sizzling fajitas. There's only one thing wrong with Freddy's Revenge. *Where the heck is Heather Langenkamp?*

You probly remember, I singled out Heather as the Best Actress Named Langenkamp last year, and also said she was the new Jamie Lee Curtis for the way she gouted blood in *Nightmare* Numero Uno. She was the only teenager left alive in the first movie, so where the heck is she?

I think we all know the answer to that one. I'm checkin it out with New Line Cinema, the turkeys that made this one, but I think we *already* know what happened here.

I bet you anything Heather got the Donna Wilks Treatment. Donna Wilks, the 16-year-old hooker in *Angel, stripped* of her dignity by being replaced by Betsy Russell, the one that looked like she had a head-on collision with a Max Factor truck in *Avenging Angel*. And why? Why does such a tragic thing happen?

Because Donna wanted a measly 8 million dollars to do the sequel.

I'm sorry, it still bothers me. And I bet the same thing happened here. They went to Heather and they said, "Hey, Heath, how much for the sequel?" And she said, "Eight million dollars." And they said, "Sorry, we can only go seven." And so we *all* suffer. We just have to wait on somebody willing to pay Heather's price. And now that I mention it, *I'm* willing to pay Heather's price.

Anyway, we start out with this new guy named Jesse moving into Heather's house at 1428 Elm Street, because Heather went crazy and murdered her mama *(sure she did!)*. And, sure enough, Jesse is havin the same kind of dreams about Freddy Krueger, the guy that got his face stuck in a Lawn Boy, and what do you think Freddy's doing? Same deal—trying to *take the little boys and girls down into the boiler room*.

But even though we got a new director doing this flick (Wes Craven, the master, had to go off and make a movie with Roger Corman, king of the drive-in), we got some pretty decent slime-spewing. Freddy jumps into Jess's dreams, takes over his body, and pretty soon we got Killer Parakeet Attacks, flying basketballs, lethal jumpropes, and a coach dressed up in leather that gets flayed to death with a wet towel, and all the usual "Kill for me" Post-Toastie teenagers getting their buns zapped into Guam. Course, Jesse feels like he's losing his mind, pigs out on No-Doz and black coffee, and gets so mentally deranged that he falls in love with a Meryl Streep lookalike. We're talking *scary*.

One breast. Nine dead bodies. Two dead birds. Two gallons blood. Seven beasts. One great transformation scene, where Freddy breaks out of Jesse. Gratuitous Hope Lange. Scene where Freddy rips the skin off his skull so we can see his brain breathe.

Freddy takes a chunk out of a bimbo's leg. Teenagers boiled alive in swimming pool. One motor vehicle chase. Exploding TV. Exploding aquarium. Exploding swimming pool. School bus fu. Snake fu. Parakeet fu. Basketball fu. Electric toaster fu. Black tongue fu. Weenie fu. Rat fu. A 42 on the Vomit Meter. Drive-In Academy Award nominations for Mark Patton, as Jesse, for wearing all that gunk on his face; Robert Englund, as the one and only Freddy Krueger, for saying "You've got the body, I've got the brain" and "Wake up, little girl" and "You are *all* my children now"; Kim Myers, the best Meryl Streep lookalike working in drive-in flicks today; and Clu Gulager, as Jesse's dimwit father, for saying "Animals just don't explode into flames for no reason."

Three stars. Joe Bob says check it out. ■

Silver Bullet: Big Steve Makes Big Deal with Big Dino

Stephen King's been rootin around in his wastebasket again, dredging up old stories he can take over to Dino De Laurentiis and say, "Hey, Dino, how mucha-roonie?" And then Dino says, "Oh yes, Stiffen, we meck in North Carolina." Dino does everthing in North Carolina now, cause he built him a studio out in Wilmington where he only has to pay 400,000 lira an hour. In Americano money, that means a full buck 50.

Anyhow, Big Steve wrote *Silver Bullet* a few years back when he came out with *Cycle of the Werewolf,* in the period of his career right before he got richer than God. And it was a pretty decent story, but the movie version is one of the best Big Steve flicks ever made. Okay, okay, it's not *Carrie,* cause who could forget Sissy Spacek shishkebobbing the senior class? And maybe it's not quite as good as *Christine.* But it's right up there in the top three or four, mostly cause Gary Busey proves his drive-in talents once again as the drunk, divorced uncle that builds motorcycles and learns to believe in werewolves. That was just a big misunderstanding when Gary made *The Bear* last year. They forgot to tell Gary that, even though Bear Bryant was dead, he was supposed to *act like* he was alive in the movie. Gary missed that part of it. He did the whole movie thinking he was supposed to be dead.

This time we got—*thwack*—total decapitation in the first five minutes, with flying head, rolling head, and maggots. Pretty soon we got a fat pregnant bimbo eaten by a guy in a wolf suit. Then we got a beer guzzler sucked through a greenhouse floor by Son of Kong. And then, when things start getting serious, we get this little kid flying a happy-face kite—Alpo City. After five or six people get eaten up, the town gets worried and the weirdo priest that looks like Christopher Reeve after a three-day drunk starts preaching on how "The time of the beast always passes," and then we get a bunch of vigilantes with deer rifles and baseball bats groping around in the fog till the werewolf can rip their eyes out.

That's pretty much the plot till this little crippled kid in a motorcycle wheelchair gets attacked by the werewolf one night and has to shoot a bottle rocket in his eye—and the next day somebody turns up in town with an eyepatch. This pretty much narrows down the suspect list, but Gary Busey can't figure it out until Corey Haim, the kid, explains the whole principle of the movie to him: "As the moon gets fuller, the guy gets wolfier."

No breasts. (Big Steve has been doing these PG numbers on us.) Two quarts blood. Eight beasts. A 46 on the Vomit Meter. Eight dead bodies. Head rolls. Head flies. Leg rolls. Two eyes roll. Three werewolf transformations, one reverse transformation. One motor vehicle chase. Baseball bat fu. Drive-In Academy Award nominations for Gary Busey, for being his ownself; Corey Haim, for killing the wolf suit; Big Steve, for getting the idea; Daniel Attias, who never directed a movie before this one but proved he has the drive-in stuff; and Everett McGill, as the werewolf, for saying "But it's not my fault!" Four stars. Joe Bob says check it out. ■

Communist Alert!

Some of the boys in the Sigma Phi Epsilon frat house down at Texas A&M started shootin the pigs in their front yard last month because "the members felt the pigs detracted from the fraternity's attraction during rush season and made female visitors uncomfortable." The Brazos County Sheriff's Office is investigating the pig deaths, but let's face it. It's only a matter of time before somebody confuses one of those pigs with one of their usual "female visitors" and some innocent pig is gonna die. Remember, without eternal vigilance, it can happen here.

A Sweet-Potato Thanksgiving in Georgia

This is a special time of year for me. This is when I get the chance to gather all my mentally-retarded cousins together at the old family homestead in Valdosta, Georgia, and force em to eat sweet potatoes and red beets until they're sick. And then, after they all clean their plates and start begging for pumpkin pie that's been cooked so long it stays in your mouth till Christmas, I say, "Now it's time for Uncle Joe Bob's story of how this great country of ours was created."

I'll never forget the sound of those little voices when I say that. All together, like little blackbirds attacking a mongoose, they say, "No! Please! Do we have to?"

And then I begin the ancient story. At first the only Americans were

Indians, and they had names like Pocahontas and Geronimo and Butch. They were extremely ugly. They never exterminated.

Then the white man came.

He got malaria and croaked.

Then the next white man came.

He killed a few Indians, got malaria, and croaked.

Then a bunch of white men came over to Massachusetts cause, as we all know, Massachusetts has full medical benefits.

The guys in Massachusetts attacked a turkey, dug up some sweet potatoes, and *forced the Indians to eat em.* The Indians fled to New York. The guys in Massachusetts started wearing extremely stupid hats and killing heretics and writing bad poetry.

Then the Indians sold New York for 23 bucks and used the money to invest in Appalachia. The guys in New York invented lawyers, sued the Indians, took the money back, and made em pay rent on the property in Appalachia.

Some of the Indians started hanging around in Alabama, but the rest of em started doing musical comedy in Cherokee, North Carolina, for tourists.

Then the white man killed a few hundred thousand Indians who refused to live in Oklahoma cause the cable reception was so bad.

Then a bunch of mean Indians in Boise swooped down through the prairies and started killing white men cause the Indians wanted to hog all the hunting grounds for theirselves.

Then the white man killed all the Indians in Boise, killed all the buffaloes, killed all the prairie dogs, killed all the otters and beavers and mooses and mountain lions and bears.

Then the white man gave the Indians some hunting grounds back in New Mexico, cause all we needed that land for was nuke tests.

Then the white man got organized and sent the U.S. Calvary out there and killed all the rest of the Indians that didn't live in Oklahoma or New Mexico or Arizona.

Then the white man sent some professors out there to write books about the Indians.

And that's why, today, in this great country of ours, we celebrate the sweet potato and the turkey and, of course, the lawyer. There's an old Indian saying that comes to mind at a time like this. Let's see if I remember it. It goes something like this: "White man resemble hind end of sick goose."

Okay, boys, come on now, let's eat up.

A couple weeks ago New World Pictures called up and wanted me to come out and meet the stars of *Grunt: The Wrestling Movie,* and so even though I never do interviews I went out to this gym in Southern Oklahoma and went a couple rounds with Steve Strong, who rassles out in El Lay, and Mando Guerrero, the best Meskin rassler ever to win the Georgia State Champeenship. Steve is roughly the size of the Empire State Building, and El Toro is roughly the size of an Empire State Building paperweight, so it's pretty intersting when their match is the best thing about the whole movie. "This movie is the *essence* of wrestling," Steve shouted down at me from his face. "This is the first *real* wrestling movie. They screened 125 wrestlers to see who could work under these conditions. They ruled out all the sickos and crazies."

How come, I asked Steve.

"Cause you need to show up on time for a movie. You've got to be dependable. We know this movie's gonna be watched and criticized by every wrestler on every circuit in this country, so we wanted it to be *authentic.*"

Course, they ended up makin it so

authentic that a guy gets his head rassled plumb off in the very first scene. That causes Mad Dog Joe de Curso, the guy that kicked the skull off, to go crazy while the rassling federation is deciding the question, "Can you lose your head and still retain your title?" And so Mad Dog drops out of sight, and the next six years they don't have a champion cause the dead guy refuses to defend his title.

Then this guy shows up called The Mask, and he looks a *lot* like Steve Strong except for you can't see his face, and everybody thinks Mad Dog is back, "the idol of children and kisser of dogs," and he's had his tattoos fried off his arms and now he's going for a title shot. But first he has to dump his Frenchie-poodle girlfriend, then he has to destroy the Grunt Brothers in Hackensack, then he has to skewer El Toro and wreck the studio of right-wing talk-show host Wally George, and finally he has to battle against The Great Pyramid, also known as four little midget rasslers that hang on his biceps like leeches until he scissor-kicks em into the 12th row.

It takes a 12-man Battle Royale at the Olympic Auditorium in El Lay to settle everthing for the "Mask Is Mad Dog" fan club, and we're talking some serious deltoid destruction.

Two breasts. Eight rassling matches. Three quarts blood. A 26 on the Vomit Meter. Seventeen beasts. Heads roll. Two dead bodies. Two Commonist conspiracies. Four brawls. Gratuitous electric wheelchair. Kung fu. Bimbo fu. TV studio fu. Midget fu. Frying pan fu. Tattoo fu. Drive-In Academy Award nominations for Steven Cepello, a.k.a. Steve Strong, a.k.a. The Mask, for throwing his meat around; Marilyn Dodds Frank, as Mad Dog's ex-manager; Robert Glaudini, as Mad Dog's geek fan-club manager; and Mando Guerrero, "El Toro," for making the flab fly with his rassling choreography.

Three stars. Joe Bob says check it out. ∎

Communist Alert!

Double death in Flint, Mich. First they ripped down the South Dort Drive-In to put up a sporting-goods company headquarters, and now they're tearing down the West Side Drive-In to build a headquarters for a bunch of osteopaths. I recommend some immediate spinal surgery. The paper says those drive-ins were worth $4.5 million, but does anybody care? Nope. Money down the drain to them.

The All-U-Can-Eat Highway Diet

It's that time of year again. It's Snow-bird Season. Time for all the population of Minnesota over the age of 84 to jump in their Winnebagos, hog two lanes of traffic all the way down I-35, and plug in their porta-toilets down at "Poncho's U-Park-It-Your-selfa," which is right across the Rio Grande from where they sell 50-cent turquoise bolo ties for $15 so the Mes-kin government can attract more American money across the border for the needs of the president's immediate family.

In other words, time to put out the signs:

All-You-Can-Eat Buffet
Next 3 Exits

Okay. Now. I ask this same question ever year, but nobody can ever answer it for me. How come the word "buffet" is all you need to make 37 million bucks a year off traveling Medi-caid patients?

There's basically three places to stop on the highway, right?

"B-B-Q": Everwhere except Texas, this means Sloppy Joes left over from yesterday's elementary school lunch menu. In Texas, it means exactly what it says: B-B-Q. It's hearty. It's American. It's Meat.

"EAT": This popular small-town restaurant chain serves two things— big ole West Texas feed-lot cow-burgers, and ground-beef-patty diet plates. Meat.

And finally, of course—

"All-You-Can-Eat Buffet": You can always spot these places by the number of 1967 Buick Le Sabres parked out front and the way it takes you two and a half hours just to get through the salad line. We're talking baby-marshmallow salad, cold mac-aroni with ugly little green olives mixed in there, the always popular chicken-liver-and-onions, circular chicken fried steak with Elmer's Glue gravy, shuckless tamales, and, of course, meatloaf-on-a-stick. All you can eat for $19.95.

My friend Chubb Fricke, the world's oldest surviving ex-profes-sional bowler, will stop at any all-you-can-eat buffet within his field of vision, even if it means driving backward on the wrong interstate, and so I asked him the question of the hour, which is "Chubb, you had your choice of a steak, a B-B-Q sandwich, a big ole cheeseburger, and a chunk of Frito pie that looks like it was used for tram-poline practice. Tell me now—*why* do you always go for the Frito pie?"

And Chubb looked at me with one of those expressions like "You little under-65 runt you," and then he said, "You never lived through the Depres-sion, did you?"

And I said no, I didn't.

And Chubb said, "That's what I mean."

And I said, "But Chubb—you didn't live through the Depression either."

"I know," Chubb told me, "that's why we need to eat this stuff—to expe-rience the way it was back then. You're not an American till you've stuffed three helpings of Spam Hawaiian down the old gut. Then you'll know the true meaning of 'all-you-can-eat.'"

Oh.

They said Sly Rocky Rambo wouldn't do it again. They said he was hanging up his lips, retiring the act, selling all but 34 of his gold neck chains. But then he said those immortal words that changed drive-in history:

"I take shirt off again?"

Rocky IV is here. And if I can get serious here for a moment, I want to say that this is the most sensitive and intelligent movie about nuclear war ever directed by Sylvester Stallone. You probly heard what the Ruskies are up to. They been shootin up all their athletes with steroids so they can beat the bejabbers out of us at the Olympics the next time they boycott it. You know, it's one thing to use drugs for what is known in the business as "mammary augmentation," or trick boobs, but I think it's pretty disgusting to take perfectly normal human beans and wire em up to Radio Shack computers and turn em into killing machines.

That's what happens when Ivan Drago comes to the Newnited States and says he wants to fight Apollo Creed. Ivan was a mere 7-foot-2, 280-pound trained athlete before the Russians started workin him over with hormones and turned him into a breathing Caterpillar tractor. So what does he do? He comes over here and turns Apollo Creed's face into a Grape Nehi fountain, and Rocky has to put on a set of Ray-Bans and deliver the eulogy:

"There's a lot I could say about this man, but I don't guess it matters now."

Course, there's only one thing to be done: fly to Siberia with Burt Young, leave your wife at home cause she doesn't understand stupidity, wrestle some oxen to get into shape, and run up to a mountaintop, throw out your arms, and start screaming like Julie Andrews during an electrolysis treatment. In other words, time for 30 solid minutes of paint-the-ring-red sequel fu.

Sly Rocky Rambo fights the Commies twice in the same year.

Two breasts (Rocky's). Nineteen gallons blood, the 1985 record. Twenty-two beasts, all Communists. A 45 on the Vomit Meter. One dead Apollo Creed. Gratuitous James Brown. Kung fu. Robot fu. Steroid fu. KGB fu. Pouring-a-bunch-of-water-on-Rocky's-face-and-watching-him-sling-it-off fu. Drive-In Academy Award nominations for Burt Young, for sitting around listening to Singing Chipmunks records; Brigitte Nielsen, as Ivan Drago's wife, for becoming Sly's new girlfriend and personally auditioning for the part; Dolph Lundgren, as Ivan Drago, "The Siberian Bull," for being humongous and saying "I must break you"; Carl Weathers, as Apollo Creed, for moonwalking to his death in Vegas; Talia Shire, for being Rocky's wife the fourth time even though she hasn't had anything to do in the last three movies; and, of course, The Rock, who starred, wrote, directed, beat some people up for world peace, and said "We're changing—we're like, turning into ordinary people."

Four stars. Joe Bob says check it out. ■

JOE BOB'S MAILBAG

DEAR CHANNEL FIVE [San Francisco]: This letter is to express my disappointment and disgust at your choice of Joe Bob as an *Evening Magazine* item.

It would be impossible to learn the extent of the damage this crude and vulgar figure has caused. He, and other writers and entertainers like him, can undoubtedly claim credit for innumerable shoddy interludes, which at the least, evoke the image of bad complexions and oily hair.

No rationalizing of his declared intent at satire can alter the reality of a semi-literate segment of your audience which is impressionable and only too eager to subscribe to filth and violence.

To feature this manipulative caricature is to insult every viewer who is looking for signs of health in this age so full of sickness.
MARY JANE JOYCE
SAN FRANCISCO

DEAR MARY JANE: Sorry it took so long to answer your letter. I was out sick, getting my face excavated. But I wanted to tell you I do NOT subscribe to filth and violence. I buy it off the newsstand.

DEAR KORA RADIO [Bryan, Tex.]: After listening to many hours of your radio station's music and programs, I must write to tell you how disappointed and upset I am after your broadcast this morning of Joe Bob Briggs and "We Are the Weird." I cannot believe the radio station I have loved and respected for years would promote such a person! Starving children are NO joke and this song is the result of very sick thinking. As I listened to the words of the song, I could not believe my ears. How any *human* could make fun of such a tragedy!

KORA has been known for its involvement in community activities, helping the people of Bryan-College Station in any and every way. WHY in the world would you smudge your reputation with an association with such a person and his sick thinking?

I hope and pray that this type of interview will never be repeated on your station. If you continue to promote such trash, your loyal listeners will not be listening any more!
Sincerely,
LYNETTE FRIDEL
BRYAN, TEX.

DEAR LYNETTE: I'd like to make it clear that I'm opposed to starvation and I won't have it in my own house.

DEAR ORLANDO SENTINEL: I would like to subscribe to the Sentinel, because it's the best daily newspaper in Orange County and maybe even some suburbs around here.

However, I would like to receive the pa-

per only on days that you do not print the Joe Bob Briggs column. Do you offer a plan or a special rate for subscribers who want the newspaper just on non-Briggs days?

I appreciate your attention to this inquiry, and I look forward to a reply.
Sincerely,
ZELDA SAYRE
WINTER PARK, FLA.

DEAR ZELDA: Yes we do, it's called the Daily Worker plan, for those who don't want to be polluted by evil capitalist running-dog American propaganda, and it's 30 rubles a week.

DEAR FRIEND IN CHRIST: Please, I must petition you in the name and love of our Lord Jesus Christ to consider the events of our day and their significance to the return of our Lord: seemingly every country is at war, terrorism flourishes openly, secular humanism is encouraged. Communism continues to grow ever more powerful, abortion, homosexuality and pornography are considered individual rights, etc. . . .
Your brother in Christ,
GREG
DALLAS

DEAR GREG: Yeah, isn't it GREAT?

What Christmas Means to My Buddies

In this holiday season of ours, I always like to call up famous people and make a fool of myself and ask all of em what Christmas means to them. I hope their answers will fill your heart with joy and gladness this year when you start hangin around the shopping mall, going, "You do that one more time and I'll cut it off."

The first person I asked was His Holiness, the Ayatollah Rohollah Shinola Khomeini. The connection was bad, but he offered these words for the holidays: "We keel meeny meeny pipples. Here come one now. Very beesy. Got to go."

Next I called up Ed McMahon for his Christmas comment: "Do I get to be in the parade again? How much? How much after my agent's cut?"

Or how about Debby Boone, the lovely and talented daughter of Pat Boone: "It was, too, a hit record. Was too, was too."

Did I mention O.J. Simpson: "Jesus didn't break any of my rushing records, even though he could have if he wanted to. Maybe."

Comedian Jackie Vernon: "Hey, the guy made *me* famous."

The evangelist Dr. Gene Scott: "You wanna talk Christmas, I'll talk Christmas. You wanna talk Christianity, I'll talk Christianity. You wanna talk IRS, I'll talk IRS. You wanna talk what this season means to me, I'll talk what this season means to me. You wanna talk . . ."

Inspirational speaker Zig Ziglar: "If that guy had just listened to a few of my tapes, he could of forced himself to come down off that silly cross and start selling Mary Kay products. You

see the complexions on those people? The man could have made a fortune."

Sylvester Stallone: "When is it?"

Soviet Premier Mikhail Gorbachek: "Jesus Christ-ski very interesting Jewboy."

Israeli Prime Minister Shimon Peres: "He was born here, but we didn't kill him."

Ann Landers: "The man was a disgrace to his Jewishness. The man was a pest. I always do Miami Beach in December. People who can't be a Jew and stay a Jew, they just make me sick."

Andy Williams: "What do you mean, Bob Hope's doing it again? I've got arrangements, I've got production numbers, I've got . . ."

Mel Torme: "Why would I ever get tired of singing it?"

In 1968, the zombies ate Pittsburgh. In 1979, they took over ever shopping mall in America. Now, in *Day of the Dead,* they've plumb took control. There's about 12 folks left, and they're all hidin down in Evergladesland, wanderin around an underground missile silo, saying the f-word a lot. But they've got a plan.

First they herd the zombies into cattle chutes and wire em up for brain research. Then they start teachin em to use Sony Walkmans and Gillette Trac 2 razors. Finally, this zoot-suit doctor in a bloody smock says, "We can *domesticate* these zombies!" But the military commander says, basically, that he's gonna turn his geek soldiers loose with Uzi submachine guns and waste the z-man population and copter himself over to Guatemala and hide out in the jungle. Only two or three *problemas,* though. One: not enough ammo. Two: not enough food. Three: only one bimbo left, and she hates his guts, so how you gonna rebuild the population?

And the big Numero Four-o: One of the chained-up zombies is startin to *understand.* He's startin to read old Stephen King novels and demand double helpings of Hamburger Helper. Too bad, though, cause before they have time to teach him to count to four, one of the wimp guerrillas starts turning into mental Jell-O, and then one of the zombies gets out of her pen and eats off the limbs of three people and for the next hour we got zombie fu, with the living fighting the dead fighting the living dead in the all-time gross-out paint-the-walls-red intestine feast of the decade. George Romero, the master, does it again.

We got approximately 1,500 zombies. A 92 on the Vomit Meter. Four hundred thirty-five gallons blood. Nine dead bodies. Thirty-seven undead dead bodies. Two dead breasts. Three and one-half heads roll. Ears roll. Fingers roll. Arms roll. Stomachs roll. Necks roll. Cheeks roll. Eyeball rolls. Guts roll. Gratuitous man-eating alligator. Hypodermic fu. One motor vehicle chase. Soldier-feeding. Drive-In Academy Award nominations for Antone DiLeo, as the wimp who says "Look! It's a miracle! He doesn't see us as lunch"; Terry Alexander, the copter pilot, who does a great imitation of an unemployed reggae singer and for saying "We been punished by the Creator"; Lori Cardille, the bimbo scientist who can't understand why her boyfriend would start having a nervous breakdown just because one lousy zombie bites his arm; Richard Liberty, as the crazed scientist who says "I don't know what's wrong, the zombie won't eat"; Joseph Pilato, as the evil commando, for making his eyes big and saying "You've given us a mouth full of

Greek salad"; Howard Sherman, as Bub the Zombie, the most lovable on-screen dead person since Rita Jenrette; and George Romero, the master, who does it again.

Four stars. Joe Bob says check it out. ■

JOE BOB'S MAILBAG

DEAR JOE BOB: I'm a big fan of yours, but I think I should set you straight on Ed Gein. Mr. Gein was *not* a grave digger. He was a taxidermist, and a damn good one, too. There was no "woman in a deer suit" (Quoting you). He did, however, have his mother's hide (skin) Tanned, and he wore that while he talked to her (via psychotic scizophrenia).

He was also an economically sound man. When he caught his prey (human) he would use all the parts of the carcass; skins for lampshades, chair leather, drumskins, and etc. and the bones for various structural devices; like split craniums for soup bowls.

He also stuffed and mounted the heads of his victims, like your ordinary hunting trophy.

He was truly an amazing individual.
LIZA MOHAWK
SANTA ROSA, CALIF.

DEAR LIZA: I don't know what came over me. I must have lost Ed's head.

DEAR JOE BOB: Hi didn't didn't, The cat and the fidn't, Came out to garb us a doon. The beemrabs came home, To a hut made of loam, And the meegraybs Burr Strabberly nags!

That is the meaning of life.
KEITH THOMAS
GREENWOOD, IND.

DEAR KEITH: Yes, but what about underwear?

Successful Lying

I want you to listen to what people are already saying about the Joe Bob Briggs motivational sales course, "Ten Days to Successful Lying."

Slim Randle, Vice President/Marketing, "Jeans for Queens," Ashtabula, Ohio: "I was skeptical at first. Then Joe Bob Briggs made a two-hour presentation to our staff, and three months later our sales declined *400 percent*! But we didn't care, because we all got divorces!"

Louise Perry, teacher, Iroquois Elementary School, Iroquois, New Mexico: "I think Mr. Briggs was the first speaker we ever had who actually assaulted some of the teachers on their lunch hour. At least four of us have never been the same since then. Our lives have changed. We carry guns now. We're going to get a great deal of money from Mr. Briggs."

Nobody believes it at first. Nobody believes because nobody *wants* to believe. You know, this world of ours is filled with so much negativism that it takes a special person to stand up and be counted and say, "Hey! I've been telling the truth all my life. I'm sick of it. I'm ready to make people buy things from me for no apparent reason. I'm starting with *you*. Hey, *buy this shirt*! The one I'm wearing. It was given to me by Prince Charles."

I didn't even have to tell that person what to say. As soon as he got in touch with his Human Potential, as soon as he knew that he was destined to be a millionaire no matter how many people he had to bankrupt to get there, then he was already a Liar in his mind. Now maybe he didn't know that. Maybe he didn't go around saying, "I'm a Liar in my mind." But once he learned the ten techniques of Lying, there was no turning back. He started losing weight, he started wearing gold chains, his wife started flashing her breasts so men would come in the house and he could roll them. And in *six short months*, he had quit his job as an accountant for a major midwestern bank and *socked away $750,000 that they'll never find even if they send Sherlock Holmes to Switzerland!*

Now I know what you're saying. You're saying to yourself, "Sure, he could do it. He was a natural Liar. He was born a Liar. But I've never had any *talent* for it."

But I'm here to tell you, If you can talk, you can lie. And to prove it, I want you to say the following words to yourself at least a hundred times every day.

"People like me. People really like me. No, really, they do."

Communist Alert!

The California Supreme Court outlawed "Ladies Night" cause some wimp in Anaheim sued for equal rights. As we all know, Ladies Night was originally instituted in this nation so women could get drunk just as often as men could, but we wouldn't have to put the extra beer money in their salary. Now we'll have to start buying em banana daiquiris again just to make em shut up.

If you can convince yourself of *that,* then you are eligible for the full "Ten Days to Successful Lying" course. Just send $1500 to Joe Bob Briggs, P.O. Box 2002, Dallas, TX 75221, and I'll call you up and show you what a real liar can do.

This is the time of year when all the drive-in movies vanish so they can Meryl Streep us to death. But if you'll just keep on driving out of town, out past the city dump, out past the trailer park, out past the last B-B-Q stand, and keep on going till you come to a drive-in that looks like God's been using it for a toxic waste dump, and then if you wait till the third feature that comes on at midnight, then maybe you can see *Superstition.*

The devil's moved into this house up in Vermont somewhere, and he's roaming around in there, possessing the microwave oven, sticking human heads in there, and then turning up the heat so the head looks like a piece of quiche that's been sprayed all over the insides. He's been doing this ever since 1692, when a witch was killed in town but the preacherman was too wimpy to drive a stake through her heart and so he just tossed her in the pond and threw a cross in there and figured, hey, it's over.

But 300 years later we still got heads rolling, bodies rolling, and this deaf-mute named Harlan is getting blamed for everthing. You gotta feel sorry for the guy. All he does is hang around the house, jumping off ledges and imitating a maniac, and the police think he's *doing* something.

Then a new priest moves into the house, and this guy is such a bad priest that he's drunk and also he forgot his vows and so he has a wife and two teenage kids. A guy like this in the house with the devil, anything can happen. So the first day he's there, *whacko!* the buzzsaw goes haywire and the blade flies right through the monsignor's body. It takes about 30 seconds to burrow all the way through and come out the back, and all the time everbody's standing around going "That's extremely odd." And then the teenage girls decide to start lounging around in their swimsuits by the *pond.* Pretty soon we got a house full of Owens Farm Country Sausage.

We're talking no breasts, but 19 dead bodies. Nine gallons blood. A 68 on the Vomit Meter. Three beasts. Exploding head. Burning lakes. Priest screwed to death on a wine press. Gratuitous rotting flesh. Face-staking. Toe-chewing. Heads roll. Body rolls (split down the middle). Microwave fu. Woodsaw fu. Drive-In Academy Award nominations for Jacquelyn Hyde, as the ugly old hag, for saying "You have a 20th-century mind—and you may soon regret it"; Albert Salmi, as the Inspector, for saying "Also, one of the victims was microwaved" and "You're an ugly old hag"; and James Houghton, as the young priest, for saying "I don't understand any of this."

Three stars. Joe Bob says check it out. ■

Top 10 Films for 1985

You know, sometimes you have one movie that just sort of sums everything up for you, a drive-in moment that says it all for the whole generation. And that moment came for me in 1985. The movie was *Barbarian Queen*. The actor: one of those South American extras in a pith helmet. The situation: I forgot. And, of course, the line is immortal:

"You are much too beautiful a girl to let yourself be broken into food for the royal dogs."

Kinda makes life seem worthwhile again, don't it?

Roger Corman, the drive-in king, made *Barbarian Queen,* but don't try to find it at your drive-in anymore. There are parts of this country that won't even get to *see BQ,* ever, and that's because of the growing Communist menace that's seepin down here from Massachusetts and startin to turn us all into homosexual Buddhists. You know what I'm talkin about. I'm not afraid to say it. It's time to name names.

I'm talkin about VCRs.

Very Cruddy Ripoffs.

Normally, this time of year, I'd give you my top 10 flicks for '85, go back over the highlights (I been saving *Gymkata* dialogue for seven months now), but we don't have time for that anymore. Most of the drive-in flicks released in 1985 went *straight to the video store* and were rented out to guys named Enzio. Last year I had to drive 250 miles to find a drive-in playin *Human Animals.* I had to go to San Antonio to see *Make Them Die Slowly. White Cannibal Queen* never did make

it to town. *Karate Killers on Wheels—* video fu.

A lot of you are out there smirkin right now, stuffin videos down your pants so I won't see em, trying to act like it's all the *other people* that are runnin the drive-ins out of business. But here's a few questions I want to ask you before I send some sumo wrestlers over to your house to check the sound quality on your I Ate-a Beta or whatever you call it.

Numero Uno: Do VCRs come with in-car heaters? No they do not. You people are gonna freeze to death trying to watch those little babies in the winter.

Numero Two-o: Do VCRs sell Milk Duds? No they do not.

Numero Three-o: Can you fog up the window on a VCR? No you can not.

Numero Four-o: Do VCRs have backseats? No way, José-can-you-see.

Numero Five-o: Do the cops come and hassle you when you're watchin a VCR?

Come to think of it, guess I'm gonna need one of them suckers.

Okay, here's the top 10 drive-in flicks for '85. Listen up.

Nightmare on Elm Street: Freddy Krueger, better known as the walking Nazi experiment, wanderin around in the dreams of nubile young teenagers in Van Nuys until Heather Langenkamp, the new Jamie Lee Curtis, paints the room red with his face.

Make Them Die Slowly: Established a world drive-in record with a 98 on the Vomit Meter. Excellent slime-eating extras. Made by Umberto Lenzi, the Italian Lee Harvey Oswald. Banned in 31 countries and Chillicothe, Oklahoma.

Breakin' 2 Is Electric Boogaloo: The year's best spin-on-your-head permanent-brain-damage musical, about a bunch of white spastics trying to tear down the Watts Community Center and put up a mall. The best scene is where the breakdancers destroy a bulldozer brigade with *menacing pelvises.*

Re-Animator: Only movie ever made where an actor gets his head cut off halfway through the movie but *finishes the movie.* Excellent laser lobotomies, plus the current gross-out champion—a scene where the headless guy straps down the medical school dean's daughter on an autopsy table, holds his head in his hands, and [this is where they always censor me].

Invasion U.S.A.: The Russians land thousands of troops on Miami Beach, invade downtown Atlanta, and wait for Chuck Norris to come roaring up Interstate 95 in his Range Rover for revolving restaurant fu.

The Last Dragon: Best black-exploitation kung-fu musical of the year. Bruce Leeroy lives in a Harlem walk-up over his daddy's pizza joint ("Justa directa yo feetsa to Daddy Green's Pizza"), worships Bruce Lee, goes to kung-fu class, wears a little Chinaman's hat, says stuff like "I am confused, master," tries to get in Vanity's pants, and teaches four Chinese guys to breakdance to the song "Suki Yaki Hot Saki Sue."

Rambo, Second Blood: What can I say?

Perfect: Jamie Lee Curtis in the best horror film of 1985.

Lifeforce: Electro-lip space ghouls in heat. A classic.

Fright Night: Roddy McDowall raises his career from the dead and attacks a recent graduate of the Richard Gere Charm School for Well-dressed Vampires.

Commando: Arnold the Barbarian gets a burr haircut, rubs some dirt on his face, and out-Rambos Rambo.

Return of the Living Dead: Zombie-Rama.

Death Wish 3: Remember the elephant gun? Remember the green-haired geek that molests 75-year-old ladies for their Medicaid money? Remember the little pile of scum at the end? The Master. ∎

Communist Alert!

Up till now there's only been one place in New York City you could see a decent drive-in movie—The Deuce, Forty-second Street. For a city that don't have drive-ins, they had the next best thing. Last month alone, they had *Doomed to Die, My Friends Need Killing, Ten Violent Women,* and *Shocking Cannibals, all showin at the same time* on The Deuce. But now somethin called the Urban Development Corp. is gonna wreck all of em—the Liberty, the Harris, the Empire, the Times Square, the Cine, and the Roxy—cause they say these are "dens of blight, crime and decay." Ever drive-in fan in the Big Apple has been writin in to me about this, and so I want the postcard fu to start *immediately.* The man's name is Ed Koch. Drop him a noose. Remember, without eternal vigilance, it can happen here.

Going to Vegas for New Year's, Baby

Usually on New Year's Eve I work the Catskills—either the Sergio Franchi lounge or the warm-up for Allen and Rossi. Course, there was that one year when I got my big shot on the Siegfried and Roy *Beyond Belief* show, but it was real tough cause they wedged me in between the basketball-playing unicyclists and Lynette the Snake Woman. I went straight to Bernie Yuman about it—Bernie's the business manager for Siegfried, but he has some kind of agent commission deal with Roy—and I said, "Bernie baby, listen to me, I can't work snake-woman warm-up anymore, it's not me." And Bernie, what a sweetheart, I'll never forget what he said.

"You're fired."

That's what I love about show business. One year you're on top, next year you're hanging around the blackjack tables in Vegas going "I did Donahue *twice,* buddy."

In fact, that's exactly what I was saying on *this* New Year's Eve when I got kicked out of the Dunes for being such a good blackjack player. You probly already heard about it, it was in all the shoppers. I didn't wanna punch the guy out, but he was cheatin. He said he thought it was suspicious that I kept hittin 20 and stickin on 11. Obviously, he just never saw a pro before. I was using the System that night.

Like, I'm not gonna give it all away in the newspaper, but here's basically all you need to know about my blackjack system:

Always do the opposite of what the dealer expects you to do.

Like a lot of people, they get two face cards—one up, one down—and they say to theirselves, "What's the chance of me getting a one-card, also known as an 'ace,' on the next deal?"

But *I never even have to think about it anymore.* You know why? I've memorized all the combinations. My mind is like a computer. I see two face cards, I just automatically say "Hit me," or, if I've had six or seven complimentary cocktails, I say "Hit me in the gut bucket."

The dealers really like it when you say "Hit me in the gut bucket." It's a sign to them that you're "cool," "hip," or "a guy that talks like Frank Sinatra when he's drunk."

Okay, here's another one. You look at your cards, and whatta you got? A six down and a five up. Add it up in your head. I'll wait. Now it may surprise you to know that 99 players out of a hundred will take another card in this situation. Not me. I just say, "I'm coolin my heels," and most of your dealers will recognize that as the international slang for "The stupid guy is back at the table again."

But here's my point again: I never think about it. It's automatic. I've *trained* myself to stick on 11. Most people can't even do it. Try it. Go to the tables, wait till you get 11, and *try to stick on it.* See how hard it is?

Next week I'm gonna show you how to count cards (hint: you start with the number "one"), but right now I got to go to the drive-in.

A lot of you been askin me about it. You been wonderin why I didn't review it when it first came out last October. And the answer is "I forgot." But now we're gonna do it cause it's the only thing out that don't have "indoor-bull-stuff" written all over it. I'm talkin about the stupidest name of the year, the only hero named after a bedpan. I'm talkin *Remo.*

Now you may be thinkin to yourself, "What is a Remo?"

A Remo is the guy that played Gus Grissom in *The Right Stuff,* only now he's a cop that gets shoved into the East River by a CIA bulldozer and fished out by skindivers so he can have his face changed by surgically removing a mustache. Once we can't recognize him, he gets bossed around by Wilford Brimley to fulfill the 11th Commandment: "Thou shalt not get away with it."

In other words, he's a Super Scum Scooper. He works for the last secret agency on earth that still believes in good honest police work and wants to make America strong again—by blowing up evil businessmen and making it look like they had a little accident with their Powerlift Skil Saw. Course, you can't just walk out there and start exploding Lockheed executives the *first day,* so first Remo gets sent to Joel Grey, who's been freeze-dried and kept in a Korean missile silo ever since he made *Cabaret,* and now he's trained his body to dodge bullets and slice corned beef without a knife. He spends most of his time puttin Remo up on 30-story ledges and takin him to Coney Island and climbing up and down the Statue of Liberty while three goonies crack lug wrenches on his skull so he can learn how to "forget fear." After he learns kung fu, karate, ninjitsu, and tofu, Joel Grey teaches Remo how to run across wet cement. Finally, he's ready.

Time to go run around missile factories with a bimbo Army major who wears high heels and says "I'm gonna file a 16-11" a lot. Since they let bim-

---

JOE BOB'S MAILBAG

DEAR JOE BOB: Two questions: 1) What are you on? and 2) Can I have some?

I'm from South Texas and down here we spell it MESCUN not MESKIN.
CHARLENE HUDSON
SEGUIN, TEX.

DEAR CHARLENE: I'm on somethin they bring up from Mesko.

DEAR JOE BOB: Hi! I would like to tell you my, how can I say this, my way of defining the meaning of life:

Life is being born then having your parents boss you around and feed you these green, mushy looking vegetables, and then they tell you "it's good for you."

After that you're finally a teenager and you think you can do anything you feel like, but you're still eating the mushy green stuff that your parents make you eat, if you don't get grounded or something overdrastic that only your parents can conjure up.

After your teens I commonly guess that you'll probably bust your butt to get enough money to retire and by then you're 60 and you probably will have lung cancer from smoking too much. And when you're a millionaire you're about 80 and you suddenly drop dead before you get to see it or even spend it on prune juice.

Well, thank you for reading my letter, if you did, and thank you for listening to a 13-year-old that guesses at everything.
ELISSA (LISSA) UNDERWOOD
KISSIMMEE, FLA.

DEAR LISSA: Pretty good for a kid—except for the part about smokes. You get the lung cancer from the mushy green vegetables. What this means for you, in practical terms, is that you're already a goner. There's nothin you can do about it.

bos in the Army now, Remo not only has to kill the meanie, but he has to shut her up, save her life, keep her from gettin a run in her stocking, fight off three killer dogs, dodge semi-automatic machine gun fire, and blow up half of West Virginia.

Why? Cause if he don't, Wilford Brimley will make him fly Braniff.

No breasts. Ten dead bodies. Two pints blood. Three motor vehicle chases. Exploding truck. Drowned patrol car. Exploding factory. Exploding jeep. Dead jeep. Gratuitous exploding Army recruit. Walking on water. Mad-dog attack. Mad-rat attack. Dog tight-rope-walking. Log avalanche. Bullet-dodging. Only a 12 on the Vomit Meter. Kung fu. Sinanju. Tofu. Bulldozer fu. Gas chamber fu. Statue-of-Liberty fu. (By the way, you can send money to the "I'm Sick of Hearing About It, Rip Her Down" Committee, P.O. Box 2002, Dallas, Texas 75221.) Chopsocky City. Drive-In Academy Award nominations for Fred Ward, the only actor capable of fulfilling the name "Remo"; his sidekick J. A. Preston, for saying "Remember—in and out, like a duck mating"; the 108-year-old Joel Grey, for saying "You move like a pregnant yak"; and Guy Hamilton, the director, who ain't made anything this decent since *Goldfinger.*

Three stars. Joe Bob says check it out. ■

Communist Alert!

New Line Cinema in New York City finally called up to explain why Heather Langenkamp, the new Jamie Lee Curtis scream queen, was *not* re-signed for *Nightmare on Elm Street, Part 2*. These guys claim Heather ran off and got married to Bob Dylan's keyboard player and hasn't been seen since. Can it be? Am I supposed to believe this? One day she's a drive-in star and the next day she's layin cross a big brass bed with some piano player? Remember, without eternal vigilance, it can happen to your mother.

Ugly-on-a-Stick Thins Out

Ever week people write in and say, "Whatever happened to Ugly-on-a-Stick?" And I wanna say right here, I think it's a little cruel of you people to refuse to use her Christian name of Chloris. Cause she has a new image now. She's lost some weight, bought her a new set of elbows, and now she's approximately six-foot-seven and weighs 44. Some people would *kill* for that figure. I saw her over at Eckerd's Drugs last week, imitating a driveshaft.

I said to her, "Chloris, why the new look?"

And she rolled her upper lip up over her gum in that way she has that makes her look like a clay Aztec Indian, and she said, "So I can put out the Ugly-on-a-Stick Workout Tape."

Some people you just can't be nice to.

What happened was she went to see this movie *Chorus Line,* and she came back home and said, "Joe Bob, most of them girls were uglier than I am."

And I said, "Well, now, let's not exaggerate, Chl . . . uh, Ugly."

And she said, "No, you go look. They had one that rented out her face for nuclear testing."

Anyhow, the whole experience convinced Ugly-on-a-Stick that she might as well quit her job at Le Bodine and go audition for a 30-million-dollar movie about obnoxious dancing weenies. And I told her it wouldn't work. I said, "Chloris, they don't make more than two, three movies about obnoxious dancing weenies a year. The odds are *astronomical*."

And she said, "But Joe Bob, you didn't see the one that looked like she'd been using her boobs for trampoline practice."

And so ever since then she's been seen all over town, hummin the theme from *Fame* and doing Ugly Yoga. She's not satisfied just to stick her heels behind her neck, like a *Dynasty* star posing for *USA Today,* but she's got to wrap her ankles around her forehead, like a *Dynasty* star posing for *Journal of the Permanent Spinal Injury Foundation.*

It's not a pretty sight.

After she finishes that, she'll generally start floppin her legs all over the lot like a tarantula that wants to be in a Bulgarian trapeze act, and then she'll reach down and grab her ankles and start doing "the Shirley MacLaine," which makes her look like she just got run over by a sem-eye, and finally she'll do reverse double backflips *without ever leaving the ground.* I have to admit, I didn't think Ugly-on-a-Stick was capable of this kind of performance, but after personally witnessing it, I only had one thing to say.

"Chloris?"

"Yes, Joe Bob?"

"You're still ugly."

A Chorus Line finally got to the drive-ins this week, and now I know what Ugly-on-a-Stick was talkin about. This is the most terrifying Danskin horror movie since *Perfect.* What we have here is approximately 17,000 creepolas that live in New York so they can go around saying "I hate my parents, I hate my life, I hate my little crummy New York apartment, I really hate these auditions," and then dancing their little hearts out.

Meanwhile, Michael Douglas sits at the back of the Broadway theater, chewing on dead rats and saying "Come on, spill your guts some more, or else I'll make this movie *ten minutes longer!*"

And so when he says that, they generally burst into tears and talk about how they became homosexuals.

Sometimes this Mick Jagger lookalike hops around onstage and gets em so excited that they sing songs, even though all of em sing like Dr. Joyce Brothers. My personal favorite was the

---

Communist Alert!

Victory over Communism! *The Gothic Times,* student newspaper at Jersey City State College, gets attacked by the student government about once ever month for continuing to print Joe Bob's movie reviews, so finally they forced em to run an election to see if it stayed in the paper or not. If the election was in Communist Russia, 99 percent of the population would of voted. But over here in the U.S., nobody likes to vote, and so nobody voted. Another all-American victory for Joe Bob.

classic "Who am I anyway? Am I my résumé?" I would put this song up there in a class with the scene in *Chainsaw* where Leatherface hangs Pam on a meat hook.

Then we have some more stuff about hating your parents and being ugly. Then we have some bimbos chiming in on the beautiful and lovely "God, I Really Need This Job!" Then we have this bimbo Cassie that keeps hangin around backstage and interrupting the movie to whine. Michael Douglas keeps dumpin on her, tellin her to go home, but she *refuses to leave,* and so finally we have to watch her do a ten-minute number called "I, I, I Am a Dancer." She, she, she is not, not, not.

Then we get a bunch of ethnic fu. A black guy, a chiquita, a little Chinawoman, a Puerto Rican transvestite, and then the big suspense moment in the film comes along, and we start squirming around in the seat and going "No! No! Don't do it! Not that! Keep em away from it!"

But it's too late. Somebody already went backstage and opened the box.

They pass out the straw hats. They give em *canes,* for God's sake. In any other hands these would be mere toys. In this movie, they are *deadly weapons.*

Then they give em the gold plastic pants!

Two breasts (see-through leotard). Eighty-one jigglers. Ninety beasts (the entire female cast). Seven gallons blood (stomach ulcers in the audience). Gratuitous goose-stepping. Gratuitous girlfriend-dumping. Gratuitous cast. Tap fu. Ballet fu. That-stuff-they-do-when-they-shake-their-shoulders fu. An 84 on the Vomit Meter. A full 10 on the Purina Dog Chow Meter. Drive-In Academy Award nominations for Michael Douglas, the best child molester since Freddy Krueger; Yamil Gorges, the chiquita, for saying "How could anyone want to be anything but a dancer?" and forgetting the answer; and for Sir Dick Attenborough, who directed this sucker and kept sayin "Just remember, no matter how many times the audience throws things at you, they *cannot hurt us.* We *will not* fight back. We are Jews, we are Hindus, we are Muslims, we are all men. We will fast until the violence stops."

Two stars. Joe Bob says check it out. ■

Ninja in a Business Suit

Sho Kosugi was in Texas last week, kick-boxing around the lobby of Doubletree Hotel and beggin for publicity, so I'd be reviewing *Pray for Death* this week even if I didn't want to. You know I've come close to saying this before, and I'm not just saying it cause I don't want Sho to beat my head in with his middle toe, but it's true:

Sho Kosugi is the best kung fu man since Bruce Lee. Forget Jackie Chan. Forget Jet Lee. Forget Bruce Lei, Bruce Li, Bruce Lea, and Bruce Leigh. It's no wonder that they're giving Hong Kong back to the Commies. They haven't turned out a world-class *thwacker* since 1974, when Bruce's head blew up.

Pray for Death—which I been trying to get released ever since I discovered it last year in France—is the first movie ever made about a Japaheeno Ninja who joins a neighborhood improvement group. All Sho wants to do is take his little Japaheeno wife to Houston, buy an old house, lay a little bathroom tile, replace some wood shingles, and play some Frisbee with his Yokohama younguns.

Unfortunately, there's this mushmouth mobster named Limehouse that gets his jollies out of pouring gasoline on people and saying "Hey, how about a Viking funeral?" And he decides a Japaheeno family would be just the right people to take the blame for some missing California nose candy. So first he kidnaps Sho's little kid, then he gets two Cro-Magnon men in a pickup to run over the other kid and Sho's wife, and then he sneaks into Sho's wife's hospital room, fiddles around with her life support equipment, and goes "Whoops!"

Pretty soon we got one p.o.ed Ninja in a business suit.

Unfortunately, we also got some Communist censorship going on here. The version I saw over in France is *not* the one that's opening up now, cause the guys on the national censor board decided *Pray for Death* needed an X for violence, and so that meant they couldn't advertise in the newspaper, and so that meant they had to go back and take out some of the scene where Limehouse burns up an old man and the scene where Sho's wife gets her plug pulled. They been doing stuff like this ever since some mommies complained about *Indiana Jones and the Temple of Scum* a few years back.

Good thing we got Sho in charge, though, cause he rises above the scissors and turns this into *Enter the Dragon, Death Wish,* and *Halloween,* all rolled into one flick. It goes immediately to Numero Uno on the JBB Best of '86 list, surpassing the previous

best horror flick—*A Chorus Line.*

We got 48 dead bodies (17 before the opening credits). Two breasts. Nine gallons blood. A 98 on the Vomit Meter (84 in the censored version). Chest-carving. Wrist-slashing. Six kung fu brawls. Motor vehicle chase. Kung fu. Ninjitsu fu. Kid fu. Hypodermic fu. Ax fu. Chainsaw fu. Lumber mill fu. Crowbar fu. Big Wheel fu. Gasoline-and-a-Bic-lighter fu. Shinto Temple rigamarole about fire and sword and death and prophets. Gratuitous mall shopping. Gratuitous Batman. Two exploding cars. Drive-In Academy Award nominations for James Booth, who wrote this sucker and also played Limehouse, a guy so mean he says "I'm gonna burn you, kid, like a roman candle"; Sho, the new master, who keeps saying "I'm sorry—my fault—so sorry"; Kane Kosugi and Shane Kosugi, Sho's kids, for excellent midget fu; and Gordon Hessler, the director, his best flick since *Scream and Scream Again.*

Four stars. Joe Bob says check it out twice. ∎

Communist Alert!

About 2,000 people showed up for the last night of the South Park Drive-In in Bethel Park, Pa., but the cops made everbody go home at midnight. Why? Merely because "rampaging youths were tearing the place apart." It took 30 cops to wade in there and throw everbody out, but congratulations to the guys that went down swingin. Remember, without eternal vigilance, it can happen here.

Nuevo Laredo: In Search of Art

Me and Rhett Beavers drove down to Nuevo Laredo last week to pick up some art. I've been depressed ever since last year when one of my Dozing Meskin Sombrero Bookends fell off the table and broke into something that looked like a sour-cream enchilada that got left out in Hurricane Amos. For six months I had to use a Rock Burro to hold up my book, and I was gettin sick and tired of it.

So we fired up the Polio Wagon and attacked the Interstate. The reason we used the Polio Wagon was that Rhett spent all last week painting fake bodies in shoulder harnesses on the rear window, so we could ignore the Communist Mandatory Seat-Belt Manifesto and *fake out the cops*. The only problem is when the paint cracks and it makes you look like you have a permanent spinal cord injury and a fire hose coming out of your neck. Other than that, though, it's perfect.

Anyhow, we got down to Nuevo Laredo and started looking for some "el bargains." Fortunately I speak fluent *Espanish,* and so we had no trouble at all. The only tough part was finding replacement parts for Dozing Meskin Sombrero Bookends. If you don't watch these shrewd "el salesmen," they'll make you buy a *pair* of Dozers instead of just the one you need. I happen to know a little bit about this market, and I can assure you that the price is the same *even if you just want one*. Most people don't know this and they end up getting "el broke-o."

After we bought a big bag of candy that looks like Pre-Fab-Crete painted brown, we decided to take in a few races at Nuevo Laredo Downs. One thing you might not know is how this is the only racetrack where the horses can run in any direction they want. Most racetracks, you point the horses down the track, they all go the same way. Boring. Or, as we say in Mesko, "el snoro." But here you get into deep horse psychology before you lose all your "dinero."

Unfortunately, there's a sad part to this story, too. You've heard about it, I know. You've wondered whether it was really true. You've always wanted to know, can such *inhumanity* and *cruelty* exist in the 1980s, when everbody drives a Datsun 280Z? Haven't we evolved beyond *this*? And the answer, I'm sorry to say, is no, we haven't. It still exists. I saw it with my own eyes.

Chihuahua racing.

You wouldn't believe the fascists that own this gruesome sport. They treat these animals like doorstops with legs. sometimes the little guys get so tuckered out they just hang their tongues out, roll their eyes, and start jumping four feet straight up in the air, begging for an old lady that will name them "Tiny." But it's too late. You should see the expressions on their little faces when they bring out the chihuahua saddles. Most of the jockeys weigh at least 250 pounds. The race itself takes seven and a half hours to go 12 feet.

And the crowd *cheers* for this kind of madness. Makes you wonder about mankind, don't it?

Speaking of mistreated house pets, Sonny Bono is in *Troll,* and he has this great scene where he gets attacked by fungus-face midgets and turns into a giant Caesar's salad with a bad singing

JOE BOB'S MAILBAG

DEAR FRIEND: What is it like to be awake and have the full use of your mind? What is mind? Why do you think the types of thought that you do? How do your thoughts affect your emotions, career success, relationships, and your awareness of the psychic, occult, and spiritual sides of your being?

For most people life is, at best, a difficult thing. Their minds are constantly flooded with random thoughts and emotions. They constantly seek happiness in their jobs, sexual relationships, homes, and hobbies. Yet very few people find real and lasting happiness. Religions, philosophies, and "successful" people tell you how to lead your life and where meaning lies. But how many of the religiously minded, philosophically oriented or glittery "beautiful" people are, under their polished exteriors, really happy?

My name is Rama. I teach courses in Psychic Development and Self Discovery. You may have heard of me. I have been teaching the mystical arts for many, many lifetimes. In this life I have been teaching for over sixteen years.

It has been my personal experience that a human life can be uncommonly happy. Naturally, in order to achieve a meaningful level of happiness and success, you need to do specific things that most persons don't do and avoid psychically draining experiences, thoughts, and emotions that most individuals indulge in.

The Only Limitations That Exist Are Those Within Your Own Mind.

[blah blah blah I'm skippin over a lot of stuff in this letter]

Normally the admission price for my seminars is $400. But you can attend your first seminar series for only $200.
RAMA—FREDERICK LENZ, PH.D.
RAMA SEMINARS, INC.
BEVERLY HILLS, CALIF.

DEAR RAMA LAMA MAN I've had the exact same experience you've had. Most people are unhappy cause they don't have the 200 bucks.

voice. This is roughly what Cher did to him in the divorce settlement, but with a lot more slime-spewing.

What happens is this family moves into a new apartment and signs a lease without asking about monsters in the laundry room first. So they deserve everthing they get when Torok the Troll possesses the body of their little snitty daughter and starts going door-to-door in the building, turning people into botany experiments and trashing their apartment with jungle vines. The little girl's brother keeps saying "Something's wrong with Wendy. I don't know—she's just not right." Usually he says this right after she's whopped him upside the head and knocked him unconscious. But they have Michael Moriarty for a daddy, so what do you expect?

Fortunately, June Lockhart is a good witch living upstairs, playing with her pet mushroom and saying "Remember when I was on *Lassie*?" June talks to the brother and decides

Communist Alert!

A bunch of people in England are trying to outlaw the ancient sport of dwarf-tossing. Lenny "The Giant" Bamford, 4-foot-4, makes a living as a human shotput, as guys in South London see who can throw him the farthest ever night in a cabaret. The record is 12 feet 5 inches, but does the British Parliament care? No way. They're trying to put Lenny out of a job by passing a law condemning the practice of "particularly robust men throwing a person of restricted growth as far as possible." Remember, if they ignore the right to bear midgets in England, they can do it here.

there's something wrong about a troll going around sticking his ring into people and turning their living rooms into Lion Country Safari. So she gives the kid a magic golden sword and tells him to kill any giant pigs with wings that come into his apartment, specially if they're trying to turn him into a house plant. Then she goes and turns herself into *Anne* Lockhart so that maybe some producer will see her and Anne can get another guest shot on *Magnum P.I.*

We're talking Condo Vegematic. Two breasts. Two quarts blood. Nine dead bodies. (Five trolled to death.)

Three great mush-face transformation scenes. Eight beasts, including Sonny Bono. No motor vehicle chases. Gratuitous Shelley Hack. Fungus fu. Drive-In Academy Award nominations for Julia Louis-Dreyfuss, as the nekkid nympho in the forest; June Lockhart, for blowing on a trumpet to stop the devil music, which makes her cheeks look like cantaloupes; and Phil Fondacaro, as a midget English professor who goes around being kind to little girls and reciting bad poetry.

Two and a half stars. Joe Bob says check it out. ■

Cleaning Up Dirty Space Talk

I can't believe these people don't have anything better to do than study Uranus. You'd think if we were givin em 19 billion bucks a year in tax money to dangle out there in space, they could start bringing in some pictures of Martians or space ghouls or something, but they're out there playing with something called a "deep space probe."

I don't know about you, but I don't want our tax money being spent on probing Uranus. It's no accident that these Jet Propulsion boys are in California.

Like last week, those guys were *obsessed*. They kept talking about two enormous moons, including one named Miranda. The more they stared at em, the more they talked, and pretty soon we had em describing the moon of Miranda as full of canyons, sprawling valleys, an "area that looks like it was swept by a broom," and, most disgusting of all, "stacks of flapjacks." Then one of these kinky scientists had the gall to say on national TV that

Miranda was attracted to the pole of Uranus.

Is this the kind of stuff you want your children listening to?

But they didn't stop there. They started describing how Uranus was tipped on its side so the "waffling" of the poles could begin. Maybe you laugh at that, but I'm telling you, I saw it done to this guy in Chihuahua City one time and it's the kind of thing that can scar you for life.

You know, this country was founded on certain principles. And one of those principles is that you don't go around talking about "gaseous rings" unless they're your *own* gaseous rings. But down at Pasadena, where all these guys stand around studying craters, anything can happen. They start making these announcements, right there next door to Hollywood where everybody's looking for an excuse to launch a deep space probe, and people just go plumb crazy.

Right after this whole thing was released to the media, there was a sad thing happened out there. You can't blame anybody really. It's nobody's fault. I don't wanna point any fingers. But I just use it as an example to show you what can happen when responsible employees of our government start talking about "interpreting our instruments" without regard for the consequences.

Three days after this happened, *Fess Parker announced he was running for the U.S. Senate.*

I rest my case.

Speaking of Congress, *Streetwalkin* finally came to town. It's the best movie about high school girls making the sign of the double-gilled anaconda since the original *Angel*. It's the ancient plot that goes like this: One morning they're sitting in biology class mutilating worms, wondering where "Mommy" went. Next thing you know

---

JOE BOB'S MAILBAG

DEAR JOE BOB: My boyfriend and I have been wondering if Bunny Briggs of the tap dancing group called the Copasetics might be related to you. And did you know that saying "Rabbit Rabbit" upon awakening the first day of any month brings good fortune for the entire month?
Good luck to you
CHERIE AND RICHARD
SACRAMENTO

DEAR CHERIE AND RICHARD: Yes, I was taken into a family of poor tap-dancers when I was a little orphan child, so yes, he's my brother. The other thing you can say on the first day of the month is "Please get off my arm, I'm sick of you being in my bed ever night." This changes your life, too.

---

they're painting a black microskirt on their upper thighs and hanging around street corners going, "I'm a person, too. Really. I just do this cause I wanna be loved."

Since *Streetwalkin* was made by Roger Corman, the drive-in master, we just skip over all that stuff and end up with Melissa Leo getting off a Greyhound in the Big Apple, so poor that all she has to her name is one Mary Kay Cosmetics bag, and then immediately falling in love with the first pimp that comes along.

Melissa used to be a hot little number on *All My Children,* but now she's starting her serious dramatic career by dressing up like Erich von Stroheim and telling old men to moo like a cow or else she'll have to punish em. Then she gives all her money to Duke the Pimp, who breathes like a mass murderer all the time, only he doesn't really *mean* anything by it. And whenever Duke decides to slap some of his prosties around, or beat them to a mushy pulp, she runs over real quick and starts demanding "What's going on here? I'm personally offended."

If any of you guys remember Wings Hauser, the pimp in *Vice Squad* that liked to play coathanger roulette, all I got to say is *Duke is ten times meaner.* This guy makes Jason look like he's collecting for the Lottie Moon Christmas Offering. And when Melissa decides to take her hairdo chemicals over to the gentle pimp across town, you can pretty much see that, when Duke finds out, he's not gonna challenge her to a game of checkers.

Listen to what we got. Twenty-two breasts. Nine dead bodies. Three quarts blood. Three motor vehicle chases. Hooker slapping. Hooker slugging. Dueling pimps. Slobbering customer. Mooing customer. Psycho apartment-trashing. Junkie-on-a-leash.

Gratuitous toenail painting. Kung fu. Garter fu. Russian roulette fu. Julie Newmar driving a killer Chrysler fu. Goodyear radial fu. Drive-In Academy Award nominations for Melissa Leo, for saying "Duke looks after us and you better learn to appreciate it!"; Julie Newmar, for running through the whole movie in a red garter belt and an abstract painting on her eyelids, saying "Someday I'm gonna quit this and go into the horse business"; Dale Midkiff, as Duke, for saying "I love you and so I'm going to kill you"; and Joan Freeman, the director, who used to work for the communistic PBS network before she graduated to the drive-in.

Three stars. Joe Bob says check it out. ■

Lack of Thingy Causes Teen Death

URGENT: OPEN THIS LETTER AT ONCE! If you don't, you could be throwing away A GIANT PICTURE OF ED McMAHON!

But if you do, you could be the next person that SUBSCRIBES TO *U.S. NEWS AND WORLD REPORT* even though you'll never read it because it's "BORING"!

For years people have been getting this same fat envelope in the mail. Why? you may be asking yourself.

The answer is SIMPLE.

If nobody sent in these little stickers, *U.S. NEWS AND WORLD REPORT* would have gone out of business 35 YEARS AGO!

IN FACT, few people know this, but the editors at *U.S. News* have been sending out THE SAME COPY EVERY WEEK FOR 35 YEARS!

That's why we're appealing to your GREED now! Right now is the time. This may be the luckiest day of your life. Or else you might die today. Yes, think of the possibilities when you shake hands with Ed McMahon on the *Tonight Show* and Ed says, "I get ten million dollars for doing this."

Think of it! TEN MILLION DOLLARS!

Or, if you are dead, Ed will come to your FUNERAL.

Maybe you're getting confused by now. Maybe you're about to take this letter and the 34 little pieces of paper stuck in the envelope with it and the stickers and the lucky numbers and you're about to STUFF it all in the trashcan.

STOP! THIS MESSAGE IS NOT FOR YOU! DON'T READ IT!

Communist Alert!

A deejay named Michael Lowe in Orlando got suspended without pay for calling Santa Claus "an obscene man" and suggesting that Rudolph the Red-Nosed Reindeer be "killed." Mike didn't know his mike was on, or else he would of included the Easter Bunny. I ask you, how much more power are we gonna allow to these fairytale minority groups before we put our foot down?

Most of you know how this game works by now. But there's always a FEW pikers that think they can just ignore all this stuff. It comes to your mailbox, you open it up, you don't feel GREEDY or GUILTY, and so you do NOT renew your subscription to *U.S. NEWS AND WORLD REPORT*.

Frankly, we're amazed. We're amazed that you would run the DANGER of being dropped from our computerized zip-code mailing list which GUARANTEES you a picture of Ed McMahon in your mailbox every three days. We're amazed that you wouldn't AT LEAST send in for 18 issues of *GRIT,* the newspaper sold exclusively by convenience-store stockboys that have been fired from their jobs.

URGENT! MILLIONS AT STAKE! Be the first to send in all nine lucky-prize-number stickers and BALANCE YOUR CHECKBOOK NEXT WEEK because you won't have time for any of your mail tonight. It's going to take you all night to figure out how to stick all the stickers on the right card.

JUST THINK OF IT! There's something way down in that envelope that you FORGOT TO DO so now you can worry that you're INELIGIBLE for the GRAND PRIZE! This is so, by this time next year, you'll know it's time to subscribe to *U.S. News and World Report* like EVERYBODY ELSE!

But meanwhile we're going to TELL ED McMAHON what you did! And you'll be SORRY!

Speaking of ripoffs, there's another son-of-*Animal House* called *School Spirit* that's been roaming around America for about a year now but it just got to Texas on account of it only made 25 cents in each city and so they didn't wanna make a bunch of copies of it. It's one of the best movies ever

JOE BOB'S MAILBAG

DEAR JOE BOB: You were right!

A couple of months ago, I wrote asking what to do about my dog, Fred, who had turned communist on me. Well, I've made him watch *Green Acres* every day. Then, yesterday, when Mr. Ziffel found out that Arnold was romping with Mr. Haney's basset hound at night, and screamed "No pig of mine gonna go out with a Haney!" I could see a light come on in Fred's eyeballs. He jumped up, tore right through the screen door and bit our pinko mailman. Then, he took his mail bag, shook it with his teeth, and scattered letters all over the yard.

Fred is cured!
Your friend for life,
MALCOLM ALCALA
WHITTIER, CALIF.

DEAR MALCOLM: *Even though the worst of it is over, you need to start some immediate post-trauma therapy. I'd recommend* Cannon *at night and* My Three Sons *in the daytime. Under no circumstances should he be allowed near* Mr. Ed.

JOE BOB: Have you ever known anybody who shaved their forehead?
CRAIG MURPHY
RIVER FALLS, WIS.

DEAR CRAIG: *I hope you're not implying that my shaved forehead is unattractive. It's the only part of my body that I shave.*

made by that great Indian tennis player Vijay Amritraj, and his brother Ashok, who are, of course, the greatest Indian tennis-playing movie producers working today.

What we got here is a college kid named Billy who gets a coed trapped in the president's office one night and starts making the sign of the three breasted wildebeest, but things start looking bad when she asks the question, "Do you have a little thingy?" He doesn't have a little thingy, but he says he can get one at the drugstore, so he tears off down the highway, gets hit by a Mack truck, and goes Tap City on the operating table. Here's the good part: He goes *back to college* as a ghost. Get it? School *spirit?* I wanted to make sure you got it.

Okay, Billy's invisible, right, so now we get Billy in the sorority-house shower, Billy throwin Seven-Up in the student president's face, Billy getting *all the girls' blouses wet*. And pretty soon you got a bunch of plot getting in the way of the story, about a Frenchie woman coming over from wherever French people live, to give 17 jillion dollars to the university, only she shows up on Hog Day (when everbody becomes a raving oinker) and then

Billy's uncle keeps trying to get him to go back to Heaven where he belongs, and all we want is for Billy to start ripping off blouses like God intended for all people with X-ray vision.

We got 29 breasts, including 19 wet ones. No blood. Two motor vehicle chases. Slime Slide. Excellent pig costuming. Gratuitous blind folk singers. Grocery groping. Chili slinging. No cheating on the shower scene. Mack truck fu. Yogurt-on-the-head fu. Water-on-a-clingy-silk-blouse fu. Drive-In Academy Award nominations for Elizabeth Foxx, as the iceberg sorority queen, also known as No Nookie of the North; Marta Kober, as the president's daughter, for going on a date with a punk band; Larry Linville, as the president, for saying "Remember me in *M.A.S.H.*?"; and Vijay Amritraj, for being such a great tennis player.

Two stars. Joe Bob says check it out. ∎

The Breasts and Beasts of '85

For the first time in drive-in history, the 4th Annual Drive-In Academy Awards Ceremonies will be televised *even if nobody shows up to accept their award as usual*. Thanks to the sickies at KGO-TV in San Francisco, we'll be handing out the Hubbies exactly one hour before the fake Oscars start down in El Lay, Monday, March 24. And in honor of this historic night, a night that will live in my memory, I'm gonna stop being a Nazi about the Hubbies like I was last year and, once again, I'm gonna let the drive-in fans of America vote on the nominees.

May I have the envelope please?

Winners will be announced *on the air* with a bunch of weirdo wimps from *St. Elmo's Fire* that were already booked before I agreed to go on.

And the nominees are:

BEST FLICK

A Nightmare on Elm Street: Responsible for 19 mass murders in Times Square alone.

Make Them Die Slowly: A 98 on the Vomit Meter, with pig torture, caterpillar eating, gratuitous furry-animal death, turtle hacking, slime-eating extras.

Rambo: Second Blood: The man's an animal.

Return of the Living Dead: Greatest face-eating gut-spewer since *Basket Case.*

Invasion U.S.A.: Body count 185, the new modern record. Best Russian invasion of Miami Beach ever filmed.

Commando: Arnold gets a burr haircut, rubs some dirt on his face, steals a shoulder-mounted rocket-launcher, 18 machine guns, and 34,000 rounds of ammo, and says "Let's boogie."

Re-Animator: Only movie ever made where an actor loses his head halfway through the movie but *finishes the movie.*

A Chorus Line: Best horror film of 1985.

BEST ACTOR

Shabba-Doo Quinones, the best breakdancer that wears big animal teeth in his ears, for *Breakin' 2 Is Electric Boogaloo.*

Sly Rocky Rambo, for liberating 47,000 missing-in-action prisoners from a mud hut in East El Lay.

Johnny Travolta, for sticking the bag of potatoes down his jogging suit in *Perfect.*

Raymond Burr, for filling up the frame in *Godzilla 85* and saying "You know, Nature has a way of reminding man just how puny we are, whether it tells us in the form of a tornado, an earthquake, or a Godzilla."

Big Chuck Norris, for wasting I-95 and exploding a Klaus Kinski look-alike in *Invasion U.S.A.*

Arnold the Barbarian, for the scene in *Commando* where he picks up a phone booth, gives the occupant some directory assistance, chases him up a mountain, dangles him over a cliff by one leg, and goes "Whoops!"

Jeffrey Combes, for wielding the green needle in *Re-Animator* and saying "Come on, why not, this is the freshest body we have."

Charles Bronson, who buys an elephant gun and says "Think I'll go down the street and get myself some ice cream" in *Death Wish 3.*

BEST ACTRESS

Sybil Danning, for performing the cigarette-burn torture, the sword-in-the-face torture, and the shut-up-you-little-animal-before-I-slap-you-again torture in *Jungle Warriors.*

Tawny Kitaen, for battling three raving horny Amazons to the death in a duel of the world's largest abalone-shell underwire support bras in *The Perils of Gwendoline.*

Vanity, for being named Vanity, in *The Last Dragon.*

Ariane, for being named Ariane, in *Year of the Dragon.*

Lana Clarkson, despite using a couple of No. 2 Faber pencils for arms, for saying "I'll be no man's slave and no man's whore" in *Barbarian Queen.*

Jamie Lee Curtis, for making the best horror film of her career—*Perfect.*

Brigitte Nielson, in *Red Sonia,* for flexing her plastic sword and saying "You slaughtered my parents! Like cattle! My brother! My sister!"

Pamela Pratt, Queen of the Amazons, for sleeping with a guy named Garth, zapping him into outer space, then hangin him up by his ankles to dry, in *Hercules II.*

BREAST ACTRESS

Remy O'Neill, for the title role in *Hollywood Hot Tubs.*

Lainie Kazan, as a singing balloon, doing the song "Let Me Take You South of My Border," in *Lust in the Dust.*

Kristi Somers, doing a donut commercial in an all-flour bra with the slogan "Eat it. Eat it all," in *Tomboy.*

Rachel McLish, the El Lay valley girl in the tiger-skin jumpsuit, who stars in *Pumping Iron II: The Women,* with immortal lines like "You're really dealing with human beings. You can't depend on them. It even says so in the Bible."

Mathilda May, for showing off her intergalactic love pouches in *Lifeforce*.

BEST BEAST

Robert Englund, the pasty-face walking Nazi experiment in *Nightmare on Elm Street.*

Soon-Teck Oh, as the evil Colonel Egg Foo Yung, for killing Chuck Norris's pet chicken in *Missing in Action 2: The Beginning.*

Godzilla, in *Godzilla 85,* doing the Tokyo Stomp.

Jennifer Beals, created out of lightning, wrapped like a mummy, and—oh God, not *that*—threatening to flash-dance again in *The Bride*.

Richard Lynch, as Rostov the Ruskie in *Invasion USA,* the guy that likes to stick his gun down people's pants and pull the trigger four times.

Howard Sherman, as Bub the Zombie in *Day of the Dead,* the most lovable on-screen dead person since Rita Jenrette.

BEST SCREENWRITING

Jungle Warriors: "You are peeg who sleeps with own sister!"

The Perils of Gwendoline: "Take your clothes off, quick!"

The Dungeonmaster: "I reject your reality and substitute my own."

The Dungeonmaster: "You have spirit, woman."

Make Them Die Slowly: "No, don't eat that! It might be Rudy!"

The Last Dragon: "Justa directa yo feetsa to Daddy Green's Pizza."

Barbarian Queen: "You are much too beautiful a girl to let yourself be broken into food for the royal dogs."

Red Sonja: "I will tell the future in your entrails, Red Woman!"

Lifeforce: "Collect the pieces of those bodies and *watch them*!"

Police Academy II: "Don't make me flare my nostrils!"

American Ninja: "What do you think I am, a jungle baby?"

Year of the Dragon: "The press is independent! Not just another undercover cop!"

Re-Animator: "I'm sorry, honey, but your dead father's been lobotomized."

Nightmare on Elm Street, Part 2: "Animals just don't explode into flames for no reason."

Silver Bullet: "As the moon gets fuller, the guy gets wolfier."

Rocky IV: "We're changing—we're like, turning into ordinary people."

Day of the Dead: "Look! It's a miracle! He doesn't see us as lunch!"

Superstition: "Also, one of the victims was microwaved."

BEST DIRECTOR

Umberto Lenzi, the Italian Lee Harvey Oswald, for *Make Them Die Slowly*.

Tobe Hooper, "Mr. Chainsaw," for *Lifeforce*.

Sam Firstenberg, the world's greatest martial arts director, who said "Excuse me! Excuse me! Could we have a little more dynamite over there, please!" and made *American Ninja*.

Stuart Gordon, drive-in newcomer of the year, for the classic *Re-Animator*.

Sly Rocky Rambo, for *Rocky IV,* the most sensitive and intelligent movie about nuclear war ever directed by a man with huge breasts.

BEST FU

Missing in Action 2: The Beginning: Rat fu. Egg foo fu.

Cat's Eye: Barbecued wife fu.

Gymkata: Pig-licking fu.

Police Academy II: Body-cavity-search fu.

Return of the Living Dead: Zombie half-dog fu.

American Ninja: Watermelon fu. Mr. Goodwrench fu.

Hercules II: Lou Ferrigno transformed into an underwater sperm-cell fu.

Year of the Dragon: Soybean fu. Egg fu yung.

Invasion USA: Range Rover fu. Knife-through-the-hand-three-times fu.

Commando: Coffee-table fu.

Stand Alone: Fat fu.

Re-Animator: Lobotomy fu. Bonesaw fu. Dead Attack Cat fu.

Death Wish 3: Two-by-four with a nail on the end of it rigged to spring trap fu. Old-man-set-on-fire-like-a-Bic-lighter fu.

Nightmare on Elm Street, Part 2: Killer parakeet fu. Black tongue fu. Weenie fu. Rat fu. Teenagers-boiled-alive-in-swimming-pool fu.

Remo: Gas-chamber fu. Statue-of-Liberty fu. ∎

Communist Alert!

"Popcorn throwing in the Showcase Cinemas, Seekonk, Mass., during a recent screening of *St. Elmo's Fire* culminated in the stabbing of two men, police said." And they say movies don't cause violence! If these guys had been watchin *Make Them Die Slowly,* instead of some wimpola prepster Malt-o-Meal epic, then this wouldn't of ever happened. But Massachusetts don't *have* drive-ins anymore. Remember, without eternal vigilance, it can happen here.

INTERMISSION

Guilty Pleasures

There's basically three ways to get nookie at a drive-in, and two of em are legal:

Numero Uno: Auto-erotic suggestion. One way you can do this is to dress up your auto like an Angora goat in Danskin leotards. Another way you can do it is to sit *inside* your car (we're gettin kinky here now), turn to your Date Specimen, and say, "Hey honey! Over here! Yeah, you! Get a load of *this*!" If you try this, be careful not to specify what "this" is. Otherwise you run the risk of a Class A misdemeanor, "Solicitation of a Public Sex Act No Woman in Her Right Mind Would Consent To." If you get a lady D.A. on that baby, we're talkin 30 days in the Lew Sterrett Justice Center. No, the best way to execute the art of auto-erotic suggestion is to pay good money for a flick that is *proven* to be so irresistible to women that sometimes just the title alone can cause em to forget the fact that you're a pervert and probly diseased and dangerous.

These titles are marked below with the international symbol "Baa." Note that none of them are X-rated. Anybody that would let you take em to an X-rated drive-in is what we call in the business a "presold commodity." This means they have fungus growing on at least three different parts of their body.

If you're not a pervert, go on to . . .
Numero Two-o: Auto-psychotic

---

12 pages to show time

101

suggestion. What this means is, you take her to see somethin so disgusting that she has no choice except to scream like a greased javelina hog or else demand to know "What kind of person would make a movie like that—I mean, what's the point?" If she screams like a greased javelina hog, I think we all know what to do. However, if she actually wants to *talk about the movie,* you have already reached a point of absolute control of the situation. All you have to do now is say the following sentence and *mean* it: "They say the director killed himself as soon as he finished making this." You see what happens here? Up to this point she's been thinking "I don't know about this movie—it's almost like somebody unbalanced made it." *Now* she *knows* she's in the hands of a genuine maniac.

These titles are marked below with the international symbol "Brf." And finally we have . . .

Numero Three-o: Auto-narcotic suggestion. Tell her you read *Film Comment* and afterward you want to talk about the "Grand Guignol humor" of *The Texas Chainsaw Massacre.* This never works.

Okay, here goes. The 10 Best Flicks to Get Nookie By are:

Hundra (1983): The first real feminist exploitation movie starring Laurene Landon in the title role as the last survivor of an Amazon tribe, determined to journey to the Land of the Bull to preserve her race. Laurene mounts a steed, grabs a broadsword, and pillages her way through half of macho Spain accompanied by nothing but her two enormous talents and a cowardly dog named Beast. Symbolism includes seven or eight lances dramatically broken in half by Hundra, who is finally shackled, tossed into the bull pit, given to a horde of mangy, raving, flesh-eating extras from Barcelona, and saved just in time to offer up her virginity to the nearest available Madrid B-movie matinee idol. Directed by Matt Cimber, the genius ex-husband of Jayne Mansfield who thinks no action stunt is any good unless someone is at least partially paralyzed, this one should be avoided by anyone with an aversion to bullwhips.

White Star (1985): You might not realize it, but a lot of women have fantasies about Dennis Hopper. They figure, "I can straighten him out, nobody's *that* scrambled, I know what he needs," and so they love it when Dennis stares into the camera and starts wildly flippin words out of the commercial blender formerly known as his brain. This flick, made in Berlin for about 25 bucks, is the best nonstop Dennis Hopper gonzo flip-out monologue ever made. Dennis plays a rock promoter who used to be the Rolling Stones tour manager, but now he's bottomed out and all he has to manage is this dimwit, blond-headed keyboardist, and he starts out to make him famous by staging a riot in a punk club, then hiring somebody to shoot at him while Dennis stands around and shouts, "Assassination attempt! Assassination attempt!" Dennis then does a 10-minute, raspy-voiced nostalgic monologue on what it was

11 pages to show time

like to spend a night with Keith Richard's groupies. She will never again think *you* are twisted.

How to Make a Doll (1968): Of all the flicks by the goremaster Herschell Gordon Lewis, this sex farce is the most valuable nookie-expediter for one reason. It gives *you* the chance to say "You know what? I think you're much more beautiful than any of the nekkid girls on the screen," *and really mean it*. Because it's true. It's the story of a math professor who invents a computer than can synthetically produce android nymphomaniacs in bikinis—and then gives the computer a human voyeur's brain. You see the beauty here? The computer now has a *personal stake* in the sexual happiness of the inventor. Unfortunately, all of the six or eight androids, including one that I swear is a male actor, look like their silicone chips were intended for a Mexican transistor-radio factory. Don't tell *her* this, though. And be sure to stay until the end, when the computer starts violating their punch cards and generates a gang rape of the professor.

The Hills Have Eyes (1977): Of all the possible cannibal dead-tourist classics, like *The Grim Reaper* and *Saw,* I think this Wes Craven stranded-Winnebago saga is the most terrifying to a female companion—because it's the closest the movies have ever come to *wasting a baby onscreen*. It's one thing to see easygoing Papa Carter get crucified on a burning cactus, but when the nuclear-mutant desert family steals that baby and starts fighting over the dinner portions on their C.B. radios, girls have been known to vaporize and

just leave a little slick spot on the upholstery. Tell her you want to see this one because you "admire the career of Dee Wallace" (the mother), but do *not* let her leave once it starts.

Billy Jack (1971): Women love it, men despise it. Tom Laughlin out on Geek Patrol, defendin wimp Indians and ugly women in Meskin dresses by kicking the New Mexico white trash into Arizona. The only reason it works is that Delores Taylor, Laughlin's co-star and wife, and the reason he has to go up the mountains and get eaten up by rattlesnakes and come back down and kickbox his way through six or seven bowling teams, is *no threat*. If Billy Jack will kick ass for *that* little whiny sniveling sprout-eating Communist, there's hope for everybody. Kick in a few BMW fenders during the movie, just to let her know where you stand politically.

Caged Heat (1974): One of the problems with takin her to see *Private Duty Nurses* or *Fly Me* or any of the nurse or stewardess or bimbos-in-cages flicks is she's gonna think you just wanna see a bunch of jigglin duffel-bags being abused and degraded by jerks like yourself. *Caged Heat* is different. First, the title disguises the fact that this is a great bimbos-in-cages classic. Second, all the girls *triumph* over their abusers and bust out of jail, which makes it all right. And third, it's full of jigglin *feminist* duffel-bags being abused and degraded by jerks like yourself. Jonathan Demme is the magician who made this one, featuring the ripaway bra queen of the Seventies, Barbara Steele.

10 pages to show time

The Wild Angels (1966): The movie that proves that, just cause you wanna ride around on your Hog, refuse to get a job, drink three crates of beer a day, bust up churches, and treat your Old Lady like a piece of dirty laundry, doesn't mean you're not a sensitive kind of guy. Why? Peter Fonda as the leader of the Hell's Angels, in this Roger Corman classic. Women love this guy. He can get away with anything, cause he looks *sooooooooooo sweet*. Make her think she's Nancy Sinatra, but lose the vinyl boots, okay? I'm not completely crazy.

The Trip (1967): Best of the LSD psychedelic crayon-on-the-lens flicks, starring the four primo acid-heads of the Sixties (Nicholson, Fonda, Dern, Hopper), it includes one moment that will *guarantee* her acquiescence to later experimentation. It's when Bruce Dern looks at Peter Fonda, offers him the acid, and says, "I'm gonna be here, man. Trust me." If she buys *that*— putting your life in the hands of Bruce—she'll let you do *anything*. Lots of kinky kaleidoscope pastel crapola floating around on the screen, so you can go "Wow! I can't believe what this is doing to me! I'm about to go *out of control!*"

Naughty Dallas (1964): For the intellectual date: a drive-in documentary on the Kennedy assassination. Larry Buchanan, who would later go on to international docudrama superstardom when he directed *The Trial of Lee Harvey Oswald* and *Goodbye Norma Jean,* started out with this inside look at the life of Jack Ruby, hiring every stripper that used to work at Ruby's club on Lemon Avenue, and revealing the answer to the question, "What would drive a man to cold-blooded murder?" Answer: false eyelashes, sagging bazoomas, and guys in flowered shirts playing snare drums. Tell her you know Ruby personally "and he would have loved this tribute to his life's work." Cry a little bit.

Funny Girl (1968): Get good and stoned before you try this, but this is the one that *can't fail*. Every woman cries at this movie. Every man calls it The Movie That Refuses to End. Take her to it and *act like you're enjoying yourself.* Talk about how "cute" Barbra Streisand is. Choke up on "People." Tap your foot on "Don't Rain on My Parade." Say something like, "Boy, does that Nicky Arnstein make me *envious.*" Put your arm around her when they take Omar Sharif to jail. In other words, act like a dork. She's yours. ∎

9 pages to show time

The Drive-In Guide to the Oscars

America's Most Shameless Movie Critic Gets Ornery About Oscar's Omissions

Ever year it's the same dang thing. They wheel in all the Academy members from Palm Springs, hook up their IVs so they can vote, and say, "Time to look at our Meryl Streep close-ups again." And a lot of em don't wanna take their medication. They fight it at first—they go, "NO! Oh, God, no, not *that*!"—and then they have to put clamps on their ears and play the soundtrack from *Chorus Line* over and over again until they lose their will to resist, and then finally, after they're broken, they'll request to see the uncut version of *Gandhi* again. It is now safe to give em an unmarked Oscar ballot.

I don't know how else to explain it. I don't know how we can go year after year without even *nominating* Big Chuck Bronson, who's grown so much as an actor that, like, last year for *Death Wish III,* he bought an elephant gun to skim the scum with. Has Eastwood ever used an elephant gun? Have you ever seen *Jack Lemmon* fire an elephant gun at an orange-haired geek trying to shake down a welfare patient? I rest my case.

Okay, let's get down to the nitty.

BEST SUPPORTING ACTOR

The first question I gotta ask here is, *where is Robert Englund,* the pasty-faced walking Nazi experiment in *Nightmare on Elm Street*? The man turns in the finest child-molesting performance in the history of movies, and what does he get for it? *Nightmare on Elm Street, Part II*—that's what. Or how about Howard Sherman, who played Bub the Zombie in *Day of the Dead,* the most lovable onscreen dead person since Rita Jenrette. But instead we got these losers:

William Hickey (the godfather in *Prizzi's Honor*), the first man to die before filming started and *still finish the movie*. He plans on sending himself to accept the award posthumously.

Eric Roberts (the wimpster convict in *Runaway Train*), who was so sleazy in *Star 80* that Mariel Hemingway said, "I don't want him touching my new bosoms."

Robert Loggia (the old-coot drunk detective in *Jagged Edge*), whose face looks like a map of Uganda.

Klaus Maria Brandauer (the baron in *Out of Africa*), who deserves a special commendation for giving Meryl Streep syphilis, but can't win cause he's from some goulash country next door to Communist Russia.

---

8 pages to show time

And, finally, Don Ameche (the horny party reptile in *Cocoon*), another veteran of the Spanish-American War and the *only nominee anybody's ever heard of.* Don was so great on the "International Showtime" circus show that he's a shoo-in at 5-to-2 odds.

BEST SUPPORTED ACTRESS

Don't even *look* for Lainie Kazan in this category, even though she turned in a great performance as a singing balloon in *Lust in the Dust,* where she did the song "Let Me Take You South of My Border." Or how about Remy O'Neill, for the title role in *Hollywood Hot Tubs*? But the number-one oversight here is Jennifer Beals in *The Bride.* Created out of lightning, wrapped like a mummy and—oh my *God*—threatening to flashdance again. Here's what we got instead:

Margaret Avery (the lesbo floozy in *The Color Purple*), who makes the sign of the double-gilled anaconda with Whoopi and grosses everbody out.

Amy Madigan (in the movie that nobody saw and nobody can remember the name of).

Meg Tilly (the nun that gets knocked up in *Agnes of God*), who gets Jane Fonda for a shrink and lives to tell about it. Meg is best known as a piece of furniture in *The Big Chill.*

Anjelica Huston (the interior decorator in *Prizzi's Honor* who keeps trying to decorate Jack Nicholson's interior), who was blessed with all the best features of her show-business parents—John Huston and Walter Huston.

And, can I have a fanfare please?—Oprah Winfrey (the big, bossy Mama in *The Color Purple*), who's a 2-to-1 favorite for her enormous performance that tested the limits of the Cinemascope screen.

BEST ACTOR

Everybody knows what a joke this one is. Sly Rocky Rambo—the man who liberated the 47,000 missing-in-action prisoners from a mud hut in Nam, including all the MIAs that Chuck Norris forgot to liberate in *his* last movie—was *not nominated.* Arnold the Barbarian was *not nominated,* even though *Commando* established new records for dead Meskins. Even Johnny Travolta, who stuck that big bag of potatoes down his jogging suit in *Perfect,* got the No-Way-José sign from the Academy. And I'm not even gonna mention Shabba-Doo Quinones, the best breakdancer that wears big animal teeth in his ears, for *Breakin' 2 Is Electric Boogaloo.* Listen to these turkeys:

William Hurt (the whining fairy in *Kiss of the Spider Woman*), for being such a bitch.

Jon Voight (the one in the bad beard in *Runaway Train*), for saying "I am too a star. Am too. Am too."

Harrison Ford (the detective in *Witless*), for hanging around the Amish people, going "I respect your right to refuse to brush your teeth for religious reasons."

James Garner (the nice guy in *Murphy's Romance*), who'll get a lot of sympathy votes for being banged up in

7 pages to show time

Darby Hinton, best Chuck Norris lookalike of the year, makes himself into a Bimbo Sandwich in *Malibu Express*.
(Artwork courtesy of Malibu Bay Films.)

Leatherface and his now immortal Black & Decker, enjoying a leisurely moment with Grandpa.
(Photo courtesy of New Line Cinema Corporation.)

Charles Durning races through the streets of Dallas in *Stand Alone*.
(Still from Stand Alone provided through the courtesy of New World Entertainment, Ltd.)

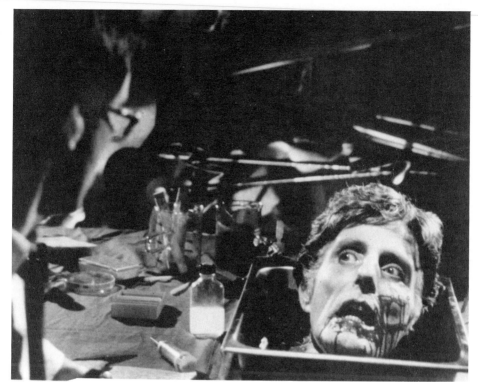

David Gale's performance seemed a little detached in *Re-Animator*.
(Photo courtesy of Empire Entertainment, Inc.)

Bub the Zombie in *Day of the Dead* demonstrates how the new Gillette Trac II razor does not perform as advertised on those hard-to-get spots.
(Photo courtesy of United Film Distribution Company.)

Future meat in
Mountaintop Motel
Massacre.
(Still from **Mountaintop Motel**
Massacre *provided through the*
courtesy of New World Entertainment,
Ltd.)

The Toxic Avenger proves
that this girl will go home
with *anybody*.
(Photo courtesy of Troma, Inc.)

Starring in the *Demons* title
role is this slime glopola
specimen who studied with
Brando; notice the
forehead.
(Photo courtesy of Ascot
Entertainment Group.)

Remember, if you see a blow-dried Dutch actor hitchhiking on the interstate, do *not* pick him up. (Rutger Hauer in *The Hitcher*)
(Photo courtesy of Tri-Star Pictures, Inc.)

A Chorus Line star Audrey Landers reciting the Gettysburg Address.
(Photo courtesy of Embassy Films, Inc.)

Jason discussing his Paramount contract. *Friday the 13th, Part V. Jason Lives.*

Heavy symbolism in the drive-in classic *When Nature Calls . . . You've Gotta Go.*
(Photo courtesy of Troma, Inc.)

It was the subtle symbolism of scenes li this one from *Sybil Danning's Adventure Video* that changed Jo Bob's mind about vid
(Photo courtesy of S. C. Dacy

Underemployed actor Tom Nolan being strangled to death in *School Spirit*.
(Photo courtesy of Concorde Pictures.)

A student at Beaver High gives free physical examinations to two students at once in *Loose Screws*.
(Photo courtesy of Concorde Pictures.)

Critters—the movie that answers the question, "What's really eating the American farmer?"
(Photo courtesy of New Line Cinema Corporation.)

Big Wayne is on the left.

stunts, injured in car wrecks, and, worst of all, sacrificing his body by jumping into Sally Field's haystack.

But the winner's gotta be: Jack Nicholson (the mumbledy hit man in *Prizzi's Honor*), cause he's a personal friend of Kareem and he promised to make the man stop scrunching up his face like that evertime the ref calls a foul. Call it 4-to-1 for Jackieboy.

BEST ACTRESS

I don't see Tawny Kitaen on this list, even though she battled three raving horny Amazons to the death in a duel of the world's largest abalone-shell underwire support bras in *The Perils of Gwendoline*. I don't see Brigitte Nielsen, who flexed her plastic sword in *Red Sonja* and uttered the memorable lines, "You slaughtered my parents! Like cattle! My brother! My sister!" And, of course, it goes without saying that once again the Academy *ignored* Sybil Danning, who performed the cigarette-burn torture, the sword-in-the-face torture and the shut-up-you-little-animal-before-I-slap-you-again torture in *Jungle Warriors*. Newcomer of the year was Pamela Pratt, queen of the Amazons, who slept with a guy named Garth, zapped him into outer space, then hung him up by his ankles to dry in *Hercules II*. But would the Academy notice a performance like that? No, they were too busy with:

Jessica Lange (dressed up like a drugstore cowgirl in *Sweet Dreams*), for getting through a whole movie without threatening to fire the director. Jessica went through long hours of preparation for the part, working with a periodontist who trained her gums to do the cotton-eyed Joe.

Meryl Streep (diddled by two guys in *Out of Africa*), for doing a different foreign accent in ever scene of the movie.

Anne Bancroft (the Super Nun in *Agnes of God*), for staying married to Mel Brooks even after he made *History of the World, Part I* and they couldn't go out to dinner for a year.

Whoopi Goldberg (the rag doll with the food-slinging younguns in *The Color Purple*), for having the world's largest teeth.

And—the bimbo favorite at 5-to-1—Geraldine Page (wandering around Texas in *The Trip to Bountiful*), cause she's real old and everbody thinks it would be *so nice* if she won right before the "Tribute to Rock Hudson" segment of the ceremonies.

BEST FLICK

Make Them Die Slowly is not on the list, even though it was directly responsible for 19 mass murders in Times Square alone and scored a 98 on the Vomit Meter. *Chorus Line*, the best horror film of 1985, was not nominated. Neither was *Invasion USA*, probly because the Academy was terrified by the scene where the Russians invade Miami Beach. *Rocky IV* is the finest film about global peace ever made by a man with enormous breasts, but it did no better than *Rambo: Second Blood*, the movie that gave a new meaning to the word *whah?* And the sleeper hit of '85, *Re-Animator*, the

6 pages to show time

only movie ever made where the star loses his head halfway through the movie but finishes the movie anyway, is a no-show at the Dorothy Chandler. Here's what the yokels gave us instead:

Kiss of the Spider Woman: Sonia Braga don't even get nekkid. All she does is wander around in Raul Julia's head while he's saying "We weel have revolution! We weel! We weel!"

Witless: The movie that makes you wanna go get some real-estate developers and send em up to Amish land to build a Burger King next door to an old mill.

Out of Africa: Me Redford. You Streep. We rich.

Prizzi's Honor: Next time, kill Kathleen Turner in the *first* scene. Start by assassinating her accent.

The Color Purple: It would be just like these Academy Bozos to vote for a movie about Crayolas. It's a done deal. ■

Working on the Chain Gang

America's Number-One Drive-In Movie Critic Goes to Pieces in *The Texas Chainsaw Massacre 2*

I was chain-saw meat for Tobe Hooper. That's Tobe "Mr. Chainsaw" Hooper to you. Tobe "I really did, too, direct *Poltergeist* even though Steve the Wimp was hanging around all the time" Hooper. Tobe, the man who saw American families turning to cannibalism in 1974 and treated it like the growing social problem it was instead of like they were *weirdos* or something. The man who made the greatest drive-in movie in the history of the universe: *The Texas Chainsaw Massacre.* The man whose parents didn't know how to spell *Toby.* Tobe was on the horn. Tobe wanted me.

On the day I showed up, on a hot, muggy Wednesday in downtown Austin, there were giant horseflies hitchin rides over to the set just to see Dennis Hopper's underarms. It was that kind of day. Somebody was sleepin on top of the rat cage, which was located next to the chain-saw-repair facility (thirty-five saws specially rigged for splatter), which was located in the loading dock of the old abandoned *Austin American-Statesman* newspaper building, which was full of 2000 skeletons trucked in from somewhere, includin a couple hundred real ones from India, and the remains of three or four city editors from the Fifties. This was the

5 pages to show time

Barbecue Pit, the place where Tobe was takin the raw material of this human existence of ours—our pain, our joy, our sadness, our desire to act like geeks all day if we can be in the movie—and turnin it into 100 minutes of cheap exploitation. I was proud to be part of it.

The most famous cannibal family in history has grown up in *Saw 2*. They've gone and got theirselves a catering bin-ness, and to handle all the meat, they had to go get this abandoned amuse-ment park by the interstate and con-vert it into a combination slaughter barn, short-order grill, dining room, and playpen. All the furniture's made out of human and animal bones, but ever once in a while Daddy (Jim Sie-dow) has to scream at em to get up off their hinies and do some work instead of just setting around all day listenin to the radio and Black-and-Deckerin the house. If you can believe it, Bill Mosely as Chop-Top and Bill Johnson as Leatherface have even lower IQs than their brothers from *Saw I*. "If I told you once, I told you a million times," Daddy yells at them, "don't saw the main support beams!"

The guy who dreamed this up is Kit Carson, the co-screenwriter on *Paris, Texas,* who spent two hours sleepin on the sidewalk the night before I got to the set. He came walkin toward me lookin like a pup tent that's been chewed up by a pit bull, danglin a por-table typewriter in one hand and trying to keep his matted blond hair from breeding. I told him he looked real ex-istential.

"Joe Bob!" he spurted. He then launched into an explanation of how *Saw 2* was the movie for people sick of *The Breakfast Club* and the little brat-pack oatmeal-face whiners that are in those flicks and how everbody that looks like Molly Ringwald is gettin a chain saw through the gizzards in this one.

"Yuppie meat," I said.

"Yuppie meat," he repeated for no reason.

Then he grinned and took me over to Tobe Hooper's trailer, and Tobe in-vited me in and chewed on a cigar the size of Montana and bustled a lot like he was demented and told me how he'd been sick for a week with the weird virus that ravaged the old *Austin American-Statesman* building and made about twenty-five people think they had AIDS. This made the movie late, which didn't make Cannon Films in El Lay too happy, and that's why they weren't gonna be finished till the Fourth of July for a movie that opens August 22nd.

I asked Tobe how much money I was gettin and how it oughta be more than a few hundred since I was gettin killed off and so I'd be unavailable for *Saw 3* and could I have a free T-shirt. He whimpered a little bit, like a mangled puppy, and I knew I had a friend for life.

Next thing, we went upstairs where there used to be the set of a radio station except Leatherface had just chain-sawed it into 97,000 pieces in an attempt to casserole Caroline Wil-liams, the star of the movie, who was

4 pages to show time

walkin around with caked blood all over her legs practicing her screams. (In an effort to outdo Marilyn Burns, star of *Saw I* and greatest screamer in drive-in history, Caroline perfected five distinct varieties of scream.) They had a screen set up where Tobe could watch yesterday's scenes and confer with his chain-saw-effects master, Tom Savini, the little guy who's pumped more blood and lopped more limbs than any man alive. Tom was sittin on a beat-up old couch and watchin footage of a chain saw moving horizontally toward a screaming head, only at the last second the guy loses control of the saw and—whoops!—just hacks off an ear. The crew groans. They had to stick a bunch of stuff back on the head for the second take, where the saw goes straight through at forehead level, destroying half the head and releasin about seven gallons of spurting blood. "Excellent," I told Mr. Chainsaw. Tobe chewed some more.

For about twenty minutes we watched Grandpa try to kill Caroline with a sledgehammer—just like the scene in *Saw I,* only slicker—and then I got bored and went to find Dennis Hopper.

I don't know about you, but I consider Dennis Hopper one of the finest gonzo acidhead raving psychotic poets of our generation. In this movie, of course, he's the establishment figure— the cop that's been searchin for Leatherface and his family for twelve years, gradually getting crazier than they are. I found Dennis over on the Dueling Chain Saws set, where a couple of stuntmen were battling to the death in a raging, sparks-flyin, smoke-spewin

struggle to see who could be the first guy to get sent straight to prison by the Consumer Product Safety Commission. One guy was dressed up like Leatherface, the other guy like Dennis, complete with a pair of chain-saw *holsters.* When the fight actually started, with both guys slinging their chain saws together like swords so you could hear the blades grind together, everbody on the crew winced and flinched. When it was over, with one guy sprawled across a table after leaping two feet in the air to keep himself from being sawed off at the knee, nobody said anything for five or ten seconds, waitin to see if both guys still had all their body parts intact. Everbody secretly hoped they wouldn't need a second take.

"Outstanding," said Dennis, staring down at his stunt double from a raised perch full of skeleton art and armchairs made with arms. Dennis rubbed his hands together, wringing the sweat. "Outstanding."

He looked at me. "That was outstanding."

Dennis has this little grin he does. It's not a happy grin or a friendly grin or even a grin that's intended for you. It's a grin that sorta flits across his face and makes these little wrinkles all around his eyes and lips, and then he goes right back into a deadpan, and when it's over you try to figure it out, and you finally decide it means something like "I have just understood something in the cosmos and I'm not gonna tell you about it." That's the Dennis Hopper grin. He did it when he saw me. Then he said, "Do you eat?"

And he motioned me to follow him,

3 pages to show time

and then he wandered out into the hot night and circled around the block and went up to this thing called the Honey Wagon, where all the grips and gaffers and other people that had been workin 374 straight hours were lined up to get some spaghetti or somethin, and he grabbed two plastic trays and handed one to me and broke in at the front of the line and ordered a slab of roast beef and a fork. I figured this was the best time to ask him about the existential meaning of his part in *Saw*.

The grin again. Then a deadpan. "They didn't want me to do it, my agents," he said. "They had a big meeting. They said, 'Why do you want to throw your career away on this?' They didn't like me doin it. I told em I wanted to do it."

Dennis was fillin up a Styrofoam cup with vanilla ice cream, to wash down his roast beef. He seemed to be finished with the story.

"So, uh, why did you wanna do it?"

"Cause I love Austin, Texas, and I wanted to spend my fiftieth birthday here."

"I see what you mean."

"I got friends here. Willie, he's a friend. I like to play golf here."

"Is that what you told your agents?"

"Yeah." Grin. "That's what I told em."

"How many agents do you have?"

"At the meeting? Seven."

"Do you like this work?"

"I have seven pictures comin out this year and next year."

"What kind of pictures?"

"Well, there's this one where I play an alcoholic father. I'm doing that one

next month. And then there's one where I'm a psychotic B-29 pilot. And then there's another one where I'm a wealthy toy manufacturer. And one where I'm an alcoholic. One where I'm crazy. This one here, where there's a lot of possibilities for me to be crazy, but my character disappears after about page thirty and doesn't come back till page a hundred, so this one really I didn't need to be here the whole time. I could have played golf."

"Dennis, do you ever have any roles where you're *not* an addict or a psycho?"

"I just told you. I play a wealthy toy manufacturer."

"Oh, yeah, right. Any reason you're doing all this work?"

"Probably because I've been off drugs for two years."

"You think the drugs hurt your career?"

"I don't know. I was on drugs, so I didn't notice. I was in Taos, New Mexico, and I think the guys out in Hollywood were probably not giving me jobs because they were doing drugs but they thought I was doing more drugs than they were."

"How do you feel now?"

"Great. Better than I ever felt in my life."

"Thanks, Dennis. Gotta go get chain-sawed."

Next thing, they sent me over to Makeup and Wardrobe to get fixed up for the big scene where I play myself gettin shishkebabbed by the Saw Family. Co-starring with me in the scene was Twinkle Bayoud, the only person I ever met who was a segment on Robin Leach's *Lifestyles of the Rich and Fa-*

2 pages to show time

mous. Robin described her as a "real-estate tigress who sells hot property to the moneyed elite" and also throws the greatest parties in Texas. Twinkle is a tall, sad-eyed blonde, thin as a string of beef jerky, who called up the production office, begged to be in the flick, and kept saying "Remember, I'm only twenty minutes away by Lear."

"Yuppie meat?" I said to Kit Carson.

"Yuppie meat," Kit said.

"I'm a personal friend of Dennis," Twinkle told me.

"Do I get to kill you or what?"

The other bimbo in the scene with me is named Victoria Powells, an El Lay actress who's beautiful and knows how to act. I told Kit this wasn't gonna work.

"Can we kill her off early? She might be a distraction."

"Just more yuppie meat," he said.

By the time we got to the scene, it was 3:00 a.m. on the Fourth of July and Kit had been away two, three hours sprayin roach killer on his hair.

"Joe Bob," he told me, "what we got here is the Saw Family ridin around Dallas on Texas-OU Weekend in a catering truck searchin for yuppie meat. They decide to wait outside a movie theater—the movie theater you're about to come out of with these two bimbos. Why don't you just write your own words? And then we'll do the Saw Fu."

I asked Kit why he was talkin like me, and he said he didn't know, and then he gave me this big "I been stayin up all night" grin. By this time the

place looked like a George Romero set—walkin zombies everwhere.

In other words, they wanted me to do this scene the Coppola way. So I scratched out some dialogue and charged em twenty extra bucks for the writing, and then Tobe came out of his trailer and we were all ready to emote. By this time Twinkle was wearing 19,000 pounds of makeup and showing signs of overacting. ("I jet to New York once a week for lessons," she said.)

We rehearsed the scene one time. I'm proud to say it's a scene written so that it can never be shown on HBO, used as a clip on *The Tonight Show,* or shown to film students as an example of anything except a disgusting little exploitation scene. The professor will probably say somethin like "This scene here looks like they shot it at three in the morning."

Ever once in a while we stopped so that Tobe could bustle around setting up lights and tellin people to rack their f-stops and focus their pullers and flog their dolphins, and while we were stopped, Twinkle would order more makeup and tell me to say her name.

"It's written in the script," she said. "Why don't you say what's in the script?"

Sure enough, I wrote down *Twink* in my first line. I told her I'd say it, so all her friends would know which one she was.

Thank God we finally got to her pay-off line, which is "You two wanna go to Austin? It's just twenty minutes away by jet." That's the signal for Leatherface to spring out of the back

---

1 page to show time

of the catering truck with a chain saw in his hand and Robin Leach this woman to death. I asked if we could cut her face in half, but they said no, there wasn't enough time to rig her head for the complete Old Faithful treatment. She had to die off camera.

We finished the scene at 8:30, as the sun was risin over deserted downtown Austin and some of the Teamsters were leavin to haul people out to Farm Aid II, which also died off camera.

I went rootin around in a trailer tryin to find Kit, but he was rentin his shirt out as a nuclear-waste disposal site.

It was hard to believe it was all over. Twinkle and me, well, I guess we were friends for life. "I hope you won't put my name in your column, Joe Bob," she said. "It's just so *controversial.*"

"Okay, Twink, long as you don't invite me to any parties."

Tom was packing up his stage-blood pumper, destined for more gore.

Tobe, Leatherface, Dennis—they were all passed out on pavements, sawing logs and limbs.

As I walked away, I thought of them all, each and ever one of them, as *my family.* And when I heard the distant whine of a chain saw, revving up for the final three scenes, I knew they would all be gone soon. Very soon. ■

BACK TO THE DRIVE-IN 2

End Chihuahua Abuse, *Now*

Ever since I first exposed the practice three weeks ago, hundreds of letters have been pouring into Joe Bob's Mailbag asking, "What can I do to stop Chihuahua Racing?"

I'm afraid it's not that simple.

Mexico is not like our country. At Chihuahua Downs in Nuevo Laredo, the life of a little rat-faced weasel-dog comes cheap indeed.

What can we do? I guess I've asked myself that question six, seven times. What can we do? What can we do? Now I've asked it 10 times.

First, we can speak out about it. I know this is not gonna be easy on you—and I would recommend sending your kids out of the room while I do this—but I've waited too long to say these things. Here are the facts:

Numero Uno: The actual chihuahua racing saddle weighs 68 pounds, while the average chihuahua weighs only one pound. So you can see, that's a difference of . . . lemme see here . . . about 65 pounds. You should see the expressions on their little chihuahua faces when the *saddleros* walk out carrying these instruments of torture. Some of the chihuahuas have to be blindfolded just so they can find a part of the little guy's body that can "take the cinch." I shudder just to think about it. When I protested to the owners of the track, they merely shrugged their shoulders and said that the saddle was necessary because . . .

Numero Two-o: Chihuahua jockeys weigh 260 pounds. This disgusting breed of savages, known as *Los Hombres Flour Tortillas* in bordertown areas, pride themselves on their ability to break the spirit of a chihuahua. During the annual chihuahua roundup, when the puppies are first separated from their mothers, the *Flour Tortillas* mercilessly spur the pathetic little canines to see who can force the "triple high C" noise out of the dog. For weeks after the roundup, most chihuahuas will whimper helplessly at the sight of any man with enchiladas on his breath.

Numero Three-o: There are four types of chihuahua-racing bets: Win, Place, Show, and the "Chihuaperfecta." The Chihuaperfecta pays off when any dog fails to finish the entire six-foot oval track due to fatigue, "breaking down" (if you haven't seen this, it looks roughly like a match-stick house gettin stomped on by a gorilla), or failing to breathe for six consecutive hours. (The race normally requires seven and a half hours to traverse the entire six feet.) I once saw a guy collect $798 on a two-dollar Chihuaperfecta parlay. It's not something I wanna see again.

What can you do? You can write your senator, write your congressman, and *maybe* that'll work. But if you want to be really effective, vote with your pocketbook and tell your local butcher that you are *boycotting all chihuahua imports from northern Mexico* until this practice is stopped. Maybe that will mean eating beef and chicken for a while, but it's just the price we have to pay.

Speaking of dead meat in Mexico, the cast of *Eliminators* is the best bunch of weirdos wanderin around in a script written on acid since the classic *Ice Pirates*. Listen close, cause I want you to get into this one.

First this airplane pilot crashes in Mexico, but before he croaks an evil scientist glues him back together into a Mandroid with body by Alcoa and starts zapping him back in time so he can find out what's going on in the Roman Empire. Then the scientist is gonna take the Mandroid down to Goodwill and collect his two-cent deposit on the scrap, but the Mandroid finds out and clamps a Patton tank on the lower half of his body and lasers 30 or 40 Meskins to death so he can escape and start planning to go back and kill the evil scientist and avenge the death of his little Chinaman friend.

Next thing, Mandroid disguises himself as Harrison Ford and meets up with this bimbo-in-a-white-smock that knows how to build levitating midget robots and grease his Mandroid axles when he starts to tucker. We're talking a horny Dorothy that likes to stroke the tin man's groceries, and they're off to see the Wizard. But first they stop off and pick up a geek scarecrow riverboat pilot doing a bad Humphrey Bogart imitation, and they chug upriver dodgin hillbilly speedboats and lesbian pirates. Then they meet a black Ninja for no apparent reason and head for the evil scientist's castle so they can stop him before he goes back to the Roman Empire and kills Julius Caesar.

We're talking the modern Fu Champion.

One breast. Three gallons blood. A 38 on the Vomit Meter. Thirty-six dead bodies. Six beasts. Three motor vehicle chases. One barroom brawl. Rambo Robot. Face-sewing. Lightning-bolt strangulation. Dune-buggy jungle attack. Demon-possessed robot. Gross-out tummy catheter. Dripping slimy eye pus. Four exploding boats. Two exploding dune buggies. Two exploding hillbillies. Gratuitous wimp masochist husband. Gratuitous Roman soldiers in leotards. Gratuitous feminist discussion during a high-speed boat chase. Gratuitous fat-man electrocution. Gratuitous homosexual cave man. Great *Frankenstein* ripoff scene where the Mandroid requests euthanasia by saying "I'd kill myself but my program

JOE BOB'S MAILBAG

DEAR JOE BOB: I was reading the paper, believe it or not, and I see where Sally Field says she *isn't* going to stay *clothed and hidden anymore.*

Sounds like to me she's ready to quit doing that indoor Bullstuff (which was boring enough to win her a couple of those gold statues) and get involved in some serious drive-in art, sort of. I figured you would have the inside story.

By the way, what do you think she does with *two* Oscars?
Sincerely, sort of,
GEORGE BROWN
DALLAS

DEAR GEORGE: Did you see Miss Pumpkin Cheeks on the cover of the new Playboy?
No thank you.

DEAR JOE BOB: Are you over your New Year's Eve hangover—got your eyeballs caged and your seat belt fastened? Well, here it is, the picture they said shouldn't be made, *Bikers vs. The Undead*!!!!! Can you dig it?? A Hells Angel type motorcycle group saves a small Western town from zombies!!! My Gawd!! Putrid rotting flesh, smelly motorcycle seats—it leaves me breathless!!!!!

Seriously, we are looking for national Drive-In distribution. Can you give us the best contacts, so we can get this puppy out there in the cow pastures—where it belongs??
Yours for the revival of the Drive-In in 1986,
ROBERT E. SANDERS
PRESIDENT, 21ST CENTURY FILM & VIDEO
MESA, ARIZ.

DEAR BOB: Sorry, but anybody that still says "Can you dig it" is not allowed to produce a movie. It says so in the Constitution.

DEAR MR. BRIGGS: I am an ex-Yankee now living in Houston, enjoying your columns, showing them to other Yankees, specially the kind that still live up in Rhode Island and other places like that.

I wish you would write about, if you haven't already, the communistic plot of the government to reduce our state names to two letters. Think about it: why cant a machine tell the difference between Missouri, Minnesota and Mississippi? Is the MO-MN-MI abbreviation scheme any easier? I think its a commie plot and I hope you can investigate.
Yours in drive in wisdom,
WILLIAM C. MURPHY
HOUSTON

DEAR BILL: Sometimes it can be dang embarrassin, too, like in the case of the eastern Maine town of Beet, and the southern Arizona village of Kicke.

DEAR JOE BOB: Who are these people with the "Baby in Car" signs? Is it safe to make eye contact with them?

My wife says they are merely stupid humans and are no more dangerous than gravel haulers or deputy constables. But I wonder . . .

Could it be they are Intergalactic spies unfamiliar with our reproductive processes?
Sign me:
CONCERNED
COLLEGE STATION, TEX.

DEAR CONCERNED: No, "Baby in Car" is merely to inform you that when you plough into their car from behind cause they're going 15 in a 45 zone, they're probly gonna whine and cry.

won't allow it." Great *Death Wish* ripoff scene where two creeps try to steal the Mandroid's car. Great *Taxi Driver* ripoff line where the Mandroid says "You talkin to me?" Great *African Queen* ripoff scene where the scarecrow tows the riverboat by hand.

Great *Quest for Fire* ripoff scene where the entire cast is attacked by monkey-suit extras. Kung fu. Laser fu. Transfusion fu. Throwing star fu. Thompson submachine-gun fu. Toga fu. Monkey fu. Electric fan fu. Colored gas fu. Neanderthal fu. Lesbo fu. Hillbilly fu. Mandroid torpedo fu. Fire extinguisher fu. Laser-to-the-crotch fu. Drive-In Academy Award nominations for Denise Crosby, the blond bimbo scientist, for saying "But you're— you're—you're human" and "I'd rather be piranha bait"; Patrick Reynolds, as the Mandroid, for saying "*You're* the one that needs body work"; Andrew Prine, as the geek riverboat pilot, for saying "This is all some kind of weird science fiction thing, right?"; and Peter Manoogian, who directed this sucker, for saying "What else can we put in?"

Four stars. Best of '86. Joe Bob says check it out. ∎

Cud U Pass Jo Bob's Verry Hard Teachur's Test?

Next month all the school teachers in Texas got to take a test to see if they're qualified to scream "Have a seat, young man" every time somebody decides to drop-kick an eraser into the water fountain. We call this Competency.

I don't really understand it myself, since we've done just fine for a hundred years using incompetent teachers and it's a little late to be changing it up now. But anyhow, I though I could make a little spare change on the side if I got an *advance copy* of the test, and so now I'm sellin em for $9.95 apiece. I'd sell em for more, but the average teacher salary in Texas is only $9.95 a month.

Anyhow, if you're thinkin about buying one, here's a few of the sample questions:

1. Who is considered the "Father" of our country?
  a. Frank Sinatra
  b. Kareem Abdul-Jabbar
  c. That guy in the picture, you know, I forget his name, but the Valley Forge guy

You'd be surprised how many peo- ple answer "b," or, worse yet, write in "Lew Alcindor." But you would never have that problem if you owned a copy of the Joe Bob Briggs Cheater Kit. Here's another example:

2. Correct the grammar and punctuation in this sentence:

Joshua fit da battle of Jericho, Jericho, Jericho, Joshua fit da battle of Jericho, and the walls comeda tumblin down.

Answer: The sentence is completely correct as an example of "ethnic English" and we better not hear any cracks about it either, is that understood? You see how they can get you on the trick questions? Now try this one:

3. True or false: We're all going to die.

True, but the football coaches always miss this one.

4. Fill in the blank: Syphilis is a disease affecting the _____ _____ glands.

You'd be surprised at what some people put in that blank. The secret to this one is to *draw a picture*. It don't matter what you draw in there, they'll mark it correct ever time cause they don't want to *think* about what it might be a picture of.

And finally, this is the one *everbody* misses:

5. In 1492, Columbus sailed the ocean ——.

You know, most people, they write in there "Blue," even though there's not any Blue Ocean. Columbus sailed the *Pacific* Ocean.

If you're taking this test next month, don't take a chance. Send in for the sample right away. Otherwise, you might have to get a real job.

Speaking of IQs in the single digits, Alejandro Rey turns in one of his finest drive-in performances as a gay swinger who gets eaten by a giant slime-dripping outer-space mutant in a hot tub. The flick is *Terrorvision,* and it stars Mary Woronov's legs (aerobic dance leotard, turquoise Naugahyde miniskirt) and Gerrit Graham's gold neck chains.

The idea is this family out in El Lay builds the world's greatest earth dish and as soon as they get it finished a Hungrybeast from Pluton ends up in their living room, chomping on Grandpa. It gets scarier and scarier as the Hungrybeast starts feeding on relatives, until finally—the ultimate horror!—Alejandro Rey tries to pronounce the word "diddling"!

The only thing wrong with this monster is, it takes him *forever* to eat the whole family.

We talking no breasts, though. Two beasts (including Alejandro Rey). Twelve dead bodies. Three quarts blood. Exploding head. Face-eating. Stomach slime. Brain seepage. Menage à five-o. Outer-space monster sex. Bert Remsen squashed into a little pile of lime sherbet. Bert Remsen vomited back up. Head rolls. Hand rolls. Gratuitous nekkid-lady art. Gratuitous aerobics. Gratuitous lizard-tail eating.

Gratuitous nipple fountain. Gratuitous Hungry Hombre frozen Meskin dinner. Lizard fu. Slime fu. Waterbed fu. Gold neck-chain fu. Drive-In Academy Award nominations for the TV repairman, too embarrassed to use his name in the credits, for saying "Say, Mr. P, mind if I guzzle another Heinie?"; Mary Woronov, one of the true drive-in queens, for saying "No, dear, your father and I might be swinging tonight"; Jennifer Richards, as an Elvira lookalike, for stuffing the world's mushiest garbonzas into a great big old parachute bra; Bert Remsen, as grandpa, for staring a 10,000-ton monster from outer space in the eye and saying "I don't know, it must be a burglar"; Gerrit Graham, the daddy of the house, for looking at all the blood Alejandro Rey left in the pool and saying "What the hell did that homo do to the Jacuz?"; Jonathan Gries, as the punk-rock metal man, for saying "You got pills? What color?" and "Hey! What's on El Tube-o?"; and, of course, Alejandro Rey, for saying "Sally Field geev me no phone call now."

Two stars. Joe Bob says check it out. ■

Communist Alert!

The Lakeshore Drive-In in Edgewater, Colo., is gonna be ripped down next summer with CITY MONEY. Why? "To improve the physical image of the city," according to wimp-of-the-year drive-in destroyer Tom Kristopeit, head of the Edgewater Redevelopment Authority. Instead of a drive-in, the Head Wimp wants a Safeway, offices, restaurants, and 250 "housing units." He's spending $16 million on it. If they'd show decent flicks, they could make that in one night.

JOE BOB'S MAILBAG

DEAR JOE BOB: It's a sad case down here. A whole continent without a drive-in. I'm working on McMurdo station, Antarctica. This time I doubt it's the communists' fault. There are a couple of technical difficulties to overcome. Numero Uno the sun hasn't set in 4 months (I hate it when they start the movie before it gets dark!) and Numero Two-o when the sun does set (soon) it tends to get very cold, we're talking 30 degrees below, we're talking frostbite-fu. If we get it together to borrow a projector, line up the track vehicles to watch, and show a movie on the side of a building, the obvious choice is *The Thing*.

Well, I'm going to need a few laughs this winter. With no sun, cold, a 13-to-1 ration of men to women, and having to watch movies off a VCR (talk about a communist plot to ruin the movie industry). A few friends are sending an occasional review of yours. Please send me your newsletter and whatever else you feel inspired to. This may be a first for you. Whatever you send will be delivered in an airdrop in June, we're talking parachutes onto the ice! If you have a book out or something send it and bill me, I'm good for it.
Thanks for the laughs,
LARRY HANSEN
NAVAL SUPPORT FORCE
McMURDO, ANTARCTICA

DEAR LARRY: I'm sending you 12 bimbos from up here that are already known as the Frigidaires. I'll put you in charge of thawin em out and then handin em over to the 12-man Nookie Patrol.

The only other way to solve your problem might be to send Shirley Stubbins, also known as The Octopus. The 13-to-1 deal wouldn't bother her at all.

DEAR JOE BOB: I'm having this recurring nightmare, and I'm hopin you can help me make sense of it.

It starts out I'm walking down a street in L.A. and I'm lookin' for one of these paper-weights with the glitter inside. Suddenly this large Oriental guy grabs me and forces me to be on *Love Connection*.

Chuck Woolery sets me up with this great-lookin wench with breasts out to here. But when I go to pick her up, she turns into Governor White's wife.

She throws me to the ground and starts whipping me with a seat belt while screaming, "Drink my bodily secretions, pleasure slave!"

Then she kills me, only she doesn't go to jail cause she tells the judge how it was her period, and it always makes her do "crazy things."

Joe Bob, what DOES it all mean?
Please hep me
RUFUS TURBOE
MESQUITE, TEX.

DEAR RUFUS: If you ever read Freud, you'd know people have that dream all the time. Don't worry about it. It means your mother had sex with a lizard and then tried to kill you.

YO! JOE (DOUBLE B): O.K., now this is serious. Is George Michael of Wham! the Anti-Christ, or is it just me?
Thanx,
KEVIN DILL
VALLEJO, CALIF.

DEAR KEVIN: You are.

DEAR JOE BOB (YOUR HONOR): I hope you can help me with one of life's little problems.

You see, Joe Bob, I have a real close friend. He and his wife paid another woman to bear his child since the wife can't have children. Well, wouldn't you know it, just last week the woman skipped town with the unborn child. My question is: can she be brought in on child kidnapping charges? I'm real concerned for my friend 'cuz there's more involved here than the 500 bucks he paid for this woman to bear his child.

What does the Drive-In Court have to say about this?
Yours truly
SPARKY MENDOZA
HALL OF SHAME ARCHITECTS, INC.
ARLINGTON, TEX.

DEAR SPARKY: It's real simple. Either the lady hands over the baby, or else she can return the sperm. One or the other.

DEAR MR. BRIGGS: One of my commitments now involves working as a part-time projectionist at a Drive-In theater in Austin, Texas. This happens to be the VERY LAST of the B-movie genra, General Audience theaters in a city that now claims some 300,000 residents.

Do you want to know what really goes on with the hamburgers and hot dogs they dont sell? You'll probably think I'm kidding, but its the basic policy to refrigerate whatever hasn't been sold on the night they were made and try to sell the next night. If they aren't sold after two nights, then the snack bar staff "spoil" them and write them off the inventory.

Pop corn keeps practically forever. I never see a batch older than a couple of days because the volume of sales stays fairly constant.

I remember once when we were showing *Friday the 13th, Part V* (you know, the "final" story?). Well the print was received with the leaders and tails all mixed up on the five reels. When we tried to show it the first night after the make-up the picture suddenly went upside down, but with the soundtrack in the right place. I simply couldnt find a way to straighten it out so I just showed the first 2 reels and went to the next picture. Needless to say that didn't go over well.

The next night, after trying to piece the film together we did manage to get the whole film together so that the image was right side up, however, the continuity went all to hell. Jason kills everybody off in the middle of the picture only to have them come back to life in the middle of the next reel. And then he's dead through the climax. I have learned to lock the door.

Once when showing *Women in Chains*, I had someone threaten to come in through the glass ports after me if I didnt fix the film. When this happens its best to turn off all the lights and skulk about in the gloom, so as to avoid being a good target. I understand the need to angrily pound on the steel door so as to make the projectionist do what ever it is that needs to be done for the movie that you paid "*good*" money for. I mean were we expecting counterfeiters? There are two sides to this story, but mine is not to reason why.
Sincerely,
KIM HILL
AUSTIN, TEX.

DEAR KIM: I was there that night at the Southside when you showed Friday the 13th Numero Five-o *that way, and it was one of Jason's greatest performances. You should be proud of yourself.*

Ferdy Flees Philippines to Join Briggs' Brigade

I am pleased to announce that, beginning this week, Ferdinand Marcos, recent president of Filipino Land, has agreed to join my company as Executive Vice President for Shotguns and Cheap Drugs. A lot of people told me not to do it. What kind of dictator *is* this guy anyhow? He just gets on the airplane and *leaves*? No Somoza deal, no Shah of Iran deal. The man just *leaves*? How do we know he can handle the pressure over here? But listen to me, the man needs a job. He deserves one shot. So Ferdy's first job will be to tally the ballots for the Drive-In Academy Awards with the help of 900 members of his immediate family and the 2,700 "regulars" in his firing squad.

"Ees honor," said Marcos in accepting the new job.

Marcos refused to discuss his salary, saying only that it will be "much less than I got for supplying geishas to the Sixth Fleet."

Marcos called the Drive-In Academy Award voting a "challenge," and indicated that he might have a "special surprise" for the voters in Tennessee and Arkansas, "especially the ones that haven't suffered enough."

Due to the unexpected hiring of Marcos, the DIAA balloting will be delayed another two weeks, so that ballots may be rejected right up until the announcement of the awards March 24 on KGO-TV in San Fran.

Unfortunately, there's gonna have to be a few changes in the voting rules now.

Message to you Crayola-heads out there in Palo Alto, Chapel Hill, and ever other place in the United States that's been took over by weasel-face computer operators:

Computerized ballots will NOT be accepted for the Drive-In Academy Awards.

There's a simple reason for this. It takes Ferdinand and the "boys" *forever* to paste those little squares over the holes that were punched out.

And another thing. All ballots from now on **must be written in the Bulimia dialect of Mindanao Island.**

And, oh yeah, I almost forgot. Each ballot must be **notarized by a man named Shecky.** Any Shecky will do, except Shecky Greene, who is disqualified for working the Catskills too many times.

And finally, I hate to have to tell you this, but I put Ferdy in charge and I've got to support him no matter how stupid the voting becomes. So remember this rule:

Anyone writing in the name "Mary Tyler Moore" in any of the categories will have his little fingers cut off.

Obviously, this last rule don't apply to people that don't have little fingers.

Okay, get those ballots in. Time is running out. And you know what happens if time runs out, don't you? Do you *know* what Ferdinand is threatening to do?

He's threatening to *go on ABC and get interviewed by GERALDO RIVERA!*

Don't let it happen here. Vote immediately.

Speaking of unemployed has-beens, *Delta Force* stars every Johnny

Carson fill-in guest since 1967, including Joey Bishop, Martin Balsam, Lainie Kazan, George Kennedy, Susan Strasberg, Bo Svenson, and, of course, the Queen of Jell-O Pudding herself—Shelley Winters. Basically, all these people are pieces of background furniture that get hijacked by a terrorist named Abdul, who constantly uses bad grammar and makes everbody live in smelly places and wears some really disgusting silk shirts until Chuck can paste Abdul's little Arab hiney with exploding missiles.

In other words, seriously, no joshing now, Joey, you hear me, put your pacemaker back in, what we got here is a Drive-In Classic. Menahem Golan, the genius himself, the man behind Cannon Films (they make the Bronsons, the Norrises, the Ninjas, and a bunch of other stuff)—Menahem dusted off his mirror sunglasses and *directed* this documentary about what *really* happened to those jerks that got hijacked last summer.

First we got some *Airport* ripoff scenes where Lainie Kazan and Shelley Winters buy a bunch of shlock souvenirs in the Athens airport to take back to their fat mothers, and their husbands Joey Bishop and Martin Balsam sit around comparing matzo-ball soup prices, and then Lainie and Shelley have a Whine-Off. (Shelley wins decisively.) Then, once they get on the plane, Abdul and his buddy Mustafa start yelling stuff like "I am tekking over airplane. You weel cooperate. Thees ees hijack. Do you heeeer me?"

Meanwhile, back at the Pentagon, General Robert *"U.N.C.L.E."* Vaughn is rubbing his chin and saying "If Lee Marvin is sober, send him over there to shoot up the plane and get all the taxpaying Americans out. No, on second thought, just send his eyebrows."

But then the Army finds out Lee Marvin has cut his eyebrows back to only two feet long, and so he has to take Chuck Norris and about 40 dogfaces with him. While all this is going on, Abdul and Mustafa are trying to figure out who's a Jew on the plane. So they round everbody up and say, "I tell Morey Amsterdam joke now. Eef laugh, shoot heem."

Then there's a whole lot more plot where they put black Ku Klux Klan hoods on everbody and stick em in the PLO Hotel, and Lee Marvin and Big Chuck have to ride all over creation and get out the pontoon boats and sneak through the sewers and go out in the Israeli desert and shoot up a bunch of camouflage dummies—until Big Chuck discovers the only way to beat the Arabs.

He buys a Kawasaki and puts nuclear-guided missiles on it. And pretty soon we got little piles of Arab mustache hair all over Beirut.

The movie that asks the question, "Why *do* the Arabs wear those stupid silk shirts anyhow?" No breasts. One gallon blood. Six terrorist beasts. Ninety-one dead bodies. Two motor vehicle chases, with crash-and-burns. Garroting. Fireball City. Sewer diving. Extended whining. Exploding copter. Exploding truck. Thirteen exploding jeeps. Five exploding buildings. Exploding dune buggy. Exploding Mercedes. Exploding Abdul. Gratuitous exploding watermelons. Gratuitous message from the Ayatollah. Gratuitous chorus of "America." Gratuitous Budweisers. Gratuitous Lee Marvin Scotch-and-soda. Kung fu. Grenade fu. Bazooka fu. Motorbike rocket fu. Shelley Winters fu. Shelley Winters screaming fu. Shelley Winters screaming and screwing up her face fu. Eyebrow fu. Beirut fu. Jew fu. Drive-In Academy Award nominations for George Kennedy, as a 350-pound Catholic priest, for saying "I'm a Jew, too, just like Jesus"; Hanna Schygulla, as the stewardess, for saying "No! Not me! I can't pick the Jews! Can't you see I'm *GERMAN*!"; Robert Forster, as Abdul the Greasy Terrorist, for saying "Everyone getting up and going to beck of plin now"; Martin Balsam, for wearing a tattoo on his wrist and saying "We survived once, we can do it again"; Joey Bishop, for saying "I was in Beirut 20 years ago—it was the Las Vegas of the Middle East"; Lee Marvin, for saying the immortal drive-in line "One minute to showtime!"; David Menahem, as Mustafa, for wearing an extremely bad mustache and saying "American Marines bomb my pipple!"; Big Chuck, for ripping the mattress off a bed, finding an Arab terrorist hiding under the springs, pointing an Uzi submachine gun at him, and saying "Sleep tight, sucker"; and Men-

ahem Golan, for telling a six-year-old kid to say "They don't like Jews, huh, Mama?" and telling one of the wounded and bleeding passengers to say "Not a *local* hospital, I hope?"

Four stars. Joe Bob says check this sucker out. ∎

Communist Alert!

The last drive-in in Tahiti, land of Marlon Brando's stomach, will be closed at the end of this month. The Drive-In Gaugin, which has been showin nekkid Frenchies for twenty years, got Video Fued. Remember, without eternal vigilance, it can happen here.

Standin Up for the Bimbos in Hot Pants

Ever since all the stewardesses went on strike against the Trashed and Wasted Airline, I've decided "Joe Bob Goes to the Drive-In" needs to show support for em. You may not realize it, but a lot of these bimbos get *half the money* I do for performing the same job they do: heatin up frozen dinners. This is totally unfair. These little gals should get about two-thirds of what a man gets.

But only if they beg for it.

So anyhow, to show my support of the Independent Federation of Stewardesses, specially the ones that still wear hot pants, I'm going on strike for one paragraph:

There are no jokes in this paragraph. You can look all day and you will not find a single joke or reference to the drive-in in this paragraph. Just forget it. Want to laugh? Go to some other *scab* column that is *not* honoring the Bimbo Picket Line. Read a little Ann Landers out loud with a Miami Beach accent. Look for the breast count in William F. Buckley's column. Go straight to the editorial page and read hilarious opinions about the Gramm-Rudman bill. But don't look here. I'm on strike. In fact, right now I'm thinking of something *extremely* funny and I'm laughing so much that I can barely keep writing this sentence,

JOE BOB'S MAILBAG

DEAR JOE BOB: My buddy Ben says 13 secretaries with big boobs and erasers can get more done in one day than a computer can in a week.
NANCY "SCOOP" WALLACE
PUBLIC INFORMATION OFFICER
COLLEGE OF LAW
WESTERN STATE UNIVERSITY
FULLERTON, CALIF.

DEAR SCOOP: Only if they're highly untrained.

DEAR MR. BRIGGS: Every Sunday morning we buy the *San Francisco Chronicle* and come home and make coffee and drink it and make hash browns and eat them and read your insightful articles on the drive in genre film industry and laugh.

We hope we are not *too* late to be considered as your future wives (bigamy is no object). We can cook but we don't like to. We can party and we like to. We can clean house but we hate to. We can go to the drive in but we don't cause we're waiting for you to bring the drive in too us.

Could we have a couple of pictures of you to hang over our beds (sigh!)

Four breasts, bar fu, pasta fu, beds roll, burger fu, bimbo fu. 3 stars. Laura and Lynne say check it out.
SHARON LYNNE
MARY LAURA
ARCATA, CALIF.
P.S. Joe Bob puleeze send us money or 2 copies of your Noozletter or come visit or 2 pictures or money.
P.P.S. We are not in jail and we are not insane. Joe we're sincere. We mean it. Let it be us.

DEAR SHARON, LAURA, MARY OR LYNNE OR ANY KINKY COMBINATION: You're just what I was lookin for—some place where I can go lay around and do nothin all day except cook, clean, and watch you eat.

DEAR JOE BOB: Please don't allow the naysayers, infidels, and the trembling, temperate, sadd and madd unbelievers to sway you from your purpose here on earth.

A life without pleasure has no meaning, and is, therefore, already forfeit. Heed the words of the immortal William Claude Dunkenfield during the Great Temperance Repression: "The joys of drunkenness are fleeting." The first thing America's bible-thumping bimbos did after being granted citizenship was to vote in a ridiculous law of prejudice against the more responsible citizens who *could* hold their liquor. Now they're trying it by insidious means. I know that, without eternal vigilance, it will happen here *again*.
DANIEL J. LINCK
SCOTTSDALE, ARIZ.

DEAR DAN: I will forever defend your right to drink until you vomit.

but I'm *not* gonna tell you what it is. Next week maybe, but only if you let my bimbos go.

Okay, that's just a taste of what's gonna happen if you make these girls beg for their groceries any longer. Next week there's gonna be *two* paragraphs like that if the Terribly Wimpy Airline don't agree to the following stewardess demands:

1. We want a more precise definition of the word "layovers," due to the recent unpleasant episodes in San Francisco.

2. We want more frequent "layovers."

3. We want all our boyfriends that used to be pilots released from the Federal Correctional Institution in La Tuna, Texas, cause it wasn't their fault they got assigned to the New York-to-Bogota flight.

4. We want more of those little whiskey bottles the size of your thumb so we can stick em in our purse and take em home to our apartment and never have to buy any and when people come over they say, "Hey, I bet you work for an airline!"

5. We want bigger carts for our luggage, so we won't look so ridiculous walkin nine miles through Chicago O'Hair Airport draggin a pull toy three times a week.

6. We want Joe Bob Briggs to fly everwhere free.

Six simple demands. Six teensy, weensy little demands. Not even demands really. Requests. Common courtesies. The kind of thing you'd do for your dog. Think of it as spoonin out a little Alpo for these gals, too.

Speaking of bimbos-in-chains, *The Nekkid Cage* is the best flick about whining female convicts since *The Big Doll House* came out 10, 15 years back. What happens is, the world's stupidest cowgirl is in love with a guy named Willie who steals Corvettes and gets involved in murder by hangin around with an escaped jailbait hitch-hiking nasty named Rita. Willie and Rita get coked up and decide to rob the bank where the stupid cowgirl works, and—whoops!—Boyfriend dies and the two skirts are off to the Crossbar Hotel. Course, Rita hates the Cowgirl for the obvious reason that the Cowgirl is totally innocent and can act almost as good as Linda Blair, who usually plays this role but was too busy cleaning her navel.

First Rita lets the Cowgirl know what she thinks of her by nailing her hand to the cafeteria table with an ice-pick. Then we get to watch the warden in some lesbo "beat me, hurt me" action, and then finally, the scene we've all been waitin for, every women-in-cages has got one—the guard named "Smiley" says "I think I'll go down to Solitary tonight and do some shop-ping." It's Nick Benedict from *All My Children*, assaulting helpless unemployable actresses.

Then Rita kills the Cowgirl's junkie friend for being a junkie, and it's time for—yes, it's been a long time—it's time for Catfight City. Hair-pulling, kneeing, eye-scratching, you name it.

We're talkin 25 breasts. Sixteen dead bodies. Two motor vehicle chases. Two shootouts. Stampede. Six gallons blood. Three brawls. One hanging. S-and-M lesbo scene. S-and-Z lesbo scene, which is even worse. Razorblade slashing. Nose smashing. Glass swallowing. One race riot. Gratuitous rhyming couplets during a race riot. Gratuitous bird with a broken wing. Gratuitous rats. Kung fu. Bimbo fu. Hypodermic fu. Icepick fu. Fire extinguisher fu. Drive-In Academy Award nominations for Angel Tompkins, as the lesbo warden, for saying "The guards are zookeepers and you're the animal"; Nick Benedict, as Smiley the Guard, for saying "You

---

Communist Alert!

The Frontier Drive-In in San Diego is history. Shopping mall. Some guy name of Paul Quon paid a MEASLY $9.4 million for it. The Frontier had three screens, 1600 parking spaces, and had the Godfather of Soul, James Brown, on hand for Opening Night, April 10, 1957. San Diego used to be a great drive-in town, but the Commies got the Aero, the Big Sky, the Rancho, the Del Mar—and now, the Frontier. Remember, without eternal vigilance, it can happen here.

broke my nose!"; Christina Whitaker, as Rita the Bad Bad Girl, for putting cocaine on her garbonzas; Shelly Komarov, for going down to Frederick's of Hollywood and picking out authentic prison uniforms; John Terlesky, as Willie, for picking up Rita on the road and saying "Mi casa es su casa"; Faith Minton, as Sheila the Big Bad Prison Mama, for smothering an in-mate in dirty laundry; Shari Shattuck, as Michelle the Stupid Cowgirl, for saying "Sometimes I have dreams about home. Like right now. I'm riding on Misty. That's my horse."; and Paul Nicholas, the director, for writing the line "You think I can't kill you? You manipulated Willie!"

A definite four stars. Joe Bob says check it out twice. ■

Joe Bob Unveils the 1985 Hubby Winners

After *weeks* countin the Drive-In Academy Award ballots, Ferdinand Marcos and "the boys" finally got all the totals to me except for South Dakota. "We'll geev later eef you need," explained Ferdy, extracting a two-thousand-dollar gold piece from his wife's bra and dropping it into my hand. I told him it was okay, cause Ferdy's been depressed lately and I didn't wanna upset him. Imelda is on his back all the time, screaming at him for forgetting to pack her 7,600 pairs of designer panty hose and *now it's too late*. He'll probly have to give her an office building in Fort Worth so they can kiss and make up.

Anyhow, I stayed up all night studying the returns, but I couldn't get anybody to tell me what a return is, so I stayed up all the next night studying the ballots. And here, at last, are the 1985 Hubby winners. (As usual, nobody showed up for the ceremonies on KGO-TV, not even Sally Field, and so I have all the Hubbies—engraved 1956 Chevy hubcaps—in the trailer house.)

May I have the envelope please?

Now may I have what's inside the envelope please?

BEST FU

The winner is *Invasion USA*, for Range Rover fu—specially the scene where Chuck Norris follows a Russian spy into a Miami Beach shopping mall, saves millions of Jewish Christmas shoppers from his exploding suitcase, kills seven or eight with a hand-held sawed-off machine gun, steals a convertible *and* a TV reporter from an auto show, drives it *through* the mall, chases the Russian spy and a girl hostage he's dangling out the window, grabs the girl away from him, and then lobs a little Christmas present into the cab of the truck.

BEST DIRECTOR

Sly Rocky Rambo, for *Rocky IV*, the most sensitive and intelligent movie about nuclear war ever directed by a man with huge breasts. A *surprise winner,* beating out the favored Tobe "Mr. Chainsaw" Hooper. The only way I can explain it—everbody felt guilty about ignoring Sly three years ago when he was *not even nominated* for *Staying Alive*. Sly pouted for the whole year, but unfortunately he looks exactly the same when he's pouting as when he's not pouting.

BEST SCREENWRITING

No surprise here. George Romero, the genius of Pittsburgh, for *Day of the Dead*, featuring such already immortal zombie lines as "Send more cops!" and "Look! It's a miracle! He doesn't see us as lunch!"

BEST BEAST

Was there ever any doubt? Robert Englund, better known as the pasty-face child molester Freddy Krueger that looks like a walking Nazi experiment with steel claws in *Nightmare on Elm Street* and *Nightmare on Elm Street Part Two-o*. Freddy is the best new teen-meat killer since Jason.

Special lifetime achievement award to Godzilla, even though we all know how *boring Godzilla 85* was.

BEST ACTRESS

Extremely weak bimbo selection this year, but the dark-horse winner is Tawny Kitaen, for battling three raving horny Amazons to the death in a duel of the world's largest abalone-shell underwire support bras in *The Perils of Gwendoline*. Also, for being named Tawny Kitaen.

BREAST ACTRESS

Mathilda May, the nekkid outer-space love ghoul in *Lifeforce*, for showing off her intergalactic love pouches throughout the movie. Those garbonzas were deadly.

BEST ACTOR

Arnold the Barbarian, for wasting half of El Lay for the second year in a row in *Commando*, and also taggin along with Brigitte Nielson while she was makin a fool of herself in *Red Sonja*. We all know why Arnold got it—because he was *passed over* last year when *The Terminator* won all the other Hubbies. Congratulations, Arnie. I know if you were here, you'd say somethin like "Thunk you."

BEST FLICK

Could we have a drum roll please? *Re-Animator*! The only movie ever made where an actor loses his head halfway through the movie but *finishes the movie*. The best hypodermic fu in history. And the best dead attack cat ever trained to infuriate the Humane Society.

Drive your Hubbies in good health.

Speaking of dead people, *House* is this flick about a Stephen King–type writer who gets a divorce and goes out to live in the haunted house where his aunt killed herself and his little boy drowned in the pool, so he can write a book about his Vietnam experiences that nobody wants to read. Hey, we've all been there, right?

The problem is, the guy can't get any work done cause he has a fat neighbor that shows up ever time he rigs up his Minoltas to take pictures of the monster that's in the upstairs closet. And then when he starts running around the house in his combat fatigues, shootin off his shotgun at a Miss Piggy slime creature, the police come to the house and tell him to stop pumpin his ammo.

Unfortunately, it's not that easy, cause the house has a 12-foot-long fish on the wall that's been zombified and starts comin back to life, not to mention the seven farm implements from the shed that start flyin through the house, trying to gouge the guy's privates. In other words, what we got here is one of those nightmares-about-my-screwed-up-life flicks, sort of a cross between *Poltergeist* and *Rambo*.

We got no breasts, cause Kay Lenz wouldn't pop her top for the camera. Three quarts blood. Just a 21 on the Vomit Meter. Five dead bodies. Seven beasts. One hanging. One drowning. Valium gulping. Closet Slime Monster. Miss Piggy Glopola Monster. Flying skull bat. Chimney Gremlins. Heads roll. Arms roll. Hand rolls. Other stuff rolls. Gratuitous reptiles in the bathroom mirror. Dead fish fu. Flying farm-implement fu. Dismembered hand fu. Grenade City. Drive-In Academy Award nominations for William Katt, as Roger Cobb the Big Steve–type writer, for trying to fix up his marriage with a shotgun; Curt Wilmot, as the Rambo Skeleton, the first soldier-of-fortune monster, for coming direct from Vietnam to kill Roger; and Harold Gorton, as the fat neighbor, for attempting to harpoon the closet monster.

Two and a half stars. Joe Bob says check it out.

Praying for Donka-Shane Wayne

A lot of people think being a drive-in movie critic is all champagne and roses.

But they're wrong.

Sometimes it can be Co-Cola and plastic daffodils. Sometimes it can be muscatel and blow-up party dolls. Sometimes it can be old Mel Torme records and Lysol. But most of the time, it's a dirty job, but somebody's gotta do it. This is one of those weeks.

I didn't wanna have to tell you this.

I got the news three, four weeks ago, but I been puttin it off. I've read the letter over and over again, and I still can't believe it. I'm surprised nobody told me before now. Maybe they were trying to spare my feelings. But there it is, plain as day, postmark Las Vegas, Nevada. I couldn't even read past the first two sentences:

Dear Joe Bob: Thank you for writing. Wayne's fan club is not completely active at this time . . ."

Wayne Newton. Big Wayne. Wayne the Huge. The man I've modeled my life after for the last 20, 30 minutes. The man that got his shot on the Sullivan show in '63, Donka-Shaned his way through the '60s, rose to superstardom and bought southern Nevada in the '70s, and in the '80s . . . I'm sorry, I'm gettin choked up, I'm gonna have to stop or I'll start blubbering like a Bob Hope Special.

"Not completely active at this time."

Six words. Six of the saddest words in the English language. What does it mean? Does it mean Wayne's off doin stuff for his tribe? Does it mean he's gone into the hospital to repair stomach damage caused by the constant wearing of a 180-pound belt buckle? Could it possibly mean his dimples are droopin after all these years?

I don't believe it.

Not Wayne. Not Wayne "I'm Not

JOE BOB'S MAILBAG

DEAR JOE BOB: What's this PG-13 I see on some movie ads? It sounds like a food additive or dye. Are they using that powdered butter on the popcorn now? If so, is the PG-13 a warning that we shouldn't visit the snack bar during certain features?

On the other hand, when I was in high school, we used PG to mean "pregnant." Is it possible that there are 13 pregnancies and/or inseminations or conceptions in these movies? If it's a pregnancy tally, it seems funny that there are always thirteen. Please explain. I'm . . .
CONFUSED IN GARLAND
GARLAND, TEX.

DEAR CONFUSED: PG actually stands for "Perry Grossman." Perry is a butcher in Queens, New York, who only goes to the movies once every 13 years. The designation "PG-13" can therefore be roughly translated, "Perry Grossman decided to pass this one up, too!"

JOE BOB: I just wanna
  Sit down
  And shut up
  Have nobody bother me
  I just wanna
  Sit down
  And shut up
  Then maybe I'll see
  What life is all about
  What life is all about
  Somebody tell me
  What is the meaning of life
GEORGE PAEZ
AUSTIN, TEX.

DEAR GEORGE: Rhyming. Rhyming is the meaning of life, George.

DEAR JOE BOB: Y'know I was watching the news recently and saw some Filipino radicals in the states pouring San Miguel (which hap-pens to be a fine Pale Pilsen beer brewed in the Philippines) into the street, to protest Pres. Marcos' election. I mean, just cause old Ferdinand gets an 80 percent cut is no reason to pour good beer in the street. The whole thing reeks of organized crime and—gasp!—Communism! What do you think?

By the way, over here in Korea we get the Observer a couple of weeks late since the Department of Defense cut out your column from it's newsletters. Horrors! Later,
DEREK GRANT
HEADQUARTERS, AIR COMPONENT COMMAND
KOREA/U.S. COMBINED FORCES COMMAND
SEOUL, KOREA

DEAR DEREK: About twice a year they try to get me back in Stars and Stripes, and some colonel comes along and says "Not over my dead hiney" and do you know what happens? Do you know what this country has to go through because of that one STUPID decision?

Yes, I'm sorry, but it's true.
We get another Bob Hope Special.

DEAR JOE BOB: My wife says your last concert drew a "definately yuppy crowd." Please, JB, say it isn't so.
Sincerely,
M. B. CHUCK
DALLAS

DEAR M.B.: Yeah, but then we threw your wife out and it was fine.

DEAR JOE BOB: How could you leave Day of the Dead off the best flick list why wasnt it called Day of the Living Dead was it called Night of the Dead or Night of the Living Dead instead of the Living Dead I'd be impressed if it was called Nightmare on Living Dead Street but it wasnt and I wasnt real impressed do you think there will be a Twilight of the Living Dead without a flyboy in it how about an Evening of the Living Dead with a really big breast count how about a Breast of the Living Dead where all those living bras

get infected and chase the lead female Since they're doing a *Texas Chainsaw Massacre* part two and want to use the original cast but cannot since most of them were killed off in the movie why dont they make it *The Texas Chainsaw Massacre of the Living Dead* could they get Bub to make a cameo appearance.
DOUG LIVING DEAD NELSON
GARLAND, TEX.

DEAR DOUG: Raleigh Hills really works.

DEAR JOE BOB: Haiku-Fu for you:
Bloody Chainsaw Pus
Oozing Down My Rubber Glove
Peckinpah I Grin
Affectionately,
CHIN HO KELLY, FIVE-O
WASHINGTON, D.C.

DEAR CHIN:
 Chinese Poet
 Stow it

in the Mafia" Newton. And to prove it, I want everbody in the Job Bob Briggs audience—I don't care where you are, what you're doing—I want you to stop right now and say a little prayer for Wayne. Maybe it'll go something like this:

"Dear Lord, I don't know what's wrong with Wayne. Maybe he got a little too big for his britches and he's tryin to lose the weight again. I don't know. Maybe he's over in Europe buying up some casinos. Whatever. Just *bring him back.* We love him, even though he recorded 'Everybody Loves Somebody Sometime' and that was always Dino's song. Amen."

And then I want *everybody*—no exceptions—I want *everybody* out there to write to Laura Martinez, WAYNE NEWTON FAN CLUB, 3422 Happy Lane, Las Vegas, Nevada 89120, and I want you to say, "I'll buy anything. I'll

send you any amount of money. I'll buy Wayne's video. I'll even buy Wayne's picture button or his '82 program book cause I know yall got a lot of those left over. But *sign me up now.* I will *not* wait. We want Wayne."

Remember when Wayne used to hold that little mike right up to his lips, and he'd raise his little pinky up, and then he'd sing "Bill Bailey" real fast, triple-time, and then he'd get that big grin on his face and he'd start dancin across the stage and winkin at the ladies? Well, that's what I want *you* to do right now, wherever you are, in your living room, on the patio. And then I want to tell Wayne you did it, just for him.

Do it for me. Do it for America. Donka-Shane for Wayne. Let's send him so much money he can go out and buy another palomino.

No excuses.

Speaking of dead space, Siskel the Simp and Ebert the Wimp have been mouthin off again about "senseless violence" and dumpin on a flick called *The Hitcher.* I was gonna pass it up, cause I thought it was an art flick like *Poltergeist,* but ever since they made *I Spit on Your Grave* famous by declaring it the scummiest movie ever made, I've depended on their recommendations. And once again, they've sniffed out a drive-in classic.

This is the finest movie ever made about why it's definitely not a good idea to pick up a hitchhiking Dutch actor on a Texas highway at night in the middle of a rainstorm, specially if he carries a switchblade, smells bad, and says stuff like "First I cut off his legs. And his arms. And his head." I don't know what it was about this guy—Rutger Hauer—I just had a sixth sense that you shouldn't give him a ride.

Most of the movie is about how this

kid shouldn't of picked up Rutger Hauer, cause everwhere the kid goes, the hitcher follows him, rammin him with a pickup, blowin up gas stations, icing ever cop in sight and framin the kid for it. Then, after they've wasted ever cop vehicle in three Texas counties and had some really disgusting cheeseburgers, Rutger Hauer decides to tie the legs of the kid's girlfriend to a pole, tie her hands to the bumper of a sem-eye, and make a wish. I'm afraid, at this point, the kid gets a little p.o.ed and we have one of the all-time great Heinz Ketchup-on-the-windshield shootout finales.

We're talking zero breasts, *but:* 20 dead bodies. Seven motor vehicle chases, with five crash-and-burns. Six quarts blood. Jennifer Jason Leigh taffy pull. Gratuitous vomit, but a 62 on the Vomit Meter. Exploding gas station. Finger disguised as a French fry. Exploding attack copter. Face-spitting. Texas State Trooper fu. Range Rover fu. Drive-In Academy Award nominations for Rutger Hauer, as the hitcher, for stickin pennies on the kid's eyes and sayin "I want you to stop me"; C. Thomas Howell, as the kid, for killing Rutger Hauer five or six times; and Robert Harmon, the director, for making Ebert and Siskel so durn mad.

Three and a half stars. Job Bob says check it out. ■

Casting for Crappie in the Gulf of Sidra

Up till last week, I never did realize that *anybody* can hang around in the Gulf of Sidra, no matter how stupid. It's the international law. I don't know, nobody ever mentioned it to me until Ronnie brought it up. Nobody ever said, "Hey, Joe Bob, let's go troll for carp over in Sidra," or, "Hey, man, that Libyan slalom skiing is a monster experience."

But, you know, this happens to me all the time on bass trips. There's always some local-yokel farmer who thinks he *owns* the river, and so he stretches a bob-war fence across it and thinks it's *so funny* when you end up with your head stuck in a muck-hole.

There's only one thing we can do with Moammar Jalopy. I'm makin the call right now. I want every bass boat, every party barge, every ski boat with little orange porpoises painted on the side, and I want every bait-shop owner in Texas, Louisiana, and Arkansas to *pony up* his overpriced, banged-up rental canoes *and* his outboards that don't work, and we're all goin over to Sidra and party.

Come on, it'll be fun. What we'll do is we'll get 97,000 boats—that's the figure I'm tryin for—and we'll put em all up right to the edge of the Twelve-Mile-Limit, and we'll set there tying flies and gettin ready to cast for Libyan crappie. If Jalopy asks us what we're doin, I'll just say "Trot line." And then when we've got all the boats all bunched up together, completely occupying the Gulf of Sidra except for the 12-mile limit cause we are *not* gonna break the law, we'll ask Chubb Fricke to come over with his Evinrude

JOE BOB'S MAILBAG

DEAR JOE BOB: I cannot believe that you reviewed the movie *Chorus Line* and for that matter I don't see how any self respecting drive-in would carry that movie. The only way it could have been more revolting is if it had starred John Travolta and the Australian bimbo Olivia Newton-John. However, I guess you are just doing it to appease your commie/pinko audience which is evidenced by the letters that followed that column. Of the five letters only one was from Texas and two were from California, the land of fruits and fags and commie/pinko/nazi sympathizers. If this trend of yours continues, can I now expect you to review *Amadeus* and the latest PBS series on albino chinchilla fur transplants.

Come on Joe Bob you are supposed to represent everything that made Texas what it is today: red necks, long necks and no necked football players. Get with it.
AL THIBODEAN
CARROLLTON, TEX.

DEAR ALL: Those chinchilla transplants were NOT albino. I can't believe you'd say that.

DEAR J.B.: You are a phony redneck. First you won't review pornos and now you don't like dog racing. You probly think orange juice is healthier than free beer. Ask the vetinarian if your glands are hangin' right.
Sincerely,
RAY ROBINSON
SAN FRANCISCO

DEAR RAY: I don't know how I can thank you. I talked to the vet, and he said you're absolutely correct-o. My glands are hanging LEFT. I'm tryin to fix the problem by walking with my right leg only.

DEAR JOE BOB—The local TV stations around here have stopped showing the late night kung fu flicks. Even though these things make us Chinese look silly, it was the only way we could get onto TV without appearing as TV anchorwomen or on Asian community access TV shows.

Life isn't the same without the weekly Run Run Shaw chop-saki production. I miss those shows like *Challenge of the Ninja, Shaolin Handlock,* and *Flying Guillotene.* If it weren't for classics such as *Death Chamber,* I wouldn't be in medical school now.

I have a feeling that my school made a deal with the local TV stations just to get back at me. What course of action should I take?
JIMMY (THEY CALL ME BRUCE) LEE
SAN FRANCISCO
P.S. Dolph Lundren is the next Arnold

DEAR JIM-JIM: Did you know Dolph is Chinese? He could probly hep you out with his new martial-arts technique—Sit-on-You Fu.

Inboard Yachtmaster and anchor it six inches from the line, and then here's the beautiful part.

We ask Chubb to take off his shoes and socks. This is somethin he does about once ever four years. (Gas masks and aqualungs will be distributed on a need basis.) And then we ask Chubb to *dangle* his feet in the water until he touches the line with his big toe and says, "Hey! You! Pimple Face! I'll give you your Sidra!"

And right at that moment, we'll all shake up our cans (sorry, American beers only), pop em and spray em. If we get lucky, and the wind direction is right, and we have all 97,000 fishin boats pullin together, we can probly get beer spray all the way to the shoreline, jammin up nuke equipment, irritatin the eyes of Russian advisers, and generally makin Libya look like a *mess.* And once they turn around and look at us and see the shape and color of Chubb Fricke's feet—believe me, they'll never bother us again.

Speaking of guys that like to play mumbledly-peg, *April Fool's Day* is another Teen Meat Weekend from the producer of the classic Friday the 13th series—Frank Mancuso Jr.—the man who rocketed to the top of his profession at the age of 27 and sold all his movies to Paramount *without even mentioning* to anybody that his daddy, Frank Mancuso Sr., is the chairman and chief executive officer of Paramount.

Little Frank slipped a little bit on this one, though, and so we *might* have to have a little talk at the dinner table this week if he doesn't straighten up, young man. What we got is a bunch of extremely talented soap-opera stars, unemployed actors, and people workin for scale, who all get invited out to an island for the weekend so that "Muffy," played by Deborah Foreman of *My Chauffeur* fame, can stand around screwin up her face and makin em disappear one by one. She dresses up a bunch of Barbie and Ken dolls to resemble the cast, then cuts off their hands, pours ketchup on em, and dumps em in a bowl of Liquid Drano, but no one thinks this is strange because all the actors already look like mutilated Barbie and Ken dolls.

We got a bunch of whoopie-cushion jokes, dribble-glass jokes, exploding cigars, trick faucets, and—the biggest groaner of all—gratuitous Griffin O'Neal.

The dramatic highlight is when we almost get to see Deborah Goodrich's garbonzas. But the final breast count is zero. No plot to get in the way of the story. Two quarts blood. Nine dead bodies, sort of. Three heads roll, sort of. Monster-in-the-box. Knife in stomach. Teenage face-crushing. Jungle snake attack. Gratuitous Barbie doll mutilation. Hanging. Paramount fu. Drive-In Academy Award nominations for Deborah Goodrich, for making the sign of the quadruple-gilled attack weasel with Clayton Rohner; Fred Walton, the director, for makin *When a Stranger Calls* seven years ago and surviving this turkey; and Little Frank, the producer, for refusing to make *Friday the 13th Part 6* and gettin in *big trouble* from his daddy.

Two Stars. Joe Bob says check it out. ∎

The Return of Bodacious Wanda Bodine

A lot of people ask me, they say, "Joe Bob, why the heck don't you write about Wanda Bodine anymore?" And then they wanna know if she shut down the Rockabilly Glamorcize salon on the Grapevine Highway, or whether she finally got married to Lute Fenwick so she could get the Western Auto in the divorce settlement, or else maybe she just took her *Family Feud* winnings and opened up a snowcone stand, or *what*.

Naw, she didn't do anything that intelligent.

Wanda Bodine is going to law school to become a professional liar.

What she did is she filed a discrimination lawsuit against the law school of the University of Arkansas at Little Rock for not havin enough unemployed bimbo hairdressers with crooked teeth in the student body, and Federal Judge J. Dilworth Scuzface ruled that they had to take her in, no matter how stu-

JOE BOB'S MAILBAG

JOE BOB: During a recent drunken tour of the Great Northeast Corridor and Industrial Waste Disposal Site, I discovered some indoor bullstuff even you might enjoy. "Direct from the Windy City . . . The Chicago Knockers . . . As Seen On National TV! The World's Most Famous Ladies Mud Wrestling Team! KNOCKERMANIA! Great Family Entertainment! Catch the '86 Tour!"

While I admit most of these cutie-pies have thighs that Elsie would be proud of, they're still a better show than anything Meryl Streep has ever been in.

Knockers Fever . . , Catch 'em!
"TRASH" BAGGS
FLINT, TEX.

DEAR TRASH: I can see from the picture of the Knockers that they've been practicing power-slams with their faces again.

DEAR JOE BOB: Greek, as we know it, was mostly written in a Byzantine script developed in the 14th Century by a bunch of monks. It is highly ornate, bearing many diacritical marks, e.g. breathings and the accents acute, grave, and circumflex.

Classical Greek is said to be "quantitative" and the poetry scans when one parses for a pattern in long and short vowels in syllables.

I don't believe this. I think Classical Greek was stress accented. I mean, like, its stressed now and everyone admits that *no one knows* how it sounded in the old days.

Gerard Manley Hopkins, The Star of Balliol, wrote in "sprung rhythm." He was a very great classicist and I think he was writing what he thought classical metrics were. Jim Bob says, check it out. What do you think?

I have big t—s and wear a size 1851Q cup. I'll show me yours if . . . I think I'm falling in love with a man.
Urp,
JIM BOB AMDAHL
DALLAS

DEAR JIM BOB: The Greeks wrote with a lithp, just like you.

MY DEAREST JOSEPH ROBERT: Why don't you ever publish your real picture with your column? From the way you write I can only imagine that you are the most handsome and virile man alive.
Love always,
LUISA HUGHES
SEATTLE

DEAR LUISA: That's correct.

DEAR JOE BOB: I just finished reading your article on Sho Kosugi. To me even though Bruce Lee is dead I don't think that any one can yet replace him. Remember Bruce Lee was king of kung fu. Sho Kosugi is not nor are the others until one can be proven to become king of kung fu. I shall always know and remember Bruce Lee as being the king of kung fu.

To bad he died he was the greatest.
CHISVU CRUZ
COLORADO SPRINGS, COLO.

DEAR CHISVU: No question, man. Bruce is still the king. But Sho Nuff Kosugi COULD be the king if he dies in the next three years.

pid she was. Then she filed another lawsuit against J. Dilworth Scuzface for calling her stupid, but she lost that one when Acting Federal Judge I. Mary Cousins listened to the testimony of three psychiatrists who said they tried to administer the Minnesota Multiphasic Personality Test to Wanda but she refused to go to Minnesota and, besides that, was "devoid of personality." Then Wanda threatened to sue the three shrinks for using the word "devoid" in her presence, and so the judge issued an official order for Wanda to "immediately, and with due process and dispatch, remove your hiney to law school."

Just before she left, I went over to see her at Le Bodine, and when I got there I found her hunched over an automatic hair-dryin machine, trying to make it hum the theme from *Doctor Zhivago,* but she was so glad to see me that she threw down her tools, ran across the room, and hugged my cheek with the flat part of her hand. Then she started babbling about how she was on her way to Little Rock this year to start learning how to "sue the pants off ever jerk that thought he could get out of the marriage and still keep his golf clubs *and* his secretary."

"It's something I've been studying all my life to do," she told me.

Then, course, I had to tell her there was more to being a professional liar than just takin husbands to the cleaners. You have to be able to keep prostitutes on the streets at all times, and make sure the board of directors of Union Carbide don't have to spend any more time in prison than's absolutely necessary (and *specially* not prison in India, where it's yucky), and you have to be able to make friends with the parents of people that get killed in airplane crashes and guys that breathe on little girls in the *Winnie the Pooh* section of the library, and you have to . . .

"Joe Bob," she told me, "you don't understand."

I told her I probly didn't.

"I'm gonna be a prosecutor. I'm gonna learn how to put guys like you where they belong. You either *get married and stay married* or else you *go to jail.* There ain't any other choice."

"Wanda?" I said.

"Yes."

"Now that you put it that way."

"Yes."

"Will you show me your torts?"

The woman then committed a Class A misdemeanor in broad daylight on or about my person and *she didn't serve one minute for it.* I can already tell, she's gonna be a great one.

Speaking of unprosecuted felonies, *Loose Screws* just came out. It's *supposed* to be a sequel to *Screwballs,* one of the greatest drive-in flicks of all time, written by the woman best known as Bootsie Goodhead in the bouncing-Chevy-van-at-the-drive-in scene, the former ripaway-bra queen herself—Linda Shayne. But here's the deal: Producer Roger Corman, the drive-in king, told Linda that he'd let her write the sequel, and act in it, too, but only if she took *less money* than she got the first time. So Linda took a hike and went to work for DISNEY (!!!), but once again, Roger, I got to hand it to you, they don't call you "Mr. Low Budget" for nothing.

Anyhow, what we got here is the four biggest screw-ups at Beaver High, who get kicked out and have to spend the summer at Coxwell Academy for Morons, where they dress up like doctors on the first day of class and give mandatory breast exams to the girls and they spend the rest of the movie trying to get private lessons from the French teacher, Miss Mona Lott. It's no *Screwballs,* but it registers fairly high on the Junior-High Grossout Meter.

Thirty-nine breasts. No blood. Two shower scenes. Bathtub scene. Gratuitous boys' locker-room scene. Gratuitous roasted weenies. Fat fu. Aphrodisiac gas fu. Golf-ball-between-the-legs fu. Drive-In Academy Award nominations for Cyd Belliveau, as Mona Lott, for discussing her new job with the principal and saying "Any position under you would be just fine"; Steve Hardman, for takin everbody to Pig Pen's Topless Bar for Grossout Night; Mike McDonald, as the evil principal, for helping Mona Lott in the mailroom by saying "Let me show you your slot"; Brian Genesse, for doing half the movie in drag and posing as a Chinese massage artist named Hung Lo; Jason Warren, as the 350-pound Marvin Eatmore, for doing Fat Boy Aerobics; Alan Deveau, as Hugh G. Erection, for stuffing Kleenex down his pants; Fred Mollin, the composer, for writing the hit song "Do the Screw" for the beach-party scene; and Stephanie Sulik, as the principal's leather-and-whips wife, for saying "No, honey, not tonight, we already did it this semester."

Three stars. Joe Bob says check it out. ∎

Dairy Queens and Nasty *Critters*

A couple weeks ago I put on my gas mask and went back to San Fran-sissy for the Drive-In Academy Awards ceremonies, and before I tell you what happened, I wanna make sure everbody in the rest of the country is seated in a sitting position and separated from any extremely sharp objects that might be layin around. It's took me this long to get to where I can actually force the words out:

Carol Doda, the most famous top-less dancer in the history of modern garbonzas . . .

Carol Doda, who served as my two cohostesses on the Drive-In Academy Awards . . .

The woman they call the Twin Peaks . . .

The only lady to ever have a histor-ical marker erected to her, in memory of the day in 1964 when she tossed her 34s in honor of LBJ's visit to San Fran and ushered in Topless as we know it today . . .

Carol Doda, the lady so devoted to her art that she went from 34 to 44 in 20 weeks, practiced her tassel-twirling in all her wakin hours, and did the Ripaway Romp on the elevator piano at the Condor Club for the next 22 years . . .

Carol Doda, the only topless dancer to have her chest sculpted in neon, with little flashing lights on each one to warn approaching aircraft—a sign that still strobes ever night on Broadway . . .

Carol Doda deflated her ticket-sell-ers.

It's true. It's already history. Carol had a "pay dispute" with the new owners of the Condor—they only wanted to pay her *one* salary, is what they wanted—and so she hit the road. For the first time in topless history, she's Not Available For Hooter Inspec-tion.

I tried to talk to her about it, even though she was mad at me for callin her a national monument the last time I was in San Fran. But after I looked deep into her grand canyon and begged forgiveness, she told me the story of how, back in '83, this man and lady went into the Condor club after it was closed and started makin the sign of the triple-jointed Guatemalan stump-

JOE BOB'S
MAILBAG

DEAR JOE BOB: I'm a misfit, hopelessly inept, socially unacceptable. compared to me, Phil Gramm is handsome, Tip O'Neill is dashing, Daniel Patrick Moynihan is coherent, Patrick Buchanan is housebroken. I'm so far gone that I think *The A-Team* has charm, *Dynasty* has wit, *Miami Vice* has depth, Barbara Walters has insight, *Murder, She Wrote* has realism, and Dan Rather has integrity. I'm so bored that I can't wait to find out what Liz Taylor said, what Sting did, what Princess Di wore, what Madonna didn't wear, and where Marcos hid the money. I have such bad taste that I think Joan Rivers is funny, Cher is sexy, Boy George is amusing, Tony Danza can act, Bruce Springsteen can sing, and Robert Ludlum can write.

My question is: what should I say in my "personals" ad?
DOWN AND OUT
DALLAS

DEAR DOWN AND OUT: *"Inquiring people want to know me."*

DEAR JOE BOB: As I watched Ronnie's speech on Nicaragua I was reminded of a movie that you missed. It was one of those po-ignaint stories about this Jew and his pet Cambodian. When I heard it was about Cambodia I figured Chuck Norris was busting out MIA's again. Anyway they had this bad bunch of dudes in it called the Come Here Ruge. These dudes were like Arnold the Terminator toward anyone who had a junior high education. I dropped out to late as a sophomore. If we don't give Ronnie 100 mil to fight the Sandy Eastas now in five years we going to be battling Meskin Come Here Ruges at our local Taco Bells and anyone who can count past ten is going to get a plastic bag over their head.
A CONCERNED AGGIE
BRYAN, TEX.

DEAR CONCERNED: *I guess that makes you safe.*

KISS SOMEONE YOU LOVE WHEN YOU GET THIS LETTER AND MAKE MAGIC

This paper has been sent to you for good luck. The original copy is in New England. It has been around the world nine times. The luck has now been sent to you. You will receive good luck within four days of receiving this letter provided you send it back out. THIS IS NO JOKE. You will receive it in the mail.

Send copies to people you think need good luck. Don't send money, as Fate has no price. Do not keep this letter. It must leave your hands within 96 hours. An R.A.F. officer received $70,000.00. Joe Elliott received $40,000.00 and lost it because he broke the chain. While in the Philippines, Gene Welch lost his wife six days after receiving this letter. He failed to circulate the letter. However, before her death she won $50,000.00 in a lottery. They money was transferred to him four days after he decided to mail out this letter.

Please send out 20 copies of this letter and see what happens in four days. The chain comes from Venezuela and was written by Saul Anthony De Croff, a missionary from South America. Since the copy must make a tour of the world, you must make 20 copies and send them out to your friends and associates. After a few days, you will get a surprise. This is true even if you are not superstitious.

So note the following: Constantine Dias received the chain in 1953. He asked his secretary to make 20 copies and send them out. A few days later, he won a lottery of two million dollars. Aria Daddit, an office employee, received the letter and forgot it had to leave his hands within 96 hours. He lost his job. Later after finding the letter again, he mailed out 20 copies. A few days later he got a better job. Dale Fairchild received the letter and not believing threw it away. Nine days later he died.

Please send no money. Please don't ignore this. IT WORKS.
ANONYMOUS
COLORADO SPRINGS, COLO.

DEAR CHAIN: *I asked my secretary to make 20 copies of the letter. Three days later, I lost my secretary.*

gopher *right there on Carol's Elevator Piano*. And one of em "accidentally" hit the lift mechanism and got pancaked against the ceiling and it was in all the papers and everthing and it was *real* icky and the result was—

"My piano was violated," Carol said, adjusting her center of gravity as she spoke. "I didn't want to dance on a dead man's grave. Maybe I'm superstitious."

After that, she said, it was only a matter of time.

Sure, there's other jobs for Carol. She told me about her new "lingerie fashions for the entertaining woman," and the new "Carol Doda Theater of the Mind" telephone service (write to me for the number). But somehow it just won't be the same, knowin that Carol, the woman I like to call the Dairy Queen, won't be up there anymore, floppin nightly for you and me.

"It's no use crying," Carol told me, "over spilled silicone."

Speaking of monstrous destructive objects, *Critters* just shot to Numero Uno on the Best of '86 Drive-In Movie Stud List, thanks to the title-role performance by man-eating porcupine tumbleweeds with enormous teeth. These are the best intergalactic monsters since Zsa Zsa Gabor starred in *Queen of Outer Space*—and they wear a lot less makeup.

What we got here is an outer-space prison ship, where the death-row inmates, the Krites, get loose, steal a spaceship, and head for Grovers Bend, Kansas, to munch on the population. So to head off disaster, the outer-space king sends a couple of bounty hunters to blow the Krites away, and all the way to Earth they watch Empty-V on their monitors, and so right before they get there, one of the bounty hunters turns hisself into a Mick Jagger lookalike and threatens to do entire scenes

from *Let's Spend the Night Together*. Anyhow, by the time these two turkeys get to Kansas, the porky-weeds are already feeding on Auntie Ems all over the lot, and they got four of the top-billed stars of the movie holed up in a house that looks like every room was specially designed by Michael Landon to reflect his hairdo.

After eating a deputy sheriff and a dork from New York, the Krites start trying to make a Billy Green Bush sandwich—and the family revolts! Pretty soon we got Dee Wallace makin love to a shotgun, a kid named Scott Grimes throwin his homemade firecracker bombs into their mouths, and the horny little family porkchop, Nadine Van Der Velde, trying to avenge her dead boyfriend with a pitchfork. Meantime, the bounty hunters accidentally demolish the Methodist church with a stolen cop car, but that's nothin compared to what *really* makes the town mad—they shoot up the bowling alley! On League Night!

Pretty soon everbody ends up out at the Brown Farm, equipped with shoulder-mounted rocket launchers, and it's time to boogie.

Outstanding slime-spewing. One

Communist Alert!

American Airlines bought up half the Gemini Drive-In, the most famous drive-in in Texas, for somethin called a "NorthDallas AAirLink"—that's right, five capital letters in two words. I think you can tell we're dealing with the American Airlines Reetard Division here. Remember, without eternal vigilance, it can happen here.

breast. Two dead bodies. Four mutilated bodies. Eight dead critters. One motor vehicle chase, with two crashes. Three tumbleweed chases. Three gallons blood. Stomach-eating. Pitchfork-chewing. Gross-out mush-face alien transformation into a Mick Jagger lookalike. Explicit cow guts, also known as bovine fu. Garbage-disposal symbolism. Finger rolls. Extra points for gratuitous toy E.T. eaten by a critter. Gratuitous Empty-V song called "Power of the Night." Gratuitous Methodist church destruction. Shotgun fu. Toilet fu. Tumbleweed fu. Aerosol can and a lighted match fu. Drive-In Academy Award nominations for Dee Wallace Stone, as the mother, for *whining,* as usual; M. Emmet Walsh, as the sheriff, for being M. Emmet Walsh; Don Opper, as Charley the retarded town drunk, for talkin to the creatures through his tooth fillings; Scott Grimes, as the kid who takes on the critters, for sayin "I don't know, I must of been thrown clean out of my room by the earthquake"; Stephen Herek, for directing and writing and hiring all the same guys who worked on *Android;* Nadine Van Der Velde, for making the sign of the twin-pronged alfalfa plow with a guy from New York in the hay barn and watching him get munched into a furry Frito; and Billy Green Bush, as the farmer, for saying "These things are vicious! They've cut out our phone, they've cut out our power, it's only a matter of time til they get in here!"

Four stars. Best of '86. Joe Bob says check it out. ∎

Oh, Thank Heaven!
Playboy-cotting 7-Eleven

Excuse me if I'm a little steamed this week. It was less than eight months ago when my Babtist brothers in the Lord, Jerry Falwell and Donnie Wildmon, came to town for the protest march on the world headquarters of 7-Eleven, and I was down there supportin em all the way. I told Donnie, hey, look, I'll help you get the *Playboy*s and the *Penthouse*s out of there, as long as we replace em with my two personal favorite magazines—*Melons Monthly* and *Mouth and Garden*. And so what happens?

Two weeks ago, without even a *phone call* to the *Melons* distributor, 7-Eleven makes a big announcement that they're rippin the *Playboy*s out of the racks. No more NFL cheerleaders trying to get kicked off the team by poppin their pompoms. No more John Derek pictures of whoever he's married to. No celebrity-breast-of-the-month close-ups. And most important of all—no more letters to *Penthouse* written by me. (Yeah, it's true, I've been the "Spanking Frito" all along.)

I think we all know what did it. The issue that finally wiped *Playboy* and *Penthouse* off the convenience store map. I'm talking, of course, about the March cover of *Playboy,* the one where the entire cover is taken up by Sally Field's thighs.

Even at *Playboy* they are gonna *have to admit,* that there are limits to

JOE BOB'S MAILBAG

DEAR JOE BOB: We have recently started a group, S.I.C.K.O., that meets to view assorted depraved films. Needless to say your weekly commentaries are sources of genuine inspiration for our group. It would probably be premature to exalt you to deity status, however might you be interested in becoming our patron saint or at least poster child?

Kick it about. Or better yet kick your dog and let us know. We'll be waiting, chain saws at the ready.
Cheers,
SHARON BALESTRA
FRESNO, CALIF.

DEAR SHARON: Only if you'll get Jerry to come out here and hug me and say "Tragedies like this are what Vegas is all about."

DEAR JOE BOB: People refuse to confront the fact that we live in a world of finite resources. These resources cannot be renewed. Someday all our clean water and air will be gone, destroyed by pollution. Someday all the precious minerals will have been mined from beneath our lands. And someday, Joe Bob, someday Ann Landers will have to retire.

And what then? Who will the guy in Oregon turn to when he suspects that his wife is having an affair with the milkman? Who can the Kansas housewife complain to about the terrible manners of that family just down the street? Who will take the social, moral, and psycho-sexual problems of the entire nation, reduce them to a set of well-worn cliches, and express Calvinistic anger on behalf of her outraged readers? Who can replace Ann Landers?

Let's examine the necessary qualifications. First, and most important, the person must be a font of moral wisdom, able to instruct the masses in the mode of behavior that is proper and correct. Such a person should be a veritable oracle, in direct communication with the Deity. Obviously, almost any American politician will do nicely, although Jimmy Carter and Ronald Reagan seem especially well-qualified.

Also we need someone who can toss out snappy one-liners à la Ann Landers ("Get off the booze and dump the jerk!"). Ideal candidates would be Don Rickles, Johnny Carson, and, again, Ronald Reagan.

And of course we must have a person in this job who is in touch with the American public, who knows and cares about our deepest fears and desires: improper table settings, teenage sex, how to write a will, what to do about the awful things the new minister said in his sermon, the care and feeding of exotic pets, permissiveness in the media, and eccentric relatives. The obvious choice here: Phil Donahue.

So who is to succeed Ann Landers? My choice is you, Joe Bob. Consider:

(1) You are even more out of touch with reality than she is.

(2) Most of her letters contain questions about drug abuse and promiscuity. And you have a *lot* of first-hand experience in these areas.

(3) Her successor should avoid overly-complex words, and should write in plain, simple language that everyone can understand. Ann Landers does this to communicate with her readers. You do it because you can't spell the big words.

(4) And you share with Ann the trait that I feel is most important for any columnist: the unerring ability to express commonly-held misconceptions as though they are absolute truths.

When Ann is gone, someone, perhaps you, will have to take her place, Joe Bob, to titillate, to castigate, to remonstrate, to speak with a certitude that has no basis in fact. So I think you should begin now to write Joe Bob's Advice to the Lovelorn, the Anxiety-Ridden, the Bewildered, and the Just Plain Weird. Think of all the good you could do. Think of all the people you could help. Think of the *big bucks* Ann Landers rakes in.
PLAINTIVE YUPPIE
DALLAS

DEAR YUPMAN: If nominated I will not run. If elected, I'll advise the bimbo to pack her *hiney off to Miami Beach and let me dish out the baby-food for a while.*

DEAR JOE BOB: Congratulations! You are the first Texan I've seen or heard of whose ego needs bolstering. It must be lonely for you out there in the land of LBJ. Just for the record, I much prefer Bierce to Tolstoi: for one thing he's briefer. I'll give you a couple of opening sentences to his short stories; you might find him to your taste also.

To "Oil of Dog": "I come from poor but honest parents: my father was a purveyor of dog oil, and my mother kept a small studio in the shadow of the village church where she disposed of unwanted babes."

To "An Imperfect Conflagration": "One morning early in June of 1872, I murdered my father, an act which made a deep impression on me at the time."
Your friend,
BOB STURGEON
OAKLAND, CALIF.

DEAR BOB: My ego don't need bolstering. In fact, I'm sick and tired of being compared to Tolstoi all the time.

taste. There are lines you simply do not cross. And Sally Field in a bunny suit, *seen from behind,* is one of those lines. I won't have the issue in my house, frankly.

Personally, I would of been in favor of a warning to *Playboy* before actual disciplinary action was taken. You know, you do have to let em know so that next month they don't try something *really* disgusting, like Barbra Streisand. But instead, 7-Eleven took the wimpy way out, and said they have "evidence" that *Playboy* and *Penthouse* cause crimes.

Granted, it did cross my mind to assassinate Sally Field, but other than that I think they're way off base here.

That's why, with great sadness, cause it used to be my favorite store, I got to announce the Drive-in-goers 7-Eleven Boycott.

If Jerry Falwell can do it, we can do it.

I want the magazines back in there. I don't think 7-Eleven realizes all the poor people in this country that *can't afford* a subscription. And until we get em back, I'm callin on the readers of this column to:

1. Buy it at the Stop-and-Go, the Quik-Sak, the Hasty-Pantry, the Whip-In, the In-and-Out, the Sack-and-Pack, and the Fill-n-Pill. I don't care if it's just one pack of Marlboros, don't get em at a *Playboy*less 7-Eleven.

2. Write a letter to 7-Eleven world headquarters in Dallas that says "Hey! You! Turkeyface big deal corporation! You're history, pal! Next year you're gonna *be* one of Jerry's Kids!"

3. Take out a lifetime subscription to *Melons Monthly.*

Together, we're gonna crush em.

Speaking of indecent exposure, *Band of the Hand* is exactly what the title says it is—only I don't know what it says it is. This is the kind of movie where you spend most of the time going "Wha'd he say?" and "What are they talkin about?" and "Why did that one dude just beat the bejabbers out of that other one with a lead pipe?" and "Why is Bob Dylan screechin like a hoot owl ever time they drive down the street?" Questions like that.

What we got here is five punkolas in Miami that get arrested and sent out into the Everglades for a little Jungle Job Corps taught by a smelly snail-eating Indian named Joe. Most of the time Joe just sits around on his hiney and spears wild boars with a stick, but then he'll start gruntin and teachin these kids how to eat live snails and wade through slime water so they'll be able to kill all the grizzly bears and mountain lions that live in South Miami Beach. Unfortunately, none of the cast gets ate before they end up back in Miami, fixin up a junkie flophouse so they can live in it with a 37-member Haitian family and fight off a killer pimp named Cream. But after a while they get bored with that and so they go back into the woods for some combat weapons training so they can blow away every extra that they forgot to kill in *Scarface*.

In other words, we got "Rambo Goes Condo."

No breasts. Four brawls. Two exploding buildings. Nine quarts blood. One motor vehicle chase, with two crash and burns. Twenty-eight dead bodies. Grizzly bear swamp attack. Fuzzy mountain lion attack. (Can't you guys *please* take the plexiglass off the zoo cage when you shoot these scenes?) One wild wounded attack pig. Gratuitous disco music. Gratuitous Indian luau. Gratuitous smilin Haitians. Excellent gratuitous armadillo lecture. Gratuitous air-boat scum-sucking. Gratuitous urban renewal funding review. Rattlesnake fu. Machete fu. Knife-through-hand fu. Doberman Pinscher in heat fu. Gopher gas fu. Limo fu. Bob Dylan fu. Drive-In Academy Award nominations for Leon Robinson, as a ghetto gang leader that wears spaghetti-strap fish-net T-shirts, for saying "We be alligator food out here"; Stephen Lang, as Tonto the Job Corps liberal, for saying "This is now—learn to live or die"; Michael Carmine, as the Meskin tough guy, for saying "I can't eat this zoo food"; Lauren Holly, as the 16-year-old nympho girlfriend of Anthony Quinn's son, for having witchcraft sex in a zebra condo; John Cameron Mitchell, as the crazy kid who killed his father, for whining

while they're walking through the slime water and forcing everybody to *see who they really are as people;* James Remar, as the meany Miami drug king, for stickin a knife through somebody's hand and sayin "You got nothin now! You're outta Miami!"; and Leo Garen and Jack Baran, the writers, for the lines "You can't change the people without changing up the environment. We cleaned up the house. We cleaned up the park. Now we clean up the streets. You kids are gonna boogie and that's okay."

Two stars. Joe Bob says check it out. ∎

Communist Alert!

Larchmont, N.Y.—When Anne McDonnell answered the doorbell on Christmas Day, it was her 65-year-old husband, James. She hadn't seen him since he bumped his head 15 years ago. James McDonnell suffered a concussion in a 1971 auto accident. One day he complained of a headache, went for a walk and vanished. Then, on Christmas Eve, he bumped his head again, and his memory returned. He checked a phone book to see if his wife still lived in the same house. She did. The guy watches a Hitchcock episode, figures out a deal like that, and then—whammo!—he blows the whole thing cause he gets a little lonely on Christmas. Wife-leaving could get a bad name from guys like this. Remember, without eternal vigilance, it can happen here.

New Mesko Mission from God

Two weeks ago I hit the road for Arizona, drove 2,000 miles to face down an auditorium full of drunks at Arizona State University, and started the Joe Bob Briggs Worldwide Drive-In Evangelism Ministry. Course, I didn't know it at the time. All God said to me on the way out of town was "Joe Bob, ye have been separated out from mankind. Go ye and seek out the rich people and ye beautiful women and make them do whatever you want them to." Course, this is the essence of evangelism. It's a lonely job, but I was prepared to sacrifice my body and my soul for all the people who deserved me.

But there was something I had to do first. Before I could start telling people how they were going to Hell, I had to go out in the desert and be tempted of the Devil. So I started out for Mescalero, New Mexico, cause that's where the Apache savages worship the ancient peyote plant and if I was gonna be tempted, I wanted to go with the hard stuff. But I only got as far as Hobbs before I started to fag out, and so I stopped in at Furr's Cafeteria to chew some beef and preach some drive-in gospel, and while I was there I met this guy named Walter Walter. His first name was Walter and his last name was Walter, and he had a little brother named Walter and a son on the way named Walter Walter Jr., and his great grandfather was also named Walter Walter, after the Walter Walter who fought in the War To Carve Up Europe Into Itty Bitty Pieces. It wasn't a very famous war, but I just mention it cause of the name Walter Walter, in case you heard it before.

Walter Walter asked me what I was doing and I told him I was looking for the wilderness and he asked me what for and so I told him I had to go be tempted of the Devil and he asked me if I was ever at Geno's Topless on Harry Hines Boulevard in Dallas and I said, sure, but that wasn't the point, I needed to go out and be threatened by some wild beasts.

"I'm looking more for a buffalo-roam kind of place. A place with a lot of mesas and steppes and greasy Meskin food."

"Well," said Walter Walter, fingering his wimp goatee and getting banana pudding all gunked up in there, "New Mexico is full of mesas and steppes."

"Walter?"

"Walter Walter to you."

"Walter, what *are* mesas and steppes anyhow?"

Walter Walter sucked the tattoo on his thumb for a minute and then he said, "The kind of place you're looking for is probably up in Albuquerque. They do a lot of wilderness up there."

"Could you be more specific. Snakes? Visions? Magic clouds? Polio juice? They got any prophets calling out in the wilderness?"

"Prophets!!" said Walter Walter, and he sat up straight and I thought he was gonna drip exclamation points all over his potato salad.

Then the cashier said something like "Mr. Walter, wanted on the telephone," and then the next thing I remember is picking a few of my teeth up off the sidewalk and staring down at some really scuffed-up Buster Browns that belonged to a guy named Clete Tankersley. Clete Tankersley has no business being in this story, so I'm not gonna bring him up again.

By now I was figuring, hey, everything's going my way so far, I was destined to meet a prophet and pretty soon the devil would be hauling my rear out in the Chihuahua Desert to tempt me to turn the stones into Amarillo Slim western shirts or make myself the manager of the biggest Western Auto in Oklahoma City or give myself two hundred dollars.

Course, I didn't know at the time that the Big Guy give me the pitifullest prophet since the turkey that said to buy vacuum-cleaner stock in 1929. He wasn't even listed in the phone book. I had to drive all over Hobbs before I found him, and I wouldn't of run across him at all if I hadn't been tipped off that he hung around near the Goodwill box. So I camped out there for a couple days, thinking he'd show up, and on the third day Otis rose.

He rose straight up out of the Goodwill box.

At first all I heard was this muffled noise that sounded sort of like "Ginflacksel screwlie."

I thought it was getting ready to rain or something, so I tilted in the chute of the box in an effort to steal some old clothes for God's purposes, and when I did that, I heard the sound again, only louder.

"Finwinkle Lollobrigida."

I got kind of excited when I heard that, thinking God was getting ready to burn a bush or maybe zap a couple New Meskins with lightning while I was watching, and so I stood straight up and waited for a sign.

It was about then that the Goodwill box rose up off the ground and flopped over and made this humongous noise crashing down on the pavement. I hit the deck immediately, prostrating myself before the Lord and doing permanent damage to my prostrate gland. I

kept saying "God, it don't matter, I'll keep prostrating as long as you want to prostrate, just don't mess with my groceries."

I don't know how long I stayed in the prostrate position, praying like Tammy Faye Bakker after a perm, but it was long enough to eat a couple coconut-covered Hostess cupcakes.

I know this cause Otis was sitting there next to the Goodwill box, eating a couple coconut-covered Hostess cupcakes.

Otis the Prophet was not the most beautiful prophet God ever shaped with his holy hands. In fact, I think God probly left out some stuff when he was making Otis. Otis was about 4-foot-6. Now you may wonder why I say it that way and I don't say "Otis was a miserable little midget." It's a good question, but I don't have time to answer it.

But I would like to make one thing clear about this. It was not Otis's fault that he was a midget. I thought it was at first. I said, "Otis, why in hell did you decide to become a midget?" But he explained that he was poor back where he grew up, in Bogalusa, Louisiana, and so when he was born, his daddy said, "You know, this is the 14th kid we've had this year, and he's gonna eat us out of house and home—unless we make him a midget." And so Otis was turned into a midget from a very early age.

This wouldn't be so bad, except Otis had a head the size of Yankee Stadium. I guess God knew Otis was gonna be a prophet, so he wanted plenty of room to stuff prophecies in there, and so he said, "Stick a elephant head on this ole boy," and so Otis had elephant-man disease from the neck up. But other than that, Otis was a very handsome guy. They said, when he was younger, he used to turn the girls'

JOE BOB'S MAILBAG

DEAR JOE BOB: My friends always say that the people who write you letters do not exist and that you write your own letters. (Like they do in *Penthouse*.) I always tell them that your letters are real and it's kinda scary that such people exist in the world. I believe my friends are a communist threat against you! Would you like their names and addresses?
A REGULAR WRITER TO *PENTHOUSE*
FORT WORTH (COWTOWN), TEX.

DEAR "NAME WITHHELD": Only if they want to hear about this INCREDIBLE thing that happened to me last week at the laundromat. I was just minding my own business when this really incredible-lookin little fox in tight-fitting jeans walked over to the dryers and . . . oh, sorry, I forgot.

DEAR JOE BOB: As you well may ask, Nevada City does not have a drive in moviehouse. However, Phil Splinkowski, who is retired, spent 27 years in the Navy and has many interesting pictures on his body. We never tire of looking at them. There is a 12 lane bowling alley down the road so we're never at a loss for action. My friend Ed Martin would like to be on your mailing list. He's a dumb redneck from Morrow, Georgia.

I am enclosing a pineapple specification guide which is a very popular item in the Motherlode country.
All best,
EDDIE FALICK
NEVADA CITY, CALIF.

DEAR EDDIE: I'll consider reviewing Phil's body if you'll tell me EXACTLY where the pictures are—and I hope they're not on his pineapples.

DEAR JOE BOB: I talked to Shark Gonzales who said I should send you a death threat for the way you refer to Hispanics as meskins. Shark says that death threats are the only things you honkies understand.

But, of course, I won't do that.

Instead, I'd like to be put on your list for that other death threat, the "We Are the Weird" newsletter. Thanks.

BTW, did you see how the New Zealanders greeted Queen Elizabeth when she visited here? One woman threw an egg at her and a Maori found it necessary to expose his tattoos to Her Royal Highness. Unfortunately for the queen, the tattoos happened to be on the Maori's bare bottom, and he had to bend over and raise his grass skirt to show them to her.
Cordially,
LOUIS GARCIA
MENLO PARK, CALIF.

DEAR LOUIE: That's nothin. They been doing that in Mesko for centuries.

HOWDY-DOO, BRIGGEROO: Say, this here Dominatrix Theory ain't no mere theory any more, JB. By gum, by now it's snowballed into the unescapable Fate of the Earth, along with bola-ties and chiropractors. Talkin bout dem snotty boy-bustin broads that just won't go away. Either we conquer Mistress Sybil Danning & her disciplinary clone-hordes now or we fight 'em at the Rio Grande. Don't say I didn't warn you, JB. And don't come whimp'ring to me when you wake up to find your sweet submissive little pixy-wife transmogrified into a heavy-leather, whip-wielding she-demon, straddlin' & paddlin' you into unendurably agonizing ecstasy, her spiked garter-belts glistening in the moonlight as the riding crop comes crashing down, and her stiletto heels doin' a hoe-down on your sacroiliac and then . . . Er, catch ya later, JB.
JUSTIN REED
PHOENIX

DEAR JUSTIN: If I ever had a sweet submissive little pixy-wife, I'd probly transmogrify her my ownself.

DEAR MR. JOE BOB: Even my shrink likes you; he says you're good for business.

Cecilia says we should send you some hippy weirdos, as balance for all them Texas perverts. Ain't no place should be all one-sided, right?

Are you a pervert?

Love,
LINDA SHABUGAE
SAN FRANCISCO

DEAR LINDA: Yes I am. Will you marry me?

DEAR JOE BOB BRIGGS: I've only read 2 of your reviews but I thought I should write you. Please definitely send me the newsletter, your newsletter, "We Are the Weird". I've been locked up since mid '84 and I'm scheduled to be here a while longer in prison. One flick they showed us here at CMC-EAST I would recommend to you as the sort of fare you go for. *Nine Deaths of the Ninja.* I don't know what the 9 deaths were but it was badly acted sleaze-garbage. I can't think of anything weird to say but I'm lonely, bored, unhappy. One drive-in type movie I'd like to see is *Streetwalkin.* I'd like also to see *9½ Weeks.*

Cinematically yours,
DAVID L. BLEVINS
CALIFORNIA MEN'S COLONY EAST
SAN LUIS OBISPO, CALIF.

DEAR DAVE: I can't believe you'd SAY that about Nine Deaths of the Ninja, *which is the finest flick ever made about an American tour bus hijacked by a sadistic lesbian terrorist and limp-wristed Nazi paraplegic, and the anti-terrorist Ninja SWAT team that tracks them down, causes a polo-pony stampede, and liberates the tourists.*

Goodies on the way.

---

heads everwhere he went. In fact, they had to make him stop doing it by threatening to send him to the Louisiana State School for the Small if he didn't leave em alone.

Otis had one problem. He had dyslexia. Dyslexia is this disease you get when Southwestern Bell comes out to do your wiring and you end up on a party line with Mel Tillis. You get these great ideas in your head all the time, but they come out sounding like vomit on a Ritz cracker.

Let me give you an example. Let's say God decides to give Otis a great idea, like "Crotchless panties for pit bulldogs." God is assuming that Otis will take that idea and run all the way to the bank with it, start up a manufacturing company, get a person of the Jewish persuasion on staff to say *"Have I got ze bulldog underwear, you won't beliv!",* hire three, four hundred Polocks to sew up the underwear, buy some pit-bulldog models to pose for Sears and Roebuck. In other words, God is saying "Otis, I'm giving you this idea, now it's *up to you* to hustle up and make it work." But what happens is, something inside Otis's brain pulls out a billy club and asks the idea for some I.D. So by the time the idea gets out on the mouth end, it comes out like this:

"Let's get a dog to dig a hole and chew up some old dirty underwear and bury it."

And so, you can see, an idea like that, everbody just goes "Otis, take a hike."

That's basically what dyslexia is. So the problem with Otis, since he's a prophet, is God is giving him these prophetic messages all the time, but he forgets em before they come out the other end. Sometimes this is Otis's fault, cause God zaps him late at night and he forgets to write em down. But most of the time it's just Otis.

People like Otis make it tough on people like you and me, who work hard all our life so we can throw old pieces of used-up plastic furniture and Hawaiian shirts in the Goodwill box, but sometimes God works in stupid ways. After this experience, I could never look at a Goodwill box without remembering Otis. And a tear would come to my eye, and I'd say, "That was the stupidest thing I ever saw."

Anyhow, I looked up at Otis and and I said, "Excuse me, but you seem to be occupying a perfectly good Goodwill box."

And Otis said, "Grimdiddle Fritos."

And I said, "What?"

And Otis said "Grimdiddle Fritos" again, and for a minute I thought he was infested with a Conway Twitty demon and I was gonna have to root around in the Goodwill box until I found a dirty tennis shoe I could use on Otis's face.

And I said, "What?"

And for the third time Otis said, "Grimdiddle Fritos." And I don't know what it was, divine intervention, fate, the destiny of the stars, but God made me to *know* and to *understand* and to *believe* in Otis, and so I instantly had a full knowledge of what Otis was saying. It was like he was my long-lost brother and we knew each other intimately, except not in a biblical sense cause it's a sin to be a swisher, and I was blessed with a perfect understanding of Otis's meaning.

He was saying "Gimme a bag of them Fritos."

I picked up the bag—there was one laying at my feet, among the broken tricycles—and I handed it over to Otis and I said, "Here, eat of these Fritos. Have all you want. Can I run get you a Pepsi or anything?"

And he said "Grimdoodle Nehi."

Which meant: "Gimmee a bottle of Grape Nehi."

And so I went and fetched him a bottle of Nehi so he could wash down the Fritos, and then I said, "Okay, Otis, you're a prophet and everything, so what the heck do I do now?"

And Otis said, "Go out hence unto all the nations, if you have enough gas money, and preach the gospel unto all the peoples of all the nations, except the ones that drive Chrysler LeBarons because they are of the Evil One, and when you come to the ends of the earth you will find a sign and the sign will say, 'Does a flush beat a full house?' and of course you will know the answer, but you will be summoned to the heavenly roulette tables and you are commanded to put three hundred dollars on a six-number parlay, the numbers are 3, 6, 9, 12, 15, and I forget the next one, and you must bet these numbers exactly cause if you don't there'll be the complete destruction of the Trailways bus stations in Fort Collins, Colorado, and it'll be your fault."

And I don't know, there was something about it, it just didn't seem quite right to me. And so I said, "Otis, aren't you forgetting something?"

And he said, "Yeah, I'm forgetting the sixth number in the six-number parlay. It rhymes with teen."

Communist Alert!

After two years of utter darkness, the 271 Drive-In in Paris, Tex., got reopened by a Louisiana boy named Jim Moss and a local guy name of David Floyd. First night back, they were set to open at 7 and they had cars lined up out on the highway at 5:30. They been sold out ever since, includin the tornado night, when they were showing *Porky's* numbers one, two, and three. They get a special commendation for promising never to show *Paris, Texas* at the 271. Remember, without eternal vigilance, it can happen here.

Ten minutes later, after I stopped beating Otis up, I realized what Otis was trying to say. He'd been waiting his whole entire life for that one moment, when he could deliver the drive-in prophecy to me. It would be years before I totally understood the meaning of the universe, like I do now. I would have to go get kicked out of Texas Tech in Lubbock. I would have to take two animal-husbandry courses. I would have to search the drive-in, study the meaning of 14,000 drive-in movies, including triple features. I would have to learn the secret of existence: "Life is a fern bar, let's get outta here." All of these things would have to happen before I could found my church, the Joe Bob Briggs Drive-In Church of the Two Living Gods.

In the meantime, I just stared at Otis and said, "You know what? You're a miserable little dyslexic midget."

And Otis prostrated himself, which is tough on a midget, and he wouldn't get back up till I gave him a quarter and promised I'd go into town and buy him a *Playboy*. And human history was forever changed. ∎

Carrie Snodgress Buys a Deadly Crossbow

In *Murphy's Law* Charles Bronson's wife has moved out on him, sent him a divorce in the mail, and started tossing her tarts at a topless bar in El Lay where the girls still work with feather boas. Excuse Chuck if he's *just a little p.o.ed*. Specially when he starts followin the cheap little Pastry Queen home to her sleazoid apartment in Tuxedo Terrace and watches her play grab-the-groceries with whatever industrial waste she's brought home from the club.

But when Chuck's ex-wife gets blown to Escondido while goosing a Jade East salesman, of course Chuck gets blamed for it, and of course he has to break out of jail while chained to a 14-year-old shoplifter so they can steal a police chopper and have many exciting adventures trying to find the maniac female weightlifter who frames them for six, seven murders. And yes, yes, you guessed it—

It's *Carrie Snodgress*, attempting to kill Bronson with those disgusting little lines round her mouth!

Course, Bronson can't turn himself in until he *finds and destroys Carrie Snodgress*, cause they have 12 witnesses that can prove he did the crime. So for the rest of the movie he's out in the Valley shotgunning dope farms and nuking motorcycles and reminiscing about old times in the cop business with a fatso crippled-up doctor, and all this time Bronson thinks it's a Mafia hood named Vincenzo that's setting him up and so he goes and pays a visit on the guy and *blows away his widescreen TV*! This makes Vincenzo extremely nasty, and so now everbody wants to kill Bronson—Carrie Snodgress, Vincenzo, the ACLU—

JOE BOB'S MAILBAG

DEAR JOE BOB: The closest thing they got to a drive-in here is slide shows on a shower curtain, but I had one question and that is have there bin any quality screamers (Chainsaw-style) with any Danish actors/actresses in em?
Yerz,
F. ZIEMBA
DANISH INTERNATIONAL STUDENT COMMITTEE
FRORUP, DENMARK

DEAR F.: I can't BELIEVE you asked me that question: Red Sonja, man! The one where the guy says "I will read the future in your entrails, Red Woman!" and then Arnold the Barbarian has to lop off his head! Her name is Brigitte Nielsen and she is ONLY the woman that's been making the sign of the razor-whisker diving manatee with Sly Rocky Rambo for about a year now. Come on, man, wake up and smell Victor Borge.

DEAR JOE BOB: Tell me something. Why do 30 and 50 thousand dollar car's signals not work? Why do only Chevy station wagons and Buick Electras (I don't own either) get tickets while that Vette or Mercedes just passed that cop doing 120? Whatever happened to Drive Freindly? Why do they (Texas Department of Safety) allow little old ladies that drive rolling smokestacks to have licenses to be stupid and stop at the end of the entrance ramp of LBJ at 4:30 in the afternoon? Why do BMWs think that the 3 second yellow left turn arrow means go for it and the hell with those who he will cut in front of? Where's a cop when you want one and where do they come from when least expect and don't want one? Why are all Cadillac's and Lincoln's brights stuck in the On position? Why do people with BMWs drive around with their halogen driving lights pointed up and why do they flash their brights back when you try to get them to turn their mal-adjusted driving lights off? I would

appreciate your full and lengthy explanation and a couple of Critter buttons.
BRUCE HATHERLY
NORTH TEXAS STATE UNIVERSITY
DENTON, TEX.

DEAR BRUCE: So YOU'RE the guy that's always gettin in my way!

DEAR JOE BOB: My cousin, "Scoop" Wallace, says you know everything about movies and Communism. Based on that, I have two questions for you:
 1. Cary Grant almost always plays an American in his movies. With that accent, exactly *what* part of the country is he supposed to be from?
 2. Does Communism have anything to do with it?
Yours for cinema excellence,
CATHERINE "FOXWALLA" MORGAN
ESCONDIDO, CALIF.

DEAR FOX WOMAN:
 1. Key West.
 2. Nope. So far they've refused to turn the Cuban nukes on him.

HERR JOE BOB: What is your valued opinion on the quality of Continuity-Control in Hollywood? I mean in John Milius's *Red Dawn* they dub the sound of a cargo plane (C-130) when they *showed* the F-111 napalmin' the Rooskies. Additionally the high-schoolers never resist from wearing *Int'l Orange* rucksacks w/ their camo's, *and* the *ultimate* flaw was Cuban troops with Belgian *Fn-FAL* .308 assault rifles *instead* of Kalaniskovas (AK-47's)!!!!
 I mean who do *they* think they're *fooling* with? EMPT-V brain-less-ness? With multimillion dollar production "budgets" doesn't the American Drive-In constituency deserve a hell of a lot *better* Continuity?
 Your continued accurate prophesies (about the downfall of Americana) are still *not* being fully comprehended [Note: the total demise of 4 (count 'em) *Drive-In's* in

Mountain View CA replaced by *Cinedomes*!]
It must be the *fluoride* in the water,
Best Regards
S. P. FERGUSON
PACIFIC FAR EAST LINE
[Note from Joe Bob: stolen stationery possible]
SAN FRANCISCO

DEAR S.P.: Not only that, but when the army finally blew away all the Nicaraguan Commies who were tryin to take over tourist areas of Colorado, they died like they were from New Jersey. No "Arriba." No "Pliz pliz Senor, do not keel us." And no "Aiiiiiiiiiiiiiiiiiiyeeeee."

DEAR JOE BOB: On a recent TV interview "Rev" Jerry Falwell was asked his views on birth-control. With his usual squinty-eyed smirk he replied, "I'm only 51; I still need it." I guess this macho-man declaration was to thrill Baptist ladies.

How did they ever miss the golden opportunity to bring *Mrs.* Falwell to the microphone so she could testify with the very apt Biblical quote, "Thy rod and Thy staff; they comfort me." (Psalms 23:4).
LYN VENABLE
WALNUT CREEK, CALIF.

DEAR LYN: I don't get it. His whole staff?

everbody! And so what happens then? I know. You've guessed it by now. Bronson has to face Carrie Snodgress's deadly crossbow in a deserted office building.

We're talking 14 breasts, most of them owned by Angel Tompkins. Sixteen dead bodies. Three quarts blood. Three shootouts. Exploding motorcycles. Exploding Cadillac. Chopper crash. Gratuitous dopehead bikers. Double-barrel shotgun fu. Divorce fu. Cellophane fu. Glass-in-back-of-neck fu. Geisha bath fu. (Blow-dryer in the hot tub.) Sony Trinitron fu. Drive-In Academy Award nominations for Richard Romanus, as the Mafia honcho, for saying "Who does he think he is, Cochise?"; Carrie Snodgress, as the killer bimbo, for pointing her shotgun at a private-eye, asking him to open his mouth wide and say "Ahhhh," then doing some dental work; Kathleen Wilhoite, as Chuck's teenage sidekick, for saying "You snot-looking scrotum-cheek donkey-breath!"; J. Lee Thompson, the best director of Bronson flicks, for doing it with *feeling* when he had lines like "That's right, you're not a cocaine dealer, you're an *importer*—and your brother's not a scum-sucking pimp, he's a *talent agent*"; and Big Charles, for busting into the Ladies' Bathroom in the line of duty and for saying "What is this, Romper Room?"; "Looks like the sewer backed up again"; and, of course, "I don't like mayonnaise."

Four stars, as usual. The man's made the same exact movie 12 times now. Joe Bob says check it out. ∎

People Who Spend Too Much Time Dancing on Their Faces

Leon Isaac Kennedy has just finished writing, producing, and starring in the most violent Denny Terrio movie ever made—*Knights of the City,* also known as "Dance Fever for People Built Like Dumptrucks."

Great plot. Leon is the leader of a Miami gang who spends all his time driving around shakin down the used-car lots for protection money and saying "Don't mess with me, man, I used to shack with Jayne Kennedy till she took me to the cleaners." Then ever once in a while a bunch of mohawk-heads from the other side of town cruise by and whack all Leon's friends over the head with tire tools, and Leon has to go organize a face-bashing party that gets em all thrown in jail.

Fortunately, the Fat Boys are members of Leon's gang, so as soon as they go to jail, they start rappin and breakin on the cellblock, and a record company executive just happens to be in another cell. Not only that, it's Cochise! Trying to revive his career from the dead!

Pretty soon Leon and the boys are headin over to see Cochise's daughter, Janine Turner, who used to be on a soap opera before somebody told her she could get nekkid with Leon, and she puts the gang down for being so poor. But then when they leave she sticks their demo cassette in her Pioneer system—and they sound *exactly* like *a cheap cover band trying to imitate Stevie Wonder.* Janine goes crazy. She's got to sign these guys. But she can't find em. So what does she do? She holds a—gimme a little *Flash-dance* music here—she holds a music contest and starts wearing dresses that have little cutouts in the middle of her chest. This makes Leon's girlfriend so mad that she goes to the *other* gang leader and starts making the sign of the triple-nostriled Motown Mutant with *him.* And pretty soon he gets so bent out of shape that he tells the bimbo she better *win* that contest instead of Leon or else he might have to get drunk on Coors and kill her.

We're talking two breasts. Three brawls. One dead body. One quart blood. One ghetto-blaster pull-toy. Extremely grisly scene where Leon dresses up like a midget Lionel Richie and sings a song called "You're Not the Only One Who Cries." Gratuitous breakdancin. Gratuitous Denny Terrio. Gratuitous Smokey Robinson. Dance trophy fu. Fat Boys fu. Leon-in-red-pajamas fu. Drive-In Academy Award nominations for Michael Ansara, as a drunk record executive who frowns a lot; Nicholas Campbell, as the gonzo gang member, for saying "I'm gonna eat your eyeballs, man!"; K.C., for getting in this movie for no apparent reason and singing like a sissy on cue; Leon, for brooding a lot, taking off his shirt, and threatening Denny Terrio with violence unless he gets free dance lessons; Jeff Moldovan, as the evil gang leader, for slapping around anybody who starts rapping in his presence; Wendy Barry, as Leon's girlfriend, for saying "Nobody dumps me, Mister Uptown!" and then puttin on some hooker wear and singing a song called "I Won't Give It Away for

Nothing, I Won't Give It Away for Free!"; and Janine Turner, for wearing a lot of tight blouses and being so nice to Leon that he put her 34th in the credits, listed after "Man in Waiting Room."

Two and a half stars. Joe Bob says check it out. ■

Howling II: Doggy Style

Howling II came through Texas for about five minutes and then went straight to 7-Eleven Video, even though it includes the most innovative use of Sybil Danning's breasts in recent years. What happened was, they asked Sybil, the former drive-in ripaway bra queen, to pop her top as Queen of the Werewolves, and so she took an extra 50 bucks and did this kinky swinging-nekkid-werewolf scene. Then they took about five seconds of actual onscreen breast exposure and did *13 instant replays* during the closing credits.

Sybil was p.o.ed about the deal, but I kinda like it myself, cause it woke me up. Most of this flick is Reb Brown and Annie McEnroe walking around Czechoslovakia staring at a bunch of tap-dancing jugglers and magicians with bad teeth and saying things like "Do you see that dwarf staring at us? Should we follow him?" so they can find out why a bimbo TV reporter in El Lay turned into a slobberin wolf-woman right before she died.

There's a lot of resemblance between *Howling II* and *The Howling*. For example, both movies have the word *Howling* in their title. That's the main thing they have in common.

Other than that, you got the suspense factor, which is basically Christopher Lee stumblin around under the full moon trying to find Sybil Danning's hideout so he can bust up the Werewolf Sabbath, drive a titanium stake through her heart (silver won't work anymore), and demonstrate some special effects that look like somebody took a green Crayola and painted a gravity field around him. In their final battle to the death, Christopher and Sybil perform Dueling Poses for the Hollywood Wax Museum.

Anyhow, we got 32 breasts, 28 of them Sybil's. Eighteen dead bodies. Thirty-two dead werewolves. Four werewolf attacks. Werewolf Sex Army. Face-eating attack bat. Intestine disgorgement. Extras from *Bachelor Party* attacked by gorilla suits. Numerous dogs in cast, if you know what I mean and I think you do. Hit-and-run werewolf. Hand rolls. One speaking midget. Additional midgets in midget parts. Exploding midget eyes. Exploding werewolf. Dwarf-on-a-stick. Gratuitous punk rock band. Gratuitous puppet show. Zipper fu. Drive-In Academy Award nominations for Christopher Lee, as Stefan the occult investigator, for saying "Even now there are werewolves living among us"; Reb Brown, for saying "That's a definite new kill technique"; Sybil, for sleeping with two werewolves and saying "Take her away and teach her discipline!" and "Finally—we meet again"; and Philippe Mora, the director, for continuing to get jobs after *The Return of Captain Invincible*.

Doggy style. Two stars. Joe Bob says check it out. ■

Slime Bucket Fu in *Killer Party*

The girls of Sigma Alpha Pi are getting ready for the annual Goat Night in *Killer Party* when what should happen but—no! oh God no! stop! don't let him get any closer!—it's Martin Hewitt, who survived sex with Brooke Shields in *Endless Love* and is now trying to sleep with every 24-year-old TV-movie actress in the cast!

William Fruet—the man who proved in *Funeral Home* that he couldn't scare Imelda Marcos if he had her tied to a tree in the jungles of Mindanao—proves it again as a demon with a boat paddle runs around whackin Greeks on the noodle and runnin 10,000 volts through Paul Bartel so he won't shut down campus hazing. Pretty decent idea, except there's so many *Poltergeist* and *Exorcist* ripoffs in this baby that it's like watchin "How Sausage Is Made" on fast forward. And

Communist Alert!

The Cayman Islands, home of bank employees with suitcases handcuffed to their arms that go down there to catch a few rays, has LOST its only drive-in. The Pease Bay Outdoor Cinema is littered with palm fronds, and fronded with litter. This is one of the most capitalist places to hide your money in the world, so we KNOW the Commies did it.

JOE BOB'S MAILBAG

DEAR JOE BOB: Do you know how hard it is to get in touch with other gay Christians in Dallas? If you go to the Babtist church they say there are none to be found, never have been and never will be—like quality restaurants in Grand Prairie. Well I eventually found some and we meet every couple weeks but we decided that wasn't good enough. We figure there's others havin trouble finding us so we thought we'd tell them about this conference groups like ours are having on July 4th weekend. We're talkin a real get together—but we forgot that we "don't exist." The High Sheriffs wont let anyone say anything bout us. They think sayin anything would be "objectionable" to the Babtists. You know Joe Bob, I was thinking maybe a conspiracy here, or do they just think Babtists are always right since they sound like God sometimes. Or then again maybe they're afraid that if they admit we exist they might find out we've been sittin next to them in church. Seein as you're the only one I know of who has fought the High Sheriffs and since you know a lot bout conspiracies and Babtists and stuff, I thought you might know what's goin on.
Signed,
LOCAL LEADER OF EVANGELICALS CONCERNED
(A NON-COMMUNIST GAY CHRISTIAN GROUP)
GRAND PRAIRIE, TEX

DEAR SWISHERS: My policy on people of the gay persuasion is the same as my policy on smokers' rights: I will defend to the death the right of the American people to put any disgusting thing in their mouth they want to.

So if the only way you little tongue-talkers can communicate with each other is through this column, then I guess the Lord will forgive me this one time even if I am a Babtist.

DEAR JOE BOB: A lot of movies you review have been made up here in my hometown: *Cujo; Dead & Buried; God Bless Grandma and Grandpa; Haunts; Humanoids of the Deep* and other classics of the genre macabre.

As a matter of fact, you are the only critic that has given these films a fair shake.
Thanks Joe Bob!
J. L. FOSSE
MENDOCINO, CALIF.

DEAR J. L.: You left out the best horror film of 1982—Mendocino: Hub of Vacationland.

while everbody is getting Jimmy-Deaned to death, this blond bimbo named Joanna Johnson keeps scraping her sorority sisters off the linoleum and saying "Oh! Oh! Oh!"

The only thing that saved this one from gettin the first thumbs down since *Halloween II* is that Fruet had enough sense to kill *everbody* in the cast.

Four beasts. Two quarts blood. Fourteen dead bodies. Two beasts. Fistfight. Heads roll. Hand rolls. Involuntary cremation. Head-in-a-box. Head-in-a-refrigerator. Girl eaten by boyfriend. Pathetic zombie attack. Hot tub scene *with towels* (Bill, you got to be kiddin). Paddle smacking. Raw-egg vomit. Zombie-on-the-ceiling. Gratuitous Empty-V. Hammer fu. Butcher-knife fu. Bathtub fu. Drive-In Academy Award nominations for Jason Warren, finest fat-boy actor in America today, for dressing up like a killer bee in flippers; Paul Bartel, Mr. *Eating Raoul* himself, as an English professor, for saying "What a pleasure deep reading can be," and "You are excused—please vacate"; and Alicia Fleer, the pledge queen, for saying "Tonight Phoebe and Jennifer are slime buckets—tomorrow they will be *goats!*"

Two stars. Joe Bob says check it out. ∎

Trouble with *Saw II*

Tobe Hooper, "Mr. Texas Chainsaw Massacre," called me up last week and said he couldn't finish *Saw II* without me.

I was expecting something like this. You try to make a cannibal sequel these days, and what happens? The union complains. They want overtime for stacking 2,000 skeletons in a basement of the old *Austin American-Statesman* building, even though the

Austin American-Statesman has been staffed exclusively by corpses for at least 20 years.

Then Dennis Hopper complains cause his role contains too many days of actual acting, instead of his usual impersonation of a gonzo Buddhist encyclopedia salesman who's looking for a peyote connection. (They solved this problem by typecasting him into a role where he can prepare for each scene by whirling around 30 times until he's so dizzy he can't remember his lines or look in the camera.)

But something was still missing. They just couldn't get the old "Saw" spirit going. Leatherface wanted too much money and complained about the "sanitation factor." So they had to pack him off and hire a new Leatherface.

They decided to switch from Black-and-Decker to Poulan, but three members of the cast refused to be carved up by a Poulan.

Tobe could of dealt with that, too, specially after they took him to a screening of *Poltergeist II* and then sat around in the motel room going "Tobe! Baby! That thing would get kicked out of Istanbul, Turkey, for offensive odors!"

But then Tobe got the news he couldn't deal with:

Brando turned down the part.

I know it's hard to believe. Everybody was sure he'd go for it. The part of "Obnoxious Person on Corner No. 3" was *written* for a Method man. They had this scene where Marlon was gonna get his lower lip whacked off *on camera* and then used to make an overpriced sausage sandwich.

But Marlon said no way—not unless they let him rewrite the part so he was an Indian being massacred by bigoted German-American bankers.

And I guess we all know what Tobe said to that. He was *not* gonna sacrifice the integrity of *Saw II*—the first script written by Kit Carson since he wrote *Paris, Texas,* and forgot to put Paris, Texas, in it—and so Tobe picked up the phone and said, "Joe Bob, we lost Marlon. Get your hiney down here and do Obnoxious Person on Corner No. 3."

And I thought about it a little bit, and he said, "Do it for the Saw spirit.

Do it for Leatherface. Do it for the drive-in. Do it for 350 bucks."

Excuse me, but I'm wanted in makeup.

I'm doing it for 350 bucks.

Speaking of idiot casting, Sly Rocky Rambo and his new wife, Red Sonja herself, are the co-stars of *Cobra,* the movie guaranteed to be an upcoming exhibit in Los Angeles County divorce court. It's basically the story of a killer army of ugly bikers that like to blow up Safeways and kill dozens of innocent people "for the publicity."

Ever once in a while, though, the El Lay police are forced to call Sly Rocky Rambo to prove he can be just as disgusting as the maniac killer mutants, specially when he chews on the end of a match while spraying semiautomatic machine-gun fire across the lunchmeat freezer.

Cobra is his name. Incredibly slurred speech is his game.

In his spare time, Cobra likes to rough up TV reporters, ram his 1950 Mercury coupe into parked cars "for

---

Communist Alert!

Edward William Joseph, father of the Texas drive-in, died a few weeks back. I went down to pay my respects at the North Austin Drive-In, the first one in the state, built in 1942, but it was *gone.* He was gone and it was gone. Don't you think that's a little strange that they both would be gone? Remember, without eternal vigilance, it can happen here again.

fun," and wear mirrored sunglasses and mangy leather jackets while somebody sings all the music-video inserts. But finally he gets *sick and tired* of these killer armies that meet every night to click their axes together and pound sledgehammers through the windshields of cars and slice up unemployed actors, and so he puts Brigitte Nielsen in the front seat of his car for bait. The idea is, the drooling geeks with pickaxes will try to blow her away or drive a two-by-four through her stomach for being Scandinavian, and then Cobra can just pick em off with an AK-47 grenade launcher. Simple plan. Approximately 784 explosions later, we got . . .

"Dirty Rocky." No breasts (Brigitte's hooters are off-limits). Two quarts blood. Three beasts. Fifty-one dead bodies. Four motor vehicle chases, with three crash-and-burns. Creep-on-a-hook. Gratuitous bonesaw. Safeway fu. Sledgehammer fu. Yet another Drive-In Academy Award nomination for two-time winner Sylvester, who wrote the screenplay on this baby, including such memorable lines as "You're a disease and I'm the cure"; "You know the problem with you is? You're too violent" and, of course, "Go ahead—I don't shop here."

Three stars. Joe Bob says check it out. ■

Let's Make Babies

Lately I been worried about my biological clock. All kinds of stuff is backin up in my system, gettin all gummed up in there, and I'm afraid if I don't get married by the time I'm 40, then somethin serious could happen, like killer hemorrhoids, or gettin a permanent subscription to *U.S. News and World Report* in the mail.

I guess you know what brought this on:

The Report. I read it. We all read it.

The Report from some cow college up in the Northeast where they studied how likely it is for guys like me to get married once we've horsed around all this time getting divorced.

I'm telling you, the numbers ain't pretty.

For example, if you're a 27-year-old man, ugly, with no job and a sixth-grade education, your chances of getting married before you die are only 28 percent. (If you live in East Tennessee or western North Carolina, your chances are 88 percent.)

Okay, that's bad enough, right? But look at the statistics once you add in a few other factors:

If you're 35 years old and dress like a toad frog auditioning for *Let's Make a Deal,* then your chances of findin somebody to marry you are 17 percent.

If you're 35 years old and wear a uniform with your first name stitched over the left pocket, that number falls to 12 percent.

If you're 35, wear Jade East, and read *Easy Rider* Magazine, we're into the single digits.

And once you hit 40, *especially* for you guys who intend to father non-retarded children, I'm afraid I have some bad news for you. Unless you live in the Greater Miami Beach area,

JOE BOB'S MAILBAG

DEAR JOE BOB: I know it's a weakness, but I'm having trouble boycotting 7-11's Slurpees. I can't stand Mr. M. Slush Puppies, and Stop And Go doesn't have anything close. I know it's no big deal—I couldn't agree with you more about the *Playboy* stuff, but the Southland Commies have got me by the artificial frozen parts and there's got to be a quick solution.
TOM
DALLAS

DEAR TOM: Go to the Whip-In and ask for a Hurpie. No, really, they're great.

DEAR JOE BOB: Caught your show at Wolfgang's and loved it. I even tried to liven it up a bit by volunteering for "someone needing a husband," but you didn't seem to like the idea. You must really be horny if a 57 year old man with white hair looks like a woman, or is the lighting really that bad from on stage?
Your friend,
BOB STURGEON
OAKLAND, CALIF.

DEAR BOB: No, I'm really that horny.

DEAR JOE BOB: My sisters & I have one wish before we die & it may sound strange as if our minds are deranged, please don't ask us why beneath the sheltering sky we have this strange obsession, you have the means in your possession: *Tea in the Sahara with You.*
NAME WITHHELD
LOS ANGELES

DEAR BIMBO POET: Unless you have at least four sisters, Lipton in Escondido is about the best I can do.

YO JOE BOB: I have been experimenting today, trying to figure out how to barbeque the San Francisco Treat. Not much luck yet; the rice keeps falling through the grill. I'll call you when I get results.
My obligatory personal question: How do you write your column so that the right edge always lines up. Isn't that hard? Did you learn to do it in Famous Writer's School?
Yours in George Jones,
DALLAS DENNY
NASHVILLE, TENN.

DEAR DALLAS: No, it took years of study and a determination to ALWAYS make it come out the right length even if it don't make sense and you have to leave out many

DEAH DEAH JOE BOB: Plz try to explain what it's all about: why the symbolic sex, the staged horror, the beautiful erotic & almost willing victims. Is it all for money only or is there just possibly a reality here which I am not perceiving.
Your Doppelganger,
MICHAEL HEDGES
SAN RAPHAEL, CALIF.

DEAR MIKE: There's a reality here which you're not perceiving: money.

DEAR JOE BOB: Yes, I was one of those who attended your Drive-In Evangelism Presentation at ASU. I hope someone revealed to you the mob madness in which you were dragged into. After one and one half hours of waiting, the crowd had picked their noses clean along with all the hardened gum blobs off the bottoms of their chairs. In the tradition of Woodstock the promoters let consigned hot dogs and Suzie Qs go for free. This answer to the late JB caused a food riot like a scaled down version of the Bangladesh happening. You did a 4 star job none the less.
JAY BOB & THE DEBBER
PHOENIX, ARIZ.

DEAR IDIOTS THAT PAID MONEY TO SEE ME: You don't understand. The hardened gum blobs are ALWAYS a part of my show. Sometimes I have to wait three, four hours before the crowd will start pickin em off and the show can start.

where desperate women sometimes marry 80-year-old commercial tuna, your chances of finding a suitable mate are .05 percent. This is less than the number of people who punched out Phil Donahue in the 1985–86 fiscal syndicated television year.

What can we do about it? Surely not *all* women are jerks. There must be a *few* hard-working executive bimbos out there stupid enough to marry us. Here's a few things that might help you find one of em:

1. Admit that we all just forgot. We forgot we were gonna get old. People told us about it, but it's the kind of thing that if it's not *emphasized* and you're kinda half listening, it just goes right over your head. So we've learned our lesson. We know. We're old. We're ready to impregnate somebody now.

2. Be willing to stay unemployed for the rest of your life. Let her work. She loves it. She gets to make like Mary Tyler Moore. And someday, if she's good at it, she'll end up making trashy movies with Dudley Moore.

3. The next time you hear the words "biological clock," tell her you're willing to go on any syndicated radio talk show and let the call-in audience decide whether she *deserves* to have a child. You'll abide by the decision.

If we all follow these three simple rules, we can make millions of women happy and maybe even sell the TV-movie rights.

Okay, come on, let's make babies.

Speaking of good arguments for abortion, the *Poltergeist* yard monsters are back, runnin around the house refusing to turn off the giant attic fans that are blowing their hair back and destroying their overpriced plastic toys. Why? Because the Indian from *One Flew Over the Cuckoo's Nest* is camped out in the backyard, trying to protect the family from the evil TV-set spirits by beating on a tom-tom and making a sound that goes roughly like this:

Hi yo yee wee
Sequel Sequel
Mo Ney

Then Daddy comes home from the office and finds out that, four years after the Steven Spielberg demon possessed the body of Tobe Hooper and forced him to make a movie starring a Munchkin and almost got a five-year-old girl killed, *there's still more plot waiting out there*. All the ghosts of Cuesta Verde are living under the swimming pool, and now they're sending an old man in a black preacher's suit to the house to try to get inside and sell spiritual Herbalife to the whole family.

After the usual rainstorms and toy attacks and zombie dreams and a great scene where Robbie gets attacked by his braces, we got the finest gross-out scene since *Alien*. Craig T. Nelson swallows a worm in a Tequila bottle, starts freakin out, and vomits up a slime demon. Too bad, though, cause this is about as good as it gets. By the time the family gets back to the suburbs to fight off the zombie army, this new *replacement* for "Mr. Chainsaw" is bored with the effects. *Very* disappointing journey "to the other side," into the endless abyss of MGM Stage 27.

Also, no breasts on JoBeth. One pint blood. Two beasts. Green barf demon. Spiritual spelunking. Skeletons. Three demon possessions. Earthquake junk. Levitating chain saw, an insult to Tobe's memory. A disappointing 24 on the Vomit Meter. Gratuitous leaf blowing. Gratuitous Geraldine Fitzgerald. Orthodontist fu. Drive-In Academy Award nominations for Zelda Rubinstein, as the psychic dwarf, for hanging around and going "Now *tell me* what you feel!"; Will Sampson, the Indian, for saying "I cahoot with no one"; Julian Beck, as The Man In Black, for giving a great gonzo performance and then dying; and Craig T. Nelson, the daddy, for saying "Tomorrow everything will be all right; we can play some miniature golf."

Two stars. Joe Bob says check it out. ∎

The History of Texas

Everbody's been askin me, "Joe Bob, when are you gonna do your part for the Texas Sesquicentennial celebration?" includin the *organizers* of the TSC who are always sendin out postcards that say stuff like "Texas— 150 Years Young!" and "Rediscover Texas" and "Happy Birthday Texas" and little historical sayins like:

"In February of 1839, a German Lutheran came over here on a boat and brought all his ugly family with him and built a big old church and wrote bad poetry and killed some Indians. Today, that church is the site of Griswold, Texas, population 35."

Okay, okay, okay, if you people will just *get off my back* for a little bit, I'll go ahead and do it. Let me have your attention now. Right here, in this *one* column, is everthing you need to know about the history of Texas.

First the Indians owned it. We killed all them and sent the leftovers to Oklahoma.

Then the Meskins owned it. We killed most of them and sent the leftovers to Mexico, then they sneaked back in.

Then the Catholics owned it. We didn't kill any of them, but we should have.

Then all the people that got kicked out of Tennessee came here and kicked the Catholics out of the Alamo and got wiped out by a really fat Meskin.

Then all the people that got kicked out of ever other state in America came here.

Then some New Yorkers came down and started Dallas and Houston.

Then some Germans came over and started everplace else in Texas.

Then the cows and the buffaloes and the goats owned it for a while, but we got rid of the buffaloes cause they smelled funny.

Then we would of killed the cows and the goats, too, but somebody invented bob wire and so we started killing each other.

Then the Texas Rangers were invented to make us stop killing each other, except when they weren't looking.

Then we struck oil and got so rich we could hire other people to kill each other.

Then we let some Meskins back in to work at Denny's.

Then we paved it.

Then we killed the president, but it wasn't our fault.

Then we got cable.

Texas. One hundred and fifty years young this year.

Speaking of people who should of been killed at the Alamo, *No Retreat, No Surrender* may be the worst excuse for a kung fu movie in the history of chopsocky. I know what you're

JOE BOB'S MAILBAG

TO THE EDITOR *(San Francisco Chronicle)*: In reference to the Joe Bob Briggs column '460-Pound Jockeys on 1-Pound Chihuahuas,' we express our strong objections. This reaches the limit of sick humor. It requires a demented mind to find humor in satirizing animal cruelty, be it actual or imagined.

We protest the piece because it makes light of cruelty to animals and may appear to foster and condone other similarly warped impressionable minds to carry out abuse and exploitation of animals for fun or profit.

Furthermore, in spite of the far-fetched premise of the column, there may have been some people who took it seriously enough to investigate and contact authorities which would have resulted in inconvenience and embarrassment to all parties.

This column is a disgrace and an insult to animals; to the people who care and work for their welfare; and to the paper itself. If you value a decent reputation, we suggest that a printed apology is very much in order. A final recommendation would be to tightly muzzle the author.
CAROLYN L. KAYE,
PENINSULA CHAPTER,
CALIFORNIANS FOR RESPONSIBLE
RESEARCH,
CORTE MADERA, CALIF.

DEAR CAROLYN: There is nothing FUNNY about Chihuahua Racing. It takes a demented mind like your own to find humor in the idea of deformed 460-pound Mexican cowboys turning innocent little dogs into something that looks like a Reese's Peanut Butter Cup left out in the sun for three days.

I suggest you observe the Chihuahua Meat Boycott until this problem is brought under control.

thinkin. You're thinkin, "Oh, come on, Joe Bob, say somethin *nice* about it, you can always find some reason to like the flick," but I think we may be making drive-in history this week. For the first time since *Halloween III*—which was put on the Drive-In Black List for failing to bring back Jamie Lee Curtis, Donald Pleasance, *and* the breather in the hockey mask—we have another candidate for the Jimmy Dean Sausage Factory.

This is the story of a wimp named Jason who runs off to Seattle cause his daddy the karate coach gets Miracle Whipped by three slick-head scuzzballs that look like they were hired to pick out clothes for Pat Riley. Then, when he gets up there, he goes to Bruce Lee's grave, promises to be a good little kung fu wimp, and then proceeds to get kicked into goat meat by the local karate club, a bunch of guys at a party for Michael Landon haircuts, and several other members of the cast. He gets saved from total annihilation when the ghost of Bruce Lee shows up, slaps him upside the head, and teaches him how to kick in a used tire.

Communist Alert!

Lilly Pond of Berkeley, California, made up this calendar of female breasts, because "I was thinking what a great thing it'd be to inspire women to give themselves breast exams." But did the feminist bookstores care? No. They *want* women to get cancer. Banned everwhere poor little Lilly tried to sell it. Remember, without eternal vigilance, it can happen here.

Oh, yeah, he also kung-fus a Russian in a *Rocky IV* ripoff scene filmed in an elementary school gym. I wanted the Commies to win it.

No breasts. Extremely pathetic breakdancing. Bruce Lee's grave, disturbed. Drink-throwing. Cake smearing. Bad robot dancing. Stunt Buckwheat. Midget chasing. Gratuitous stuffed bunnyrabbit. Alleged kung fu. TV rassling fu. Fat fu. Country-western fu. Yuppie pool party fu. Drive-In Academy Award nominations for Tim Baker, for saying "Karate is *not* to be used aggressively" and "From now on the garage is *off limits!*"; Kim Tai Chong, as Bruce Lee, for demonstrating the principles of kung fu with a glass of Diet Coke and showing the kid how to draw Chinese letters and slapping him around a lot like Cato; and Keith W. Strandberg, the writer, for lines like "Stick with me and you'll never go hungry" and "L.A. karate! I'm impressed!" and "Don't worry! I'm nobody's lunch!"

One star. Joe Bob says . . . oh, do what you want. ∎

Rapping Youths Upside the Head

You ever notice how nobody ever has anything good to say about child abuse? Maybe it's my imagination, but I just don't think the newspapers are tellin *both sides of the story.* Like, for example, if I was to take a 10-year-old kid who was doing can openers off the high board and gettin chlorine in my Juarez Sunrise cocktail, *despite the presence of a paper umbrella,* and if I was to like take this kid and stuff him into a six-foot stack of life preservers and then throw him in the deep end and offer the other kids five dollars if they could push him down to the drain—it might be hard for you to believe, but I've just committed a felony *unless I can prove he's my little brother.*

Little brothers can be permanently maimed under Texas law without any penalty whatsoever, as long as you'll remember this rule. When your mother gets home, say, "Why would I do somethin like that? What's my motive for somethin like that?" Parents always expect a motive. There's not any motive, but that don't matter, cause they'll buy this.

Okay, here's another example. Kid named Drew is chunkin rocks at the tires on my mint-condition '74 Toronado and some of em are gettin up under the chassis and makin a terrible sound. What would you do?

Tire tool? We're talking 20 to 30 hard time.

Hit-and-run? I'll put you down for 35.

No, you only have one alternative in a case like this. It's to grab the kid by his ratty haircut, put your lips so close to his ear he can feel your breath in the crevices of his brain, and say the following words:

"Do that again and I'll remove it."

Now one thing you need to keep in mind. *Never,* under any circumstances, should you define what "it" is. If the little weenie says "Remove what?" which he probly won't cause he'll be too scared, just drop him in the

JOE BOB'S MAILBAG

DEAR JOE BOB: My eye was caught by your use of the word "Bimbo." I regret to inform you "Bimbo" is the male version of the english word "bim" which connotates a wanton woman with large mammalian protruberances. Since you have visited San Francisco in the past you may have picked up a literary perversion or two of this most gentile expression of a woman's virtues.
DAN SCHICK
CAMPBELL, CALIF.

DEAR DAN: *You ain't seen these gentile women, or the Jewish ones either.*
They're bimbos.

DEAR JB2: Well, I've been sitting here for weeks now awaiting your wonderous revelation to the great unwashed a/k/a your adoring fans.

That's right, 'fess up, come out of the closet and make that bold announcement—
JB2 MAN IS SUING THE *DALLAS SLIMES HERALD!*

Well sport, here is some unsolicited advice from a person who has that mystical, imitation sheepskin bearing the oft misunderstood initials, J.D. on his red meat, white bread office walls:

Numero Uno—Wear the gaudiest, loudest, widest bow tie (yes, the one with the blinking lights) you own into Court;

Numero Two-o—Do not refer to the Judge as "J-Man";

Numero Tres-o—Expect the following: 0 Breasts, 1 Beast (the *Slime Herald*'s attorney), 5 quarts blood (your own), gavel fu, pijamas under black robe fu, nudum pactum fu, illegitimi non carborundum fu

Well good luck JB2 Man. (Especially paying those *reasonable* attorney's fees.)
HAMPTON GREYLING DUNN IV
COUNSELOR AT LARGE
DALLAS

DEAR PROFESSIONAL LIAR: *Yeah, that's right, the* Slimes Herald *is claimin they own the name "Joe Bob Briggs" and so I have to go get my identity back or else move to Arkansas, where they don't have names.*

But don't worry. My new lawyer, Al Conant, better known as Conant the Barbarian, has been in court for the last 30 years proving that the Hunt brothers own all the oil in the world, and he once did so much Legal Fu on Moammar Jalopy that the man paid his bills.

I rest my case.

nearest Dempster Dumpster and say, "Wait here till I get back and I'll show you."

You see the beauty here? Instant results. No prosecution. *Intelligent* child abuse.

There's only one exception to this, and the best way to explain it is to ask the question: Have you ever been sittin at a movie and a kid behind you starts kickin your chair and sayin "What's he doing? What'd they say? Can I have a quarter? I don't like this popcorn," and "This place is grody," my personal advice would be to forget the above and go ahead and risk capital punishment. I have a good lawyer, can probly get you off. If not, it'll be worth it anyway.

Speaking of justifiable homicide, Arnold the Barbarian just keeps gettin better and better, and I'm gonna go ahead and say it here: after *Terminator, Commando, Red Sonja,* and now *Raw Deal,* Arnold is the No. 1 Drive-In Actor in the World. Forget Sly Rocky Rambo Cobra. Forget the two Chucks, Norris and Bronson. The guy that's really doing it, year in, year out, is the A-Man. One more drive-in hit and he'll already be eligible for the Drive-In Hall of Fame. *Raw Deal* has more plot in it than Arnold's ever attempted before, and it even includes about 100 words of Arnold dialogue, compared to his usual 10, and it has a *full three minutes* of pec-poppin and deltoid-dippin and tricep-trippin in front of the mirror, but here's the best part:

Arnold *successfully* speaks the following sentence.

"He molested, murdered, and mutilated her."

Arnold finally got the M-sound down. He worked out five, six hours a day until he got ready for that one line of dialogue, and he did it. Sort of.

Anyhow, Arnold is a small-town sheriff with a wife that whines all the time and gets drunk in the afternoon and throws chocolate cakes and wants to move back to New York, only first Arnold has to go undercover and infiltrate the Chicago Mafia so that Darren McGavin can get revenge for the murder of his son and the cancellation of his series. So Arnold goes up there and gets a job workin for the world's meanest character actor and drives a wrecker through a building like in *Commando* and takes Kathryn Harrold home with him even though she's a drunk bimbo and busts up a female-impersonator bar and destroys three guys in a boutique and then packs up 18,000 rounds of automatic weapons ammo, jumps in his convertible, and puts "I Can't Get No Satisfaction" in the tape deck. Pretty soon, we got:

Forty dead bodies. No breasts. Two quarts blood. Three motor vehicle chases, including the best one of '86.

Communist Alert!

This guy went to see Bo Derek and told her he could get 21 million bucks to give to her husband for her next three films so she could keep gettin nekkid onscreen. Unfortunately, the guy was out on bail after getting convicted of 94 counts of fraud, perjury, and tax evasion. Bo got suspicious when the guy said he controlled 66 CIA companies, but she didn't decide to go to the police until he said *Bolero* really smelled.

Arnold destroys an entire building by himself. Exploding refinery. Schoolbus machine-gun attack. Maniac SWAT Team. Steam shovel attack. Gratuitous Rolling Stones. Boutique fu. Coke machine fu. Cake fu. Drive-In Academy Award nominations for Darren McGavin, for his "oh my God I can walk again" scene; Kathryn Harrold, for saying "The only way you'll end up lying next to me, Max, is if we get run over by the same car"; and Arnold the Barbarian, for saying "You should not drink and bake" and "Who do you think I look like—Dirty Harry?"

Four stars. Joe Bob says check it out twice. ■

Adventures Beyond Water Wiggle

Put on your rubber Bullwinkle life vests. Time for the annual Joe Bob Briggs Summer Vacation Guide.

PART UNO: WATER SPORTS

1. **General Elmo Randolph Lincoln Reservoir and Dam:** This out-of-the-way fun spot, just off State Route 22 south of Selma, Alabama, is maintained by District XVIII, U.S. Army Corps of Engineers, for your boating and swimming pleasure, but plan to stay an extra day or two for side trips to the vulcanized zinc pottery factory in Gastonburg and, of course, the ruins of Old Junius. The ruins date from May 23, 1957, the day the Corps first released water from the dam and forgot Junius, an 87-year-old muleskinner, was still sleeping in his prefab fishing shack located in a part of the flood plain they "forgot" to mark on the map. Pay the extra two bucks for the glass-bottomed boat ride, and *look closely* at the famous "Mystery Window" of Old Junius. Is that an eyeball or just a finger? Families have been arguing about it for years.

2. **Long 'n' Slippery Water Amusement Park:** You know that long stretch between Salina, Kansas, and Lincoln, Nebraska, the one where the kids always say, "You call this a *vacation*? Get with the *program*, dude," and then start playing the "Let's Scare Daddy" game? Well, you don't have to worry about it anymore. Just veer off on U.S. 136 to Red Cloud, Nebraska, turn right at the Bo Diddley Pioneer Museum, and say to anybody on the street, "We're lookin for Long 'n' Slippery." They'll take you to the world's most disgusting mud slide, courtesy of the Webster County Irrigation District, which opened for business in 1983 with the slogan "We'll tucker the little suckers out." Parents can stay next door at the Dirt Plaza. (Watch any cable movie free that has the word "Hookers" in the title.)

3. **Wet 'n' Deep:** Owned by the Long 'n' Slippery people, operated in Vero Beach, Florida, and Heritage Village, North Carolina, for Christian families who are morally opposed to abortion but have no qualms about sending their children to play in Alligator Falls, the only water slide with genuine man-eating reptiles waiting at the bottom.

4. **Canoeing the Titaluk:** Pack an extra thermos for this one! Head 400 miles north of Fairbanks, Alaska, take a left at Deadhorse, and if you get to the Beaufort Sea, you've gone *too far*. Ask for a guide named Nunchuck at the last liquor store on the Trans Alaska Pipeline, and tell him you're ready to "Shoot the Titaluk." Also say the following words: "Joe Bob expects his cut." Don't worry about what the words mean. It just means that you'll get the real "Eskimo Treatment."

Speaking of frigid, Karen Black stars in the *Invaders from Mars* remake as the dimwit school nurse that helps the kid go get the National Guard and start zappin aliens before the Martians can fry the brains of everybody in Kansas with Roto-Rooter neck drills. In fact, Tobe "Mr. Chainsaw" Hooper assembled one of the finest casts of brain-damaged character actors in Southern California for this tribute to the one that started it all, the original Martians-have-landed classic, the 1952 version starring Jimmy Hunt as the kid who sees a Martian spaceship landing in his backyard, but *nobody believes him.*

Tobe hired Jimmy Hunt for this version, too, then he remembered that Jimmy was 34 years older and he said, "Oh yeah, I forgot, I guess that won't work," and so Jimmy had to be the police chief. So he hired Karen Black's son, Hunter Carson, but he wanted to give Hunter typical middle-American, clean, decent, wholesome midwestern parents, and so what did we end up with? You guessed it.

Laraine Newman and Timothy Bottoms.

By the time Timothy wanders "over the hill" and comes back in a shabby bathrobe with a little puncture wound on the back of his neck, it gets pretty scary. We're thinkin, "Sure, all the Martians want *now* is the Paper Chase guy and one of the Coneheads. What happens when they go after Bob Hope?"

But it gets worse. This time the Martians have a great plan to take over the world: Send Louise Fletcher. Nurse Ratchet herself, the frog-eating biology teacher. By now we're screamin at the Martians, "Take em. Take all of em. Especially Louise Fletcher. Just *don't touch the kid.* He might have a career!"

But it's too late. Hunter and Karen are the only two people that have it figured out about the Martians takin over the bodies of washed-up character actors and terrorizing entire nations with mutant green tomato-head people and drunk two-legged buffaloes that look like they just spent six months inside a nuclear reactor. These are some of the best outer-space mutants since *Ice Pirates.*

We're talkin zero breasts (and we should thank the Lord for that, considerin our only choices were Laraine, Karen, and Louise). Six quarts blood. Thirty-seven beasts. Nine dead bodies. Six undead bodies. Thirty dead Martians. Testicle architecture. Neck Roto-Rooting. Two-legged water-head-baby buffaloes. Sand crater whirlpool sucking. Disgusting eating habits. Frog throwing. Mutant green tomato heads. Louise Fletcher-eating. A 74 on the Vomit Meter, enhanced by gratuitous Laraine Newman scarfin raw hamburger meat and Louise Fletcher stuffin a frog down her throat. Two exploding spaceships (ours and theirs). Exploding buffaloes, Kung fu. Drive-In Academy Award nominations for Bud Cort, as the NASA scientist, for looking at the Martian buffaloes and saying "You do understand me, don't you?" and then gettin lasered into a little pile of ashes; Hunter Carson, for scream-

---

Communist Alert!

"Los Angeles—One of three men who held up moviegoers at a drive-in was shot and killed yesterday by one of the victims in a gun battle outside the theater, police said. Detective Chuck Worthen said the trio robbed two people at gunpoint as they sat in a car at the Centinela Drive-In Theater shortly after midnight. A man identified as Carlo Bettis, who police said was one of the robbers, was chased and fatally shot. The other two robbery suspects escaped, Worthen said." We do *one-third* of the cop's work for him, and they *still* can't stop the Commie attacks.

ing at the Supreme Marshall of Martian Intelligence "You can't do this to people!"; James Karen, as General Wilson, for saying "Don't worry, boy! Marines have no qualms about killing Martians!"; Dan O'Bannon and Don Jakoby, the genius screenwriters who did last year's *Lifeforce,* for writing the line "We don't carry loose change into combat, sir"; and Tobe Hooper, for Remake Fu.

Three stars. Joe Bob says check it out. ■

El Cheapo Summer Fun

C lamp on a cheap bolo tie made by filthy rich Indians with big thumbs. The Joe Bob Briggs Summer Vacation Guide continues.

PART 2: DUDE RANCHES

1. **The Lewd, Crude, Nasty Dude Ranch:** Located in the wilds of Wickenburg, Arizona, it's that "special" retreat for those special little friends of yours in flamingo shirts looking for a place to "swish away the summer" according to their rights and privileges as Americans to do any disgusting thing they want to with their bodies, if you know what I mean and I hope you do. The lewd, crude, nasty dude himself is a guy named Leotis who comes out of his bunkhouse once a day to administer bullwhip punishment and perform the "bucking bronco fandango" (no kiddies allowed).

2. **Velvet Vista Verde Valley:** Five miles east of Bakersfield on State Route 178, this one is perfect for that "budget" vacation. Fifty dollars for six people for two weeks (room and board not included). Complimentary irrigation materials available on request. How can they do it? Easy. They have no horses. All recreation is goat riding. (Goat-riding lessons available at a modest charge, but don't try Goat Peak on the first day. Head for Cabrito Training Hill.)

3. **Blue Lagoon Guest Ranch:** At this secluded mom-and-pop hideaway near Bandera, Texas, each room is papered with glossies of Brooke Shields and, for the kinky, Brooke Shields' mother. For a surcharge of $200 per week, Brooke will personally come to your room and recite lines from *Endless Love* to prove she was in that movie. For a surcharge of $300 per week, Christopher Adkins will *not* come to your room.

4. **The Roy-and-Dale Love Ranch:** Try this one for your golden wedding anniversary, specially if you're trying to put the old whinny back into the marriage. At the Love Ranch, 28 miles west of Pie Town, New Mexico, on U.S. 60, the sky is orange all day, just like in Roy's movies. This is because the ranch is part of the White Sands Missile Range nuke-testing facility, home of the rarely seen iridescent antelope and the strobe gopher. Ladies: Don't let Roy help you onto your horse under any circumstances. Trust me.

5. **Rancho Enchilada:** There are actually two Rancho Enchiladas operated by the Mexican government. Make sure you get a booking at the

JOE BOB'S MAILBAG

JOE BOB: Yesterday, which will be 2 days ago tomorrow, my mother said "I feel like a victim." I sat back and let these disturbing words sink in. I thought to myself "victim of egg and sperm uniting." She was incinuating that I, her child, was victimizing her. I was immensely disturbed. I soon thereafter became verbally abusive, morosely uncommunicative, and once again reclusive. I mean . . . I dont know what I mean. It's not my fault I was born, so why should she blame me. It was her damn fault for not using a contraceptive devise in the first place, right Joe Bob?
Yours,
AMIKA MOORE
EULESS, TEXAS

DEAR AMIKA: You had a choice, young lady, when you were still a contented little microegg. Did you run away when that spermatozoa hit on you or did you secretly beg him to puncture your protoplasm? I think we all know the answer, and I think it's time for you to start taking a little RESPONSIBILITY around here, is that understood?

JOE B: Hey, I'd like to see you dress up like a girl in front of Otis Sistrunk the football player turned porno movie stud. Minnie Pearl's what kinda girl you'd look like. Freckle splotched flat-chested old thing. Rumpled elbow pads. Just a suggestion.
MR. CHASE
SAN FRANCISCO

DEAR CHASEMAN: Hey, I'd like to see Minnie Pearl dressed up like Otis Sistrunk on your front porch.

Monterrey branch, *not* the one in Ciudad Mordida, which is located in the jungles of Yucatan. Many people make this mistake every year and we're expecting to hear from all of them any time now. What can you say about the Rancho Enchilada that hasn't been said already? It's the granddaddy of them all, the Hasta La Vasta, home of the all-you-can-eat Bean Plate. Remember to stop in Juarez three days on the way back. You'll avoid the "bends" later.

Next week: Historic Sites.

Speaking of people that look like a grilled fajita, I just saw *Demons* and once again, the Eyetalians are doin it to us. Just when we think we know what the word "gore" means, some Eyetalian comes along and says, "I bet you never saw somebody do *this* on the screen," and so we got, once again, the most disgusting movie in the history of movies. Automatic four stars.

We shoulda known this one had potential, cause it's directed by Lamberto Bava, who's the son of the late great Eyetalian master, Mario Bava, the guy who made *Black Sunday* in '62 and went on to impale every single body part onscreen in the years before he croaked from drinkin too much of that drillin mud they call coffee over there. Anyhow, Lamberto has this idea of "What if you went to see a horror movie, and some zombies *bricked you in* while you were watchin the movie, and pretty soon they started clawin the audience into linguini noodles and there was *nothing you could do*?" That's basically the idea, but I'm not tellin nothing else about it because there's absolutely no way to tell what happens next in this flick and so it satisfies the first rule of Drive-In Classics: Anybody can die at any moment. One breast. Twenty-six dead bodies. Two hangings. Seventeen gallons blood. One motor vehicle chase. Slime spewing. Eyeball clawing. Projection-booth smashing. Razor slicing. Boyfriend eating. Finger chomping. Classic transformation scene, where a demon crawls up out of a guy's back. Bloody zit popping. Purple jugular vein tumor throbbing. Hand rolls. Head

hacking. Gratuitous cokeheads. Coke machine fu. Yamaha fu. Grapple hook fu. Drive-In Academy Award nomination for Lamberto Bava, the kid director, who wrote the line "It's not the movie—it's the *theater*!"

And we do have a new record: 97 on the Vomit Meter.

Joe Bob says check it out. ∎

On the Road Again

All together now: "How many miles to Stuckey's?" And so the Joe Bob Briggs Summer Vacation Guide continues.

PART 3: NATIONAL HISTORIC SITES

1. **Old Stone Cannon National Park, Berkshire, Massachusetts:** In 1627, just a few years after the landing at Plymouth Rock, several Pilgrims journeyed west to this beautiful valley, where they discovered a small colony of Bulgarians spitting tobacco juice onto a roasting beaver. No one has ever explained how the Bulgarians got there. Two weeks after being seen, the Bulgarians were wiped out by three blasts of an enormous stone cannon dragged all the way from Plymouth for the purpose. The cannon has been preserved and can be seen high atop White Man's Peak.

2. **Tonkawa Gardens, Dothan, Alabama:** Many of your early American Indians were not warlike at all but simply wanted to be *left alone to diddle around*. Part of that culture has been preserved in this giant rock chess set, each piece hand-crafted by the Indians in the shape of a television game-show host. The Gardens were also the scene

of a three-day protest and siege in 1968 by the American Indian Movement, which claimed that the Chuck Woolery "queen" had been deliberately mangled by Chickasaw stonecutters, who protested its being placed alongside the Bob Barker "king." The dispute was mediated and eventually resolved by a group of nomadic Kickapoo devoted to the memory of *Queen for a Day,* who pointed out that the late Jack Riley is the only true "queen."

3. **Fort K-Mart, Laramie, Wyoming:** Scene of the only race riot in the history of Wyoming, this burned-out shopping mall, first occupied in 1957 and abandoned in 1974, held out for five days under the repeated assaults of Jewish merchants infuriated by the importation of Mexican digital watches. On Black Thursday, the day when four members of the Wyoming National Guard and five junior vice-presidents from the Denver office lost their lives, they say the smell of scorched orange polyurethane sofas reached all the way to Cheyenne. When you tour the ruins don't miss "Shivert's Corner," the place where a 33-year-old employee named Buster Shivert held off invaders single-handedly, equipped with

JOE BOB'S MAILBAG

DEAR JOE BOB: To answer your questions about my Esperanto translations of your columns in the French humor magazine *Cancer Clinic:*

In issue 35 someone disagreed with my translation of the expression "pop your top." In this instance I leaned toward a literal translation, letting the context supply any meaning that might be missing. The other person wished to tie the meaning down to "become braless." The accompanying cartoon shows the editor telling his female assistant to "become braless." She replies that she can't. He asks why not and she opens up her blouse and shows him that she is *not wearing a bra*. He then tells her to go put on a bra and come back. She does and he tells her again to "become braless." She then demonstrates that it is possible for her to take off her bra without exposing her breasts, which is certainly not the intention of the original expression. The editor then tries my expression, telling her to "burst" her top. She does so, but a piece of the exploding material strikes him in the eye.
REGARDS,
MICHAEL K. JONES
CORAL GABLES, FLA.

DEAR MIKE: The next time you send some of my stuff over to France, use the expression "diddled her fiddle." Just try it, see what they do.

DEAR JOE BLOB BRIGGS: You are the yellow-belliedest, low-downest, underhandedest, most sorriest excuse for a human bean this side of the Greater Dinuba drive-in. Yes, them's fightin words, but they ain't nuthin compared to the GOOBAR wrath you have brung down upon your cruddy self by statin' as you did that our hero Bo Svenson is a hasbeen.

We GOOBARS (Good Old Oakies, Beerdrinkers And Rednecks,) have as part of our goals in life watching out for pinkos and obvious un-American types like you who cast smarmy shadows on the pure and untainted images of true blue types like our boy, Bo.

For the life of ourselves, we cannot figger how anyone who calls hisself (or in your case, "itself") an American can defame, defile and defuse the man who played that all-American hero, Tennessee's legendary sheriff and self-serving opportunist Buford Pusser in two (count 'em, two) movies.

You have earned a spot in our armpit of our clubhouse, Job Blob, and we are submitting your name for National GOOBAR Poophead of the Year.

Until we hear from you, pal, our chapter is using the new GOOBAR slogan:

Joe Bob Briggs—FU!!
KATHY YOUNG
GOOBARS ARE FOREVER
STOCKTON, CALIF.

DEAR KATHY: I'll apologize just as soon as I tell Joe Don Baker what you said and where you live.

---

nothing but Wilson's Sporting Goods equipment and spare Hoover Vacuum Cleaner Parts. Shivert's grave is located 200 yards from the broken Perry Como records.

Next Week: Recommended summer reading.

Speaking of historic sites, the career of Timothy Bottoms gets a big boost in *In the Shadow of Kilimanjaro,* the best movie in the last month about vicious African baboon attacks. Evidently some Indian Buddhist producers went down to the San Diego Zoo and went inside the monkey cage and tried to make *Molars,* but unfortunately they put Timothy Bottoms in there as the Richard Dreyfuss "Evacuate the Population Before It's Too Late" character and so what we end up with is *Baby Teeth.*

The whole deal was filmed on location at a roadside stand in Kenya, so we got a lot of worm-eating natives throwin spears up in the air and killin cobras with their bare hands and takin the cast on rhino hunts and makin a lot of Zulu noises and then sayin "That will be two thousand dollars please." But Timothy is not interested in that. All Timothy wants to do is hang around the camp and put Murine in hippopotamus eyes and play footsie with the cheetahs. But then his wife comes and takes her clothes off and this turns into a *real* horror movie when, for the first time I'm aware of, we actually see Timothy's Bottom.

Then the baboons get hungry and start killing off the natives by stalking them until their cars break down on the highway and then throwing themselves against the windshield to break inside and chew their faces off. This makes everbody scared except John Rhys-Davies. His plan is to shoot about a thousand of the baboons and *leave their bodies for the rest of the baboons to eat.*

Good plan, but then John assembles all the tribesmen to go on a baboon hunt, and when they get out there, he says, "How are we gonna tell the monkey leaders from the monkey fighters?" So they shoot a few monkeys, slap the Africans' little hands when they try to eat the monkeys, and go home to watch some more baboon attacks, including one where a baboon stows away on an airplane and hides in a World Hunger Relief box. Finally Timothy Bottoms screams at the local policeman: "They're organizing! The baboons are organizing!" And after that we got Monkey Meat City.

Two breasts. Ten dead bodies. Forty-five dead baboons. Two quarts blood. Motor vehicle and jungle animal chase. A 56 on the Vomit Meter. Worm eating. Cobra attack. Rhino hunt. Man-eating baboons. Baboon-eating men. Baboon-eating women. Women that look like baboons. Baboon-baiting. Timothy's bottom. Baboon's-eye camera. Eight baboon attacks. Leftover arm. Tribal monkey dancing. Leg rolls. Baboons that throw rocks at the windows. One baboon-induced plane crash. Tour-bus baboon attack. Baboon bonfire. Exploding factory. Exploding baboons. Gratuitous Peace Corps worker. One gratuitous baboon. Baboon fu. Drive-In Academy Award nominations for Irene Miracle, for gettin strangled by a baboon; and John Rhys-Davies, for fighting off 30 baboons with a stick.

Two and a half stars. Joe Bob says check it out. ■

A Guide to Great Summer Literature

Sometimes we just don't have the time to go get in our personal automobiles and drive around America in the summertime makin' ourselves miserable on vacation. If you're in this position—in other words, if you're old and crippled-up—then you'll be interested in the Joe Bob Briggs Summer Reading Guide. Or maybe you won't, but here it is anyhow:

PART 4: SUMMER READING

1. *How to Force a Man to Make Up His Mind and Marry You,* by Wilhelmina Bonner: This self-help guide is extremely popular with homely women over the age of 46. It includes such chapters as "Sometimes it's better to tell him he's fat and he's not gonna find anything better," and "The case for lethally injecting 20-year-old secretaries." If you have ever asked yourself the question, "What weapons do I have left and who can I use them on?" then this one is for you.

2. *Wild Savage Loincloth,* by Rhonda Russell: This is a three-generation historical saga of a proper young English schoolgirl who goes to the Bahamas to study Greek literature, but ends up being thrown to the ground and gettin her clothes ripped off by a dark brown stranger with blazing eyes who starts to rape her but stops at the last minute and then decides to marry her. Then he rapes her.

3. *It Only Hurts When I Stutter,* by José Miguel Antonio Salazar: The former Cleveland Indian outfielder tells the inspirational story of his long struggle back from being struck directly on top of the head by a fly ball

---

JOE BOB'S MAILBAG

MR. BOB: I must disagree with your fundamental premises of what constitutes happiness in the "Great Outdoor Drive-In." Are we put there merely to enjoy "spectacle?" Merely to enjoy the "pleasures of the flesh?" I believe not.

Man/Womankind must strive for excellence to progress and must progress to survive. We must learn ancient and future languages. We must be able to count (and count well!) using the hexadecimal number system. We need to Think Metric! Your column, for example, should be written in iambic pentameter. We should not concern ourselves with blood bucket numbers. We need to stay ourselves against the sirens' song of vomit on Ritz crackers! Let's have National Geographic and Encyclopaedia Brittanica at the drive-ins!!
Pithily Yours,
SCOTT DOWNIE
KANSAS CITY

DEAR SCOTT: I looked up garbonza under "G" in the encyclopedia and it said "a chickpea grown in the West." How would you like to go to the drive-in and watch chickpeas floppin around up there all night? No thank ya.

DEAR JOE BOB: I work in land development (that's a "land butcher" to some) and occasionally it's my sad task to convert a perfectly good drive-in to another use—like a "business park" (what kind of euphemism is that? Are there swings & slides for the executives?). On advice of counsel I can't name names but I hope you'll speak out on this desecration and abuse of our national heritage!

Save the Drive-Ins! Support the right to Arm Bears! Nuke the Whales! Send your newsletter!
KEVIN LARROWE
LOS ANGELES

DEAR SPINELESS WIMP TOOL OF THE OP-PRESSORS: You touch one more drive-in in Southern California and I'm sending Lionel Richie over to compose songs in your front yard.

DEAR CRYPTO-COMRADE JOE-BOBSKI:
Ukraine Acres is no place to flee
Farm-living is the half-life for me
Fallout spreading out so far and wide
Keep the Manhatten Project—just gimme that country fried.
DOODLES GORBACHEV
HOLEY RUSSIA

DEAR JOE-BOBSHEVIK:
No, Murmansk is where I'd rather stay
I get allergic from decay
I just abhor a Day-Glo view
Dahling I love you but give me passport for two.
RAISA GABORCHEV
MUTHUH RUSSIA
(TRANSLATED BY JUSTIN REED, PHOENIX)

DEAR JUSTINSKI: Don't forget Uncle Joe. He's movin kinda slow. At Chernobyl.

he explained was "lost in the smog." Salazar, now a star player in the Dominican Republic State Hospital League, told his story to Father Salvador Sierra of the Cathedral of Nuestra Senora de Estacionamiento, Miami, Florida.

4. *How to Deal With Terrible, Gruesome Tragedies in Your Life,* by Dr. C. Wilkerson Sturtivant, Ph.D.: Very popular with people who feel great when something horrifying happens to somebody else, but also a *must* for the home first-aid cabinet. The chapter on decapitation destroys a lot of myths about that particular type of

home accident; they can do a lot with plastic surgery these days. But you'll probly make the most use of the parts on "Absolutely Fatal Diseases With No Chance of Recovery So Don't Even Lie About It." Just one example of Dr. Sturtivant's advice: "Always remember that there might be a God and if there is then who cares?"

Speaking of great train wrecks, Forrest Tucker gives a great performance in *Thunder Run* as a trucker who decides to kill some terrorists by driving plutonium across the Arizona desert in the hope that they'll attack him and he can blow up their camouflaged Volkswagens. If he does this little job for the government, he gets $250,000 and a promise that nobody will mention *F Troop* anymore.

Oh yeah—his little weenie grandson gets to go along with him in "Thunder," a cab-over 18-wheel sem-eye equipped with machine guns, rocket launchers, grenades, bombs, dynamite, nitrous oxide accelerator, heat-seeking missiles, and a tape deck. As soon as they start out, the weasel-faced Palestinian runts come after em with motorbikes, choppers, Trans Ams, laser tunnels, and about 30 minutes' worth of other stuff, but unfortunately, Tucker the trucker survives to grin again.

One breast (but probly a sneak breast, in violation of blond bimbo Cheryl Lynn's no-boob contract). One pint blood. Seven motor vehicle chases, with 11 crashes and nine crash-and-burns. Fifteen dead bodies. Forrest Tucker doing the cotton-eyed Joe (raising this to a 38 on the Vomit Meter). Pool-playing terrorists. Mashed convertible. Fireball cycles. Missile-launching Beetle. Automatic Molotov-cocktail ejecter. Sem-eye jumping. Laser lasagna. Cattle guard fu. Drive-In Academy Award nominations for Alan Rachins, as the acne-face terrorist, and Forrest Tucker, for saying "Where's the damn cavalry?"

Two stars. Joe Bob says check it out. ■

The Most Horrifying Vacation of All

Strap on the old Wolf Brand Feed-bag. Time for the final installment in the Joe Bob Briggs Summer Vacation Guide. You know what it is. I don't have to tell you. It's the most horrifying vacation of all.

PART 5: SUMMER CAMPS

1. **Camp Buckpie, Lima, Ohio:** Home of the famous Intestinal Bake-off, this three-week funfest has turned out more female Marines than any nonmilitary institution in the Midwest. Founded in 1947 by Madeline Strop, whose remains were chopped into replicas of "Halloween Surprise" cupcakes and interred directly underneath the cafeteria line, Camp Buckpie is know all over Ohio for its Sadie Hawkins Day, in which, for one day and one day only, the animals get to choose.

2. **Camp Leavenworth, Lansing, Kansas:** For those "developing inner-city youths" who want a "head start" on life after "junior high," this camp lasts all summer long and features intensive training in school-bus repair, license-plate printing, small-weapons manufacture, and six other "electives" so that, three or four years from now, when these youngsters return to start their adult lives, they'll have a big advantage over those who haven't "learned the ropes." A special feature of this camp is the "good time" option, whereby a student who expects to return soon may begin counting his work toward a degree. Word of warning: if you child elects to use a "camp counselor," avoid the court-appointed ones.

3. **Happy Little Fellers Camp for the Emotionally Disturbed, Plainfield, Wisconsin:** For children who have murdered one or both parents, this camp is highly recommended over its chief competitor, Camp Manson of Barstow, California. For one thing, these children have the benefit of Spaghetti Night (Wednesdays only), a tradition that has been pretty much abandoned except here, where spaghetti is used for "Jackson Pollack therapy."

4. **Leona Bodkin Camp for the Extremely Rich and Fat, Cheney, Washington:** For a mere $5,000 a week, your child will be trussed, harnessed, and dipped in a patented "Blubber Bath" of highly toxic chemicals while soothing Neil Sedaka songs are piped through his brain. Miss Bodkin, a former Richard Simmons lookalike who spent several years having her face steamed off and replaced with the features of David Bowie, will personally lead your youngster through the brutal third week—Tuna Casserole Training.

Time is runnin short. Get rid of the little yard monsters *now*.

Speaking of excess meat, *Dangerously Close* has ever guy in it that tried out for *Breakfast Club* and lost. You know the ones: They went to some high school in Marin County, California, where everybody leaves class at 2

JOE BOB'S MAILBAG

DEAR JOE BOB: We understand that members of the academic community of Shreveport take pleasure in degrading you and drive-in movies (i.e., Caddo Magnet High School Debate Squad). Their un-American activities make us wonder why you don't move to Alexandria where your talents could be correctly appreciated.

As members of the Bolton High School Debate Squad, we look forward to the Friday *Times* and being able to quote you as a reliable expert of American films.
SINCERELY,
THE BOLTON HIGH SCHOOL DEBATE SQUAD
ALEXANDRIA, LA.

DEAR DEBATERS: Pro or Con—The drinking age in the state of Louisiana should be lowered to 14 so American youth can learn to use alcohol in a responsible manner while still under the influence and care of responsible adults and before they go off to LSU and get nekkid.

DEAR JOE BOB BRIGGS: I wish peace to all peoples, races and creeds and to whatever one soul does with another sexually or otherwise in their agreed upon space of privacy. WE ARE SOCIALIZED ENOUGH. The areas of the heart, i.e., forgiveness, seem to be ready to be addressed, the healing through recognizing our good in being and then opening this to larger groups outside of ourselves in seeing the good of all. My mother used to always say, "Look for the good in someone, it's easy to see fault or the bad." What is that bad part. How do we address it?
SINCERELY, SINCERELY,
NANO MAN
SAN FRANCISCO

DEAR NANO NANO: Address it in care of Abigail Van Buren, 4900 Main, Kansas City 64112.

o'clock so they can study Arabian horse breeding and "do a few TV commercials." Only the plot of this baby is how a punk-rock razorhead and his buddy transfer in with their K-Mart clothes and start causin problems for The Sentinels, which is this gang of child Nazis that make sure all the graffiti is scrubbed off the sidewalk ever morning. When these guys get bored they go out in the woods and string the geeks up in hangman's nooses and spraygun their faces and then go to a private club where they can drink five-dollar vodka spritzers with their Frigidaire blondie girlfriends.

The head Sentinel is John Stockwell, who was pretty decent in *Christine,* and he does stuff like put dead animals in people's cars "for the good of the school." But Eddie Peck shows up and starts investigating why his razorhead buddy Krooger got his ear ripped off and why the wimp vice principal won't do diddly about it, and so pretty soon you got Dead Students turnin up, and as you can probly see by now there's way the heck too much plot in this mother.

One breast (on the body of Deedee Pfeiffer, the sister of Michelle *Scarface Grease 2* Pfeiffer). Two dead bodies. One dead squirrel. Seven beasts. One pint blood. A 4 on the Vomit Meter. Throat slitting. One cafeteria brawl. Ear rolls. Drunk driving fu. Spraygun fu. Graffiti fu. Student Council fu. Yuppie fu. Drive-In Academy Award nomination for Bradford Bancroft, the gonzo razorhead; and Jerry Dinome, the lead Sentinel jerkhead, who says "Brian, you know what happens to deserters, don't you?"

Two stars max. Joe Bob says check it out if you want to. ∎

Experimenting with the Wonder Wet

Last week Chubb Fricke's new Wonder Wet Machine came in the mail. It sharpens, it chisels, it grinds and dresses and hones. You can edge garden tools with it, point icepicks with it, restore nicks, repair a jack-knife. Your cleavers will be like new. Old drill bits will bore happily through any surface. You can sharpen scythes, dress planers, grind the blades on Lawn Boys. Easily and professionally, too, with a convenient six-foot cord and removable plastic water tank.

"Chubb," I told him, "you been watchin too much TV again."

Chubb didn't say nothin.

We all went over to Chubb's to watch him take it out of the box.

There it was, black and shiny, ready to hum. Chubb plugged it in.

Clete Tankersley said, "What you gonna sharpen up first, Chubb?"

Chubb grunted somethin about how he was gonna sharpen up his pocket knife first.

"Shame to waste a Wonder Wet Stone Machine that ain't never been used on a pocket knife," said Clete Tankersley.

Chubb stopped fumblin in his pocket and hesitated a second.

"Meat cleaver," Chubb said.

"Meat cleaver's good," Clete Tankersley said. "Meat cleaver's pretty good."

So Chubb went off to find his meat cleaver, and while he was gone me and Rhett Beavers started testin out the Wonder Wet Stone Machine by stickin our fingers inside it and spinnin knobs that said stuff like "Precision Protractor Calibration" and pullin the rubber suction-cup feet off the bottom of it and lickin the bottoms of em and stickin em on Chubb's refrigerator door.

"Couldn't find it," Chubb said when he got back. He had a set of double-handle garden shears in his paws. Before Clete Tankersley could object to a set of double-handle garden shears bein used to test out a Wonder Wet Stone Machine, Chubb walked over and rammed em in the front of it, plugged her in, and started buzzin and sharpenin his little heart out. About a half hour later, he pulled the shears out and showed us the blades, which looked like three hunnerd dollars worth of dental work. Unfortunately they wouldn't cut bushes worth a flip.

After that we went all over Chubb's house, lookin for stuff to sharpen, until we found Chubb Junior's baby tomahawk, and Clete Tankersley set the "Steel Gauging Adjustment Knob" on "Kitchen Cutlery" and crammed her in there before we could any of us say anything, and the machine started huffin and woofin and throwin baby-tomahawk slivers all over the kitchen and finally she just sort of tuckered out and spewed out some water and died on us.

"Ten-day money back?" Clete Tankersley asked Chubb.

"Yep," Chubb said.

"Guaranteed on TV?" Clete said.

"Yep," Chubb said.

"You been watchin too much TV again," said Clete Tankersley.

Speakin of stupid machines that don't work, *Maximum Overdrive* is Big Steve King's directing debut and I already know what you're thinkin.

JOE BOB'S MAILBAG

DEAR JOE BOB: Remember . . .
When there's no more room in the ocean, the trout will walk the Earth.
DUCHESS OF DISASTER
MORAGA, CALIF.

DEAR DUCHESS: We already have quite a few people that look like carp runnin around out here.

DEAR MR. BRIGGS: Millions of People are Going to Be Tormented Day and Night For Ever and Ever.
The third angel followed them, saying with a loud voice, "If any man worship the beast and his image, and receive his mark in his forehead, or in his hand, the same shall drink of the wine of the wrath of God, which is poured out without mixture into the cup of His indignation; and he shall be tormented with fire and brimstone in the presence of the holy angels, and in the presence of the Lamb; and the smoke of their torment ascends up for ever and ever; and they have no rest day nor night, who worship the beast and his image, and whosoever receives the mark of his name." Rev. 14:9, 10, 11.
After you have thoughtfully read this in its entirety; please hand it to a friend.
J. A. TARRES,
PHOENIX

DEAR J.A.: I'll hand it to my friend as soon as he gets back from prayin to a buffalo.

You're thinkin, "Oh, sure, Joe Bob, you're gonna say it's *not Steve's fault* when the movie starts peterin out after about an hour, cause he's *just a writer.*"
That's just so wrong it makes me want to puke.

There's a good reason *Maximum Overdrive* drops its transmission after the first hour, and that's because *Steve tried to direct a love scene.*
Think about it. Everything was fine up to that point, right? I mean, we got the machines slowly trying to take over the world. We got the bank sign flashin the f-word. We got the great scene where the drawbridge goes up by its ownself and destroys eight, ten motor vehicles, including the famous Watermelon Fu shot. We got the maniac cigarette machine, the attack diesel pump, the leapin electric carving knife, video game electrocutions, a little kid on his bike gettin Aunt Jemimaed by a steamroller, Coke-can brain surgery, various forms of deranged lawn-care equipment, exploding 18-wheeler aliens, and, of course, Pat Hingle runnin around shootin off a bazooka he happens to keep in the basement of his truck stop. Great stuff. Great flick.
Then what happens? Emilio Estevez and Laura Harrington do this pathetic little kissing scene, and a couple

Communist Alert!

Michael Nanosky, manager of the Lauderdale Surf Days Inn in Fort Lauderdale, said he suffered $200,000 damage last spring break, because "The kids are great until they get those 25 beers in them. Then they want to show their strength, punch a hole in the wall." I hope Nanosky is NOT suggesting a 25-beer limit, cause I happen to know most of those kids limited themselves to 22 beers per night this year and it would be unfair to penalize everbody for the actions of one or two of the "25-beer men."

of scenes later they start makin the sign of the four-legged spouting walrus, and you know what that adds up to?

A Perry Como music video.

The flick sorta hunkers down after that, while we wait on the eighteen-wheelers to stop trying to take over the world and let some special-effects man blow em all up, but it takes forever cause we got about 20 minutes too much plot in here.

It's okay, though. I still want Steve to do it again, cause he gets three stars first time out of the box and a 93 on the Twisted Metal Meter.

One breast (I think). Twenty dead bodies. One dead dog. Twenty-eight dead motor vehicles. Six quarts of blood. Decent AC/DC tunes. Twelve exploding trucks. One exploding ice-cream truck. Two motor vehicle chases. Wrist carving. Random video-game electrocutions. Little Leaguers massacred for no reason. Steamrolling of small children. Ventilated Pat Hingle. Filthy restrooms. Gratuitous version of "King of the Road." Vending fu. Diesel fu. Garbage truck fu. Bazooka fu. Drive-In Academy Award nominations for Yeardley Smith, as Connie the whining newlywed, for saying "Curtis, are you dead?" and "Oh, honey, you're bleeding like a stuck pig"; Ellen McElduff, as Wanda June the waitress, for gettin drunk and screaming "They can't! We made them!"; and Big Steve, for landing a part in his own movie.

Three stars. Joe Bob says check it out. ■

Getting Aholt a Some Bad Beef

A couple of weeks ago Chubb Fricke and me went over to Bridgeport, which is out west by the gravel and ceement pits, for the Texas Sesquicentennial Barbecue Luau and Sweet Potato Bake-off, but once we got out there we realized they weren't gonna have the usual Face-Stuffin Contest and so Chubb just had to hang out by the swingsets and tell the kids he'd give em a quarter to go "around the world" until one of the little monsters did a 40-foot Geronimo into Velda Weaver's striped cupcakes and we had to send the poor woman to the emergency room.

I love barbecues.

Anyhow, after we listened to some Meskins play accordion music, Chubb wanted to go watch the Little Leaguers beat each other up for no reason, but I said no, you can see that anywhere, and so we dropped by the Brisket Line for some cowmeat to chew on. Got it from a guy named Fred. Chewed on it quite a while.

I guess it was about four days later when I started to turn the color of a turquoise Naugahyde sofa. Then I started shakin inside like somebody was ridin a log-flume ride through my intestines. And finally I fell plumb over on my back and started kickin my feet like Joey Heatherton when she don't get her way. I tell you, it wasn't a pretty sight.

Then what happens? They go and announce on the radio in Bridgeport that the whole town needs to go get inoculations for hepatitis, even though nobody in Bridgeport knows how to *spell* innocculations, cause Fred has

JOE BOB'S MAILBAG

DEAR JOE BOB: Who died and made you Richard Simmons. Why do you have to pick on Roger Ebert? Roger's got something you may never have—freedom. He can travel this great country of ours unplagued by visions of Carl Malden lamenting his ignorance after some sleezewad, Oxy 5 Before picture, has stolen his travelers checks, drivers license, and his list of campsite numbers at the KOA Miwok Villages he's planned to camp at. *He can feel secure that all those things, as well as a pack of Juicy Fruit, his car keys, and a few Oreos are safely lodged beneath his clothes in the folds of his flesh. Fat people make America great, Littleman.*
DENNIS (JUGS) KARTER
CO-Z 8 MOTEL
MOUNTAIN VIEW, CALIF.

DEAR JUGMAN: I got nothin against Roger, as long as he don't sit on my lawn chairs.

DEAR MR. BRIGGS: This is to inform you that the corset you ordered is in. Although this is always a classic in black, we also have versions in peach & lilac . . . purrfect for summer!!

Since you are such a special customer, we have a pair of cute flamingo pink swimming fins that are ½ off this month only. (Of course, we know how charming they'd look on the little "toot-toot" you bought from us last Christmas.)

You will be receiving our new catalogue soon.
Regards,
SHARON, LUCY'S LACE
SAN FRANCISCO

DEAR SHARON: Stop accessorizing my toot-toot.

hepatitis and it might be a Communist Plot to wipe out the entire southern half of Wise County includin the 300 people that drive gravel trucks for a living. And so I called up Chubb to see how he was feeling, and sure enough, he had the *exact same symptoms.*

I told him to come get me cause we had to get down to Grapevine Memorial and get shot up with gam-mahemoglobulin or else this could turn into somethin serious like tongue-in-mouth disease, so we went down there and got examined by a doctor named Fred (no relation).

Doctor Fred looked us over and stuck his finger in several places and then he said, "I don't know, I don't know, I don't know."

Even though I was enjoyin this diagnosis, I told Doctor Fred to elaborate just a little bit.

"Have you ever felt like someone was riding a log-flume through your intestines?" he said.

"Yeah! Exactly!"

"How about skin color? Do you always look like a piece of half-chewed crab meat, or have you ever resembled a turquoise Naugahyde sofa?"

"Naugahyde! Absolutely!"

"Uh oh," he said. "You don't kick like Joey Heatherton, do you?"

"Oh my God, *what is it!*"

"I hate to tell you this, Mr. Briggs, Mr. Fricke, but you both have con-juntovitis, also known as Bridgeport Syndrome."

"What is it? What can we do? How long have we got?"

"It's normally spread by bad Mexican accordion music being played in the outdoors. Have you been exposed to any of that lately?"

"God, yes, I forgot all about it."

"We'll need to quarantine you. Stay away from all the cable channels. No Nashville Network. Don't venture into any Mexican neighborhoods—that goes without saying, since some of them never close their windows. And do not under any circumstances rent any Joey Heatherton videos. Is that understood?"

"Yes sir."

"In about nine, ten weeks, you'll be fine."

"Thank God."

Speaking of viruses you can't get rid of, *Friday the 13th Part VI: Jason Lives* is the movie that asks the question "Why should we try to kill him anymore?" You know, Jason's always had the ability to levitate himself all over Crystal Lake, jumpin out of refrigerators if he has to, in constant

search of Teen Veal. This time, though, you can just forget it, cause he can't be killed by a) metal gatepost plunged through ever part of his body, includin his head; b) eight pistol shots; c) three shotgun blasts; d) boulder dropped on his head; or e) drowning.

I've come up with the only *real* way to kill Jason. What would happen if you did the *one thing* that Jason couldn't *stand,* the *one thing* that would be just as deadly to Jason as Kryptonite is to Superman?

What if Paramount refused to renegotiate Jason's contract?

Would that make him mad or what? I can see him now, tryin to get through backlot security to *enforce* his sequel clause, to *resurrect* his videocassette rights, to *bludgeon to death* his severance rider. Now we're talkin movie.

In the meantime, what we got is Jason gettin zapped back to life by a bolt of lightnin, stickin his fist through Horshack's stomach, and then sayin "Let's boogie."

No breasts. Fourteen dead bodies, includin one girl who tries to buy off Jason with an American Express card. One dead undead body. Four gallons blood (low for the series). Face-eating worms. Corpse-staking. Teen shishkebobbing. Two motor vehicle chases, one with crash-and-burn. Bimbo's face shoved through a cheap prefab wall. Knife through head. Paint-the-room-red bimbo-jerking. Head ripping. Police officer head-compacting. Dart through the forehead. Sheriff crushing. Head rolls. Stomach rolls. Arm rolls. Leg rolls. Gratuitous Boy Scout lesson. Gratuitous June bug squishing. Lightnin fu. Whiskey bottle fu. Repeated machete fu. Winnebago fu. Evinrude fu. Drive-In Academy Award nominations for Thom Matthews, as Tommy, for calling Jason a maggothead; Jennifer Cooke, as the sheriff's daughter, for drivin a '77 or-

Communist Alert!

Ellen Newman at the San Francisco Zoo is advertising a "Fu" exhibit of Siberian tigers, Bengal tigers and a rare white tiger, claimin that the word "Fu" means "big cat" in Cantonese. El wrong-o. I quote from *A Handbook to Literature,* fifth edition, by C. Hugh Holman and William Harmon, Macmillan Publishing Company, 1986, p. 217:

"FU: A technical term used in the Briggsian school of alfresco FILM CRITICISM; appropriated from the Chinese "kung fu," the Briggsian application of *fu* means mindless violence. The term seldom appears alone; instead, it is used as a suffix appended to the instrument or perpetrator of the violence, as in "firehouse *fu*," "chain saw *fu*," or "bimbo *fu*."

ange Camaro and facin Jason in the final death struggle; and Tom McLouglin, the writer/director, for havin the gravedigger say "Some folks have a strange idea of entertainment."

Three stars. Joe Bob says check it out. ∎

Pigskin Payoffs
Mean Pigskin Playoffs

It's that time again. Time for all the Southwest Conference football players to report for practice driving *Trans Ams they bought with their own money they earned this summer workin at the post office*.

I wanna make this clear right now, cause last year we had to start usin Latin teachers as offensive tackles. All because a few *small-minded, envious* people claimed we had players on salary at eight of the nine SWC schools. (I'm not countin the University of Arkansas, where they had players on $278-a-day "meal allowances," because the players at the University of Arkansas normally do eat grain sorghums shipped in from Iowa.)

Don't you think it's just a little bit of a coincidence? Look at the statistics:

Number of salaried players in the SWC (averaged over the past five years): 487

Number of salaried players in all other football conferences: 2

Number of SWC athletic departments with bank accounts in the Cayman Islands: 8 (doesn't include Texas A&M, which maintains bank accounts in Bahrain and Calcutta for "routine accounting purposes")

Number of active players enrolled in at least one taxidermy course: 174

Number of current players named "Bubba": 343

Number of players last year that "just happened to find hundred-dollar bills rolled up in my sweat socks": 786

Now are we gonna quibble over a few numbers like this? Numbers you could find at *any* school in America if you just looked hard enough? Why are these people pickin on a guy like Jackie "I Ain't Done Nothin" Sherrill, the Texas A&M Head Cheese, when he has stated publicly many times that he *turned down* Darrell "Rutabaga" Swenson, the first 340-pound Swedish running back to come along in years, when Rutabaga suggested that he should receive a $100-a-week "subsidy" from the Texas A&M Alumni "party fund." Rutabaga ended up attending A&M anyway, on a Medieval Literature Scholarship, and should be able to speak English by his junior year, but there's an example of a fine young boy who played football and *will* get his college degree in 1998.

I'll just give out one more example of the kind of discrimination goin on here—Jimbo "James" Slackman, TCU's fine strongside linebacker and the man destined to set a new conference record for the infliction of career-ending tackles. James didn't always have that winning attitude. When James arrived at TCU all he wanted to do was sit on the bench and engage in belching contests. That all changed when James received the 1984 Wilbarger-Brumbaugh Challenge Grant, which was started by two Wichita Falls businessmen dedicated to "the challenge of challenging challengers in athletics today." Under the terms of the grant, James must write a five-page paper during each semester on "What Sticking My Helmet in Somebody's Gut Means to Me." At the same time Wilhelmina Estes of Abilene Christian University is asked to write five pages on the same topic. The two papers are then graded by an impartial panel of ex-linebackers from *both schools,* and the winning paper receives a $5,000 "research grant" and the use of a brand-new Chrysler LeBaron for "field trips."

This is just one of the purely *academic* programs that would be killed if this relentless persecution of the conference continues. Don't let it happen. Write your state legislator today. Enclose a hundred bucks.

Speakin of repeat killings, I went to *Psycho III* about a month ago but I forgot everthing in it the next day, and so now people been writin in and wonderin what happened. All I remember

---

Communist Alert!

The U.S. Supreme Court upheld the law in Winnebago County, Ill., that says "sexually explicit scenes" can't be shown at drive-ins that are "visible from any private residence or public street." The perverts CAN'T SHUT THEIR WINDOWS!

---

is how Tony Perkins moons around the Bates Motel, sewin up bodies and talkin to Mama a lot. He keeps Mama upstairs, where she's fallin apart on him and makin a lot of *long* speeches about who Norman needs to slice up next. Diana Scarwid wanders into the motel after gettin kicked out of a convent and almost gettin raped in a rainstorm by Jeff Fahey the slimeball guitar player. Then a reporter shows up to prove to the sheriff that Tony is still missin a few knobs on his satellite dish, and it's enough to make Mama say stuff like "Stand up straight and wipe your snotty little nose!"

Then Norman goes on a date with Diana "I Look Just Like Janet Leigh" Scarwid, and pretty soon we know Mama is gonna insist on some Justice. They let Tony direct this baby, and so the main thing wrong with it is Tony lets his Mama talk a lot and it gets *real* boring listenin to the old bag, which is literally true—she's an old bag.

Way too much plot gettin in the way of the story.

Six breasts. Seven dead bodies (one technically a dead undead body). One motor vehicle chase. Three quarts blood. Two slit wrists. Corpse sewing. Throat slitting. Stomach gouging. Ashtray bashing. Gratuitous fatty orgy. Hitchhike fu. Phone booth fu. Drive-In Academy Award nominations for Jeff Fahey, for doing a sex scene with a lampshade; Diana Scarwid, for saying "I'm afraid I did leave the bathroom a mess," settin up Tony's line "I've seen it worse"; and Tony, for saying "My hobby is stuffing things" and "Well, I can't have that sort of thing going on in my motel."

Two and a half stars. Joe Bob says check it out if it's still around. ∎

Evelyn Is Very Disturbed

Anna Chappell is this creepy mush-face old Bette Davis lady named Evelyn that runs the Mountaintop Motel in *Mountaintop Motel Massacre,* the movie that, as we all know, is the latest from Jim McCullough, the second greatest filmmaker in the whole state of Arkansas. Jim wrote the ad that says "Don't disturb Evelyn . . . She already is!" And so you can just about see what's comin here. The old bag kills her little girl with a Commie sickle before there's five minutes gone, and then one by one the entire membership of Screen Actors Guild, Arkansas Chapter, checks into this old ramshackle motel up in the Ozarks and gets turned into Chicken McNuggets.

Evelyn spent three years in the Arkansas State Mental Hospital, but they couldn't cure her of bad gardening habits, like Weed-Eating the guinea pigs. And she keeps a lot of weird knickknacks in her closet, old corncob pipes and Aztec gods and rubber doll-babies and stuff, like she's been shoppin up around Eureka Springs at one of those places that says "Hillbilly Souvenirs" on the front door, only she burns candles around the knickknacks down in this underground tunnel and says stuff like "I summon thee!" only we don't ever see who thee is cause they didn't have enough money to build one.

Anyhow, they don't really find out about the Dollbaby Shrines till the end, after she's gone around stickin snakes in the rooms and dumpin cockroaches and rats everwhere and then poppin up out of holes in the floor and stickin garden tools through their faces. This has happened to me at quite a few seven-dollar-a-night motels in the Midwest.

What we got here is: One breast. Seven dead bodies. Three quarts blood. Electro-heart massage. Sickle in face. Sickle in chest. Sickle in neck. Bad Loretta Lynn imitation. Snake striking wimp in the eye. Stuffed bobcat in attack position. Dollbaby Shrine. Gratuitous gardening. Gratuitous "Help Me Make It Through the Night." Head rolls. Snake fu. Rat fu. Guinea fu. Drive-In Academy Award nominations for Jill King, as Evelyn's

---

JOE BOB'S MAILBAG

DEAR JOE BOB: Did you know Dr. Ruth Westheimer wears a Cross Your Navel bra?
SHELBY FRIEDMAN
DALLAS

DEAR SHELBY: Let's not think about it, okay?

JOE BOB: You are like a Godlike being who lives on the edge of town. Years from now pilgrims will pay homage to you at a drive-in in Texas. The whole world will grovel at your feet. Then again, maybe not.
YOUR FRIEND & FOLLOWER IN THE WILDERNESS
TRENT TRULOCK
INDIANAPOLIS

DEAR TRENT: There's a reason God put you in Indianapolis.

little girl, for lookin at a picture of her dead father and sayin "Daddy, I think Momma's gettin *sick* again"; Bill Thurman, as the Reverend Bill McWilley, for sayin "We got everthing we need right here—Old Crow, and Vieena Sausage"; Major Brock, as Melvin Crenshaw the repairman, for sayin "They oughta call this a roach motel" and for nailin Evelyn under the floor; Will Mitchel, as Al the traveling salesman, for pickin up two girls and sayin "You girls ever hear of Columbia Records? That's mine—that's my baby—Barbara Mandrell, she's made me a million" cause I can never think of stuff that good to say; Greg Brazzel, as the dimwit newlywed, who gets gangrene of the brain; and James Bradford, as the sheriff, for saying "Six bodies in there? Sorry I was so late in getting here."

Best All-Arkansas Film of 1986. Two stars. Joe Bob says check it out. ∎

JOE BOB'S MAILBAG

MOST PRECIOUS: Please come back to me. I promise I'll only use the paddle—no more whips. Sorry I bruised more than your feelings, but I didn't realize how tender you are.
Love,
BUTCH
NEW ORLEANS

DEAR BUTCH: I have no idea what you're talkin about. The ones with the foam rubber pads?

DEAR JOE BOB: Since you're hitting the local Borscht circuit, I thought you'd make a hit with your very own theme song "The Meaning of Life." Did you know that the reason "Thou shalt not commit adultery because he who is without sin never misses."

"THE MEANING OF LIFE"
The meaning of life, the truths we hold dear
Virtue does have no reward
Now listen my son go forth with these truths
Virtue has never a virtue been
Eat lots of spinach, don't talk to strangers
Keep your eyes open and your mouth shut
Drink lots of water, don't pick your pimples
Don't loan your vibrator, don't pick your nose
You surely must know the grease that is used
To make the earth spin on its axis,
For if we ran out the earth would stand still,
Just barnyard excretions pure bull manure

When one asks your age you must tell the truth.
A woman is much like a redwood.
Just count the growth rings round the rear end.
Like counting the growth rings on a tree stump.

Don't fake your climax, relax and enjoy
One thing you can't fake is an erection,
So early to bed and early to rise
Makes a man healthy but gives him bed sores.

YOUR DEVOTED FAN,
BIG DAVE THE CHICKEN FARMER
DAVID L. ICHELSON, M.D.
CORNING, CALIF.

DEAR DOCTOR DAVE: That song was worth every single patient that died while you were writing it, and don't let ANYBODY tell you different.

Vomit Jubilee in *The Fly*

David Cronenberg's finally put out his drive-in masterpiece. Going *immediately* to number one on the Best of '86 List is *The Fly,* which is even better than the one Dave *already* has in the Drive-In Hall of Fame, *The Brood.*

What we got here is the same story as the 1958 version with Vincent Price, only this time the fly is fused with Jeff Goldblum and so *we feel sorry for the fly.* Actually what happens is Jeff deserves it, cause he's tryin to pick up Geena Davis by telepoddin stuff all over his apartment—nylons, baboons, stuff like that—and so she falls in love with him and he ends up gettin drunk one night and jumpin into the telepod machine without *checkin for flies* cause evidently he didn't see the first movie. And so what happens?

Insect fu.

At first Jeff is so charged up he flies around his crummy apartment doin scenes from *Gymkata,* but pretty soon his face starts to change. We got your basic Pizza Face look. Then we got Cream-of-Wheat Cancer Face. And finally, when things *really* get bad, we got your Vomit Jubilee Face. These may be the best drive-in makeup effects *in history.*

We're talkin one breast. Two beasts in one body. Six quarts blood. Seven quarts vomit. Eight quarts undecided. Unsuccessful Norelco cure. One compound fracture. Baboon zapping. Nylon stocking zapping. Jeff Goldblum zapping. Baboon turned inside out. Purple fingers. Excessive body hair. Huge maggot birthing. Ceiling walking. Ear rolls. Fingernails roll. Teeth roll. Hand rolls. Foot rolls. gratuitous fly puke. Arm wrestling fu. Shotgun fu. Drive-In Academy Award Nominations for Jeff, as the scientist and fly, for sayin "I must not know enough about the flesh; I'm gonna have to learn" and "I won't be just another tumorous bore, talking about his hair falling out and his lost lymph nodes"; Geena, as the girlfriend, for sayin "You look bad, you smell bad, and you have these weird hairs growing out of your back"; and Big Dave, the director, for writin the line "I'm an insect who dreamed he was a man and loved it."

Four stars. Joe Bob says check it out. ■

G. Gordon Liddy Answers When Nature Calls

Everybody's been writin in all summer to say, "When the heck are you gonna review *When Nature Calls?*"

Course, this shows how much the average layman knows, since the correct title is *When Nature Calls . . . You've Gotta Go,* and it's the movie that played for one entire week in several drive-ins in northern Jersey before going directly to several cable stations in western Kansas. This is the finest drive-in movie starring G. Gordon Liddy and John Cameron Swayze of the entire year. The movie was so short they had to stick 20 minutes of filler on the front end of it. The movie is about a New York City family that moves to the wilderness, loses track of the plot, and features the famous bear-rape sequence (the daughter rapes a bear). The movie is so bungled that G. Gordon Liddy volunteered to take the blame.

No plot to get in the way of the story. Blind-O-Vision (subtitles for the blind). Two dead bodies. Hand rolls.

ceptable in downtown San Francisco. A Symbolic Confrontation. Symbolic of what? Who knows? That's not the point, man.

Look at what the movies of today have to offer: a guy goes to a small town for yet another confrontation with rural decadence. But this time, he's dressed in Ivy League clothes, like he could be William F. Buckley's son, or something. And why are the rednecks angry? Because he wants to *dance,* man. It's like Fred Astaire Goes to Mayberry.

We've come a long way since the '60s. And it's all been downhill, man.
SID
DALLAS

DEAR SID: Groovy.

DEAR JOE-BOB: I don't care what anyone says. I think very highly of you! I think your the Burito-Supreme of life! Your top Banana in my Book! I work at Taco Bell and read your column on my Break.
SUSAN E. GOETZ
KANSAS CITY

DEAR SUZIE: I'll always think of you as a quivering frijole dinner.

DEAR JOE BOB: Young, paunchy VCU dropout seeks attractive male to drive her to bars and on road-trips because of D.U.I. The more fun we have, the more drinks I will invest.
THOMASINA JEFFERSON
VIRGINIA COMMONWEALTH UNIVERSITY
RICHMOND, VA.

DEAR THOMASINA: Don't even think about usin your DUI in a moving car if you ever think you might wanna bear children.

JOE BOB'S MAILBAG

DEAR JOE BOB: They don't make movies like *Easy Rider* anymore, man. Now there was one of your great Youth-Oriented movies. The adventures of 2 brain-dead dope smugglers as they parade around in Redneck America in clothes that would barely be ac-

Two breasts. Nine hundred eighty-seven sight gags, a new modern record. Seven gallons bleeding ulcers. Gratuitous Morey Amsterdam doing jokes about Eleanor Roosevelt's breasts. Weejun the Kaopectate Indian. Camping Iranians. Stag film starring stags. Willie Mays in a felonious sight gag that takes place in a maize field. Cougar attack. Outstanding Jerry Lewis imitation. Indian roasting. Gratuitous Myron Cohen. Acid dog. By the people at Troma Pictures, the same guys who brought us *Waitress.*

Two stars. Joe Bob says check it out. ■

The Drive-In of the Future

Dead End Drive-In is an attempt to show what happens when the Commonists take over the world and keep everbody locked up inside a drive-in where you have all your basic necessities: corny dogs, really loud Empty-V music, Arkansas Polio Weed, lots of spray paint, movies about exploding Australians, and your very own car to live in. It's in the 1900s, and this guy named Crabs takes a foxy girl named Carmen to the drive-in, and once they get there they rip off their clothes and start makin the sign of the triple-snouted aardvark and while they're doin that the cops come and "requisition" both rear wheels and so they become Numero 192 and Numero 193 in Drive-In Dachau.

This is fine with dumb-as-a-box-of-rocks Carmen, who spends all day long eatin Hormel Chili and havin her hair raked into a bean sprout sandwich like Pat Benatar, but Crabs figures, hey, there's something *not quite right* here and so he starts plannin to escape. This is harder than it sounds, cause everbody keeps tryin to get him to go to the Ku Klux Klan meeting instead of workin on the engine of his '56 candy-apple-red Chevy. Pretty soon about 150 *Road Warrior* extras start makin fun of Crabs for being *such a weenie* and refusing to pay Mel Gibson's fee to come waste the Commies.

What we got here is "Mildly Perturbed Max Beyond Thunderdome." Four breasts. Ten dead bodies. Two motor vehicle chases, with three smash-ups, one three-ton-truck jump, two crash-and-burns. Aardvarking. Tree-trunk impaling. Australian-rules cricket-bat skull-smashing. Bad dangling earrings. Really bad shiny leather jackets. Really really bad leopard-skin blankets. Gratuitous banana fritters. Gratuitous boat people. Drive-In Academy Award nominations for Ned Manning, as the crabby Crabs; Natalie McCurry, world famous as the 1983 Miss Young International of Australia, who plays Carmen and utters the classic line "But I thought you wanted to be with *me*"; and Peter Smalley, the screenwriter, for the line "How long till one of these zipheads tries to rape one of our women?"

Australia fu. Two stars. Joe Bob says check it out. ■

A Video Wake for Gordon McLendon

Been pretty bummed out ever since Gordon McLendon died last week. Father of the drive-in, king of the twin screen, producer of *Attack of the Killer Shrews* and *Giant Gila Monster,* Gordo was the guy who built more drive-ins in the '50s than were built in the entire previous history of civilization. He built his last drive-in in 1983—the six-screen I-45 Drive-In in Houston. He was the last guy that *believed* the drive-in will never die. Only *he* died. And how much credit did he get? Ten seconds. Ten lousy seconds on *Entertainment Tonight* where they called him the "father of Top Forty radio."

Anyhow, I haven't been out of my trailer house in a week now. There's a permanent oil slick on top of my TV where the fried-chicken box leaks. My Lazy-Boy recliner is locked in stretch position. Ever once in a while my friends come by to check on me, slide some Beenie Weenies under the door, but I can't even sniff em anymore.

I couldn't face it, the shame of it, the drive-in ignorance confronting this country today. I brooded about it. I sniffled a little. I rolled it around in my brain. I undressed it. I drew some graffiti on it. I spray-painted a happy face on top of it. I snorted it. I free-based it.

And then I finally did it.

I called up Clete Tankersley and told him to come on out and install a 480-inch, 748-channel "Mr. Martian" backyard satellite dish. I don't know why. I guess I had to have something to do in my time of mourning. I wanted to be alone on my sofa with a lot of nek-kid women. I wanted to see what all

JOE BOB'S MAILBAG

DEAR JOE BOB: The first time I ever went to a drive-in movie was a disaster. My buddies and I went to see Bruce Lee's *Enter the Dragon* on a hot muggy Houston night. We drank warm rum & Cokes, got sick and popped my tires sneaking into the drive-in through the exit by running over those little daggers that stick out of the cement. After reading your reviews for the last 2 years in my school paper (*The Daily Texan*) I feel the urge to go back to a drive-in. What should I see & what should I drink?
JOHN MacDOUGALL
AUSTIN, TEX.

DEAR JOHN: What you should see is the sign that says "Enter Here."

DEAR JOE BOB: How come under the new, self-policing cinema morality you can tear someone's still-thumping heart out and eat it in living, close up color, but if the plot requires a shot of a half dressed bimbo, (a plot we don't see much of lately, come to think of it), it's taken at twilight and 150 feet away?
Yours,
BRUCE NORTHRUP
CORVALLIS, OREGON

DEAR BRUCE: Cause the bimbos got lawyers and started stickin in Nookie Clauses. If the hearts ever get lawyers, we're in major trouble.

the Babtists out in the boonies are watchin ever night on satellite so they can demand their removal from dirty bookstores. I did the commercial thing. I sold out. I went Video.

It took Clete three days just to pour the concrete foundation for the dish, and as soon as we turned it on three kids had to go to the emergency room for minor brain lesions. (I got the model that picks up Cuban talk shows and Yugoslavian tractor demonstrations.) Then we hooked it up to my nine-year programmable Very Cosmic Recorder and started poppin in plastic boxes and starin at the screen and sayin "That's boring."

Then we plugged it in.

I hadn't had a feelin like this since 1957, when Dede Wilks rearranged my beads at the Valhalla Drive-In outside Sudan, Texas. Drive-in movies that were *banned in Texas* for 15, 20 years were available in little plastic boxes that *you* have to pay money for but I get *free* cause I just call up people and say, "I'm Joe Bob Briggs and I'd like to abuse my privileges as a famous movie critic by demandin you send over a copy of *Bloodsuckin Freaks* so I can look at it." It's great. You can watch this stuff and *never leave the trailer.* It's unreal.

The first week I watched 46 drive-in classics that've been shrunk up and put in little plastic boxes. Here's the ones I recommend as true drive-in material.

1. *I Spit On Your Grave:* This flick is considered "the most disgusting movie ever made" by Ebert the Wimp and Siskel the Simp, who went on TV for two, three years tellin everbody that it makes men want to rape women, which is why the theaters quit running it. But it's the most *feminist* drive-in movie ever made. The most likely thing that'll happen after a man watches this flick—especially the bathtub scene—is

he won't be able to walk straight for a week. A combination of *Deliverance, Death Wish,* and *Straw Dogs,* this one has the second best title of the '70s (best is *The Texas Chainsaw Massacre*) and is a category all unto its ownself. Camille Keaton, Eron Tabor, and Richard Pace all give Drive-In Academy Award performances, but *specially* Eron Tabor, who is the finest crudhead slimeball woman-hater ever portrayed on the big screen. The speech this guy gives about why it was necessary for him to rape Camille is a classic, and Meir Zarchi—one of those directors who is world renowned for just *one* movie, this one—develops ever single scene so that, even though you already sorta know what's gonna happen, you're always surprised by what really *does* happen. Also has the best ad line in history: "This woman just chopped, burned, maimed, and mutilated four men beyond recognition—and no jury in the world would convict her." A 94 on the Vomit Meter. Screenwriting Hall of Fame, for the following line, spoken by a drunk rapist standing over a battered corpse-like woman: "Total submission. That's what I like in a woman. Total submission." Best Drive-In Picture 1978. Four stars. Only on video.

2. *Sybil Danning's Adventure Video:* This is a bunch of drive-in movies with ripaway bra queen Sybil Danning stuck on the front end of em, and usually Sybil is the only decent thing to look at on the whole reel. One exception: *Fast Money,* the ultimate dope-deal movie, made in Austin in 1981 for about 50 cents, never seen in theaters, featuring an incredible gonzo acidhead performance by Lou Perry, recently seen as the dead-but-still-blubberin radio-station engineer in *Saw 2.* Only on video.

3. *She-Devils on Wheels:* Hard-to-find 1968 classic about a female biker

gang called the Man-Eaters, who wear pink pussycats with bow ties on their leather jackets and have a daily race to see who gets first pick from the "stud line." This bothers the sensitive new recruit Karen, who says "We treat men like they're slabs of meat, hanging on a rack at a butcher shop," and she thinks about running away to be married. Especially fine performance by 300-pound Miami biker Pat Poston, who screams "Up your Magic Dragon!" when she's not terrorizing small towns by sweeping past small children on her bike and stealing their snowcones. By the neglected master, Herschell Gordon Lewis, the Chicago genius who made the first explicit-gore flick, *Blood Feast,* in 1962. Only on video.

Joe Bob says check em out. ∎

Communist Alert!

It took em 46 years, but they finally bulldozed the South 29 Drive-In on Wilkinson Boulevard in Charlotte, N.C. This one hurts more than usual—one of the first in the South, with a screen supported by 16 huge logs. First picture in 1940: *Vivacious Lady,* starring Ginger Rogers and Jimmy Stewart. Last picture in 1986: front-end loader rippin it down with a steel cable. This leaves Charlotte, one of America's drive-in capitals in the '50s, with one measly drive-in—the Fox on Old Stateville Road.

The Video Siege Continues

Special editor's note: Mr. Briggs, who normally mails in his column from the tawdry, weed-infested suburb of Grapevine, Texas, remained incommunicado for the second straight week, refusing to come out of his trailer home despite the appearance of a small, foul-smelling group of curiosity-seekers on his front lawn. After 10 straight days, he finally agreed to speak with a pale-faced negotiator from the Universal Press Syndicate, who flew in from Kansas City accompanied by an overpaid contracts lawyer, only to be turned away with the phrase "Send more video." Questioned about what he saw on the inside of the trailer, the negotiator recalled mountains of videocassettes, many of them wrapped in TV-dinner tinfoil, a five-foot-high "Still the King" gold-plated Elvis clock, and copies of virtually every magazine not sold at 7-Eleven. The UPS negotiator did manage to extract the following "column" from Briggs after threatening to deface a Bill Dana My Name José Jimenez *album. We are printing it here for legal reasons that will become evident at a later time . . .*

[first page missing]

. . . and then she uses her pelvis to conjugate some Iranian verbs. Available on Thunder Thighs Video for $29.95, unless you're really fat and you need to get *Stop Eating or I'll Kill You Very Slowly,* for just $24.95 from Teamsters Pension Fund Video Entertainment.

The next 36-hour viewing segment was devoted to made-for-video-horror-movies-cause-we're-too-cheap-to-buy-any-ads-and-my-girlfriend-wants-to-be-in-it-anyhow. Pick-of-the-week in this category is . . .

Breeders: Nobody can figure out why a giant plastic one-eyed lizard in a rubber suit is raping virgins in New York City until a cop and a bimbo doctor discover that *every victim is covered with a strange eerie unknown substance.* They take it to the lab and find out—no, it can't be! no! not that!—it's *brick dust.* It's the *exact* same kind of brick dust they used 200 years ago to build Manhattan "but they ran out of it." That can mean only one thing: Giant alien grasshoppers are living underneath the subways, boiling virgins in larva love juice, then bustin their bodies open to create masters of the universe. As one of the actors says, "What happened is an alien life force drifted to Earth on a spore. They can't figure it all out yet." Nekkid aerobics. Forty-one breasts. Five lizard rapes. Nine bodies. Special Video Drive-In Academy Award nomination to Tim Kincaid, the writer/director, for having the imagination to conceive of virgins in New York City. Two stars.

If you been wonderin where all the Attack-of-the-Stupid-White-People flicks went, you *haven't been runnin those VCRs enough* or you would of found . . .

Malibu Bikini Shop: Actually released in *grown-up moviehouses* for about five minutes, this is one of the best movies about brain-damaged body parts with tans, twitching on the beach, since *Hardbodies.* The first hour is bikini crotch shots, followed by bikini boob shots, followed by some three-minute flashing-flopper Southern California "we can't sing but we made a video" beach music, followed by three hot-tub scenes featuring 34 actresses who constantly use the word "party" as a verb. In the big final sequence, the world as we know it is saved by the sewing-together of 250 camouflaged *Apocalypse Now* bikinis. Last movie of the late Frank Nelson, Jack Benny's "Yeeeeessss" man. Best Rita Jenrette movie since *Zombie Island Massacre* (Rita's onscreen five seconds, as a picture on the wall). Sixteen breasts. Trapeze bed. The video equivalent of a wet T-shirt contest. Three stars.

And finally, my buddy Dino DeLaurentiis, king of the modern drive-in producers, ordered one of his lackeys in El Lay to send me a video of *Manhunter,* assuming—correctly—that I would refuse to actually drive to the drive-in to watch it.

Basically what we got here is Bill Petersen as an FBI agent chasin a sex-

---

Communist Alert!

Another tough one. The luxurious Empire Theatre ("ALWAYS 3 GREAT KUNG FU HITS") on 42nd Street in the Apple has been *boarded up!!!* This is the place where they've been runnin *Mad Monkey Kung Fu* nonstop for two years. This is the site of the American premiere of *Lee's Killer Kids, Little Rascals Kung Fu, Super Ninjas,* and *18 Chambers of Shaolin.* This is the place where the Guardian Angels have a *permanent sentry.* This is the closest thing to a drive-in Manhattan ever had or ever will have. And it's over. Gone. Part of Ed the Kochman's sorry "urban renewal." Remember, without eternal vigilance, it can happen here.

ual deviate murderer, but if he's gonna catch the deviate, Bill has to *become* a deviate—think like a deviate, act like a deviate, read my column. And then once he gets on the guy's trail, he requests $340 billion worth of technical assistance from FBI headquarters—30 guys who don't work on any other case but this one—Learjets, satellite hook-ups, and, best of all, an art director so the sexual deviate kills everybody against colorful pastel backgrounds so Bill can turn on *his* VCR and watch. Great scene where the deviate puts panty-hose over his face, sets a guy on fire, and rolls him down a parking-garage ramp in a flaming wheelchair, but way too much plot constantly gettin in the way of the story and not enough scenes of Kim Griest exposing her . . .

[rest of pages missing] ∎

Selling My Soul for Indoor Bullstuff

Last week three letters with rabies poured in. The first one said, "No! No! No! Joe Bob, you've finally sold out to the video wimps, haven't you? You've sold your soul to the itty bitty indoor bullstuff screen!"

Thank you for givin me an opportunity to respond to this charge. If you are implyin that I can be *influenced* by wealthy video distributors who want to send me free movie tapes in the mail all the time, then the answer is:

Yes, that is correct.

The second disgruntled drunk said, "How can you expect to keep the few remaining drive-ins alive when you contribute to the problem by giving aid and comfort to the enemy?"

As I have said many times, I will never do anything that violates my personal and professional code of journalistic ethics. However, I will do anything for money.

But I am *not* abandoning the drive-in. Next month, I hope to blackmail my congressman into sponsoring a bill for federal payments to drive-in owners. The system I have in mind would work exactly like what the dairy and tobacco farmers get. Ever time they kill a cow or burn some crops, they get money, right? Okay, same deal. Ever time we close a drive-in, *even for one weekend,* we get $10,000. This will act as an incentive for us to sit around on our rear-ends like the farmers do.

Finally, I got this letter:

"Joe Bob, I've always dreamed of 'doing it' at the drive-in, but I'm a generation too young. There aren't even any guys in my high school who *want* to do it at the drive-in. Now you tell me that you—the man who holds the world record—won't even be doing it there anymore. Couldn't this be dangerous?"

I know it sounds kinky, but people are doing it in *beds* now. I don't understand it. I don't like it. But no one ever calls Joe Bob Briggs old-fashioned.

Let me say it one more time, too.

Great drive-ins never die. They just get knocked down with a big old cee-ment wreckin ball and smashed into little bitty pieces and carried off to the city dump.

To prove it, I actually left my trailer house this week for *three hours* and went to see *Reform School Girls* cause

JOE BOB'S MAILBAG

DEAR "SPANKING FRITO": My wife and I are answering your ad in the swingers magazine. You stated that you are seeking "some swingers who like drive-ins and mud wrestling." Well, that's us. We also enjoy streaking and listening to Phil Donahue say the word "stimulation."

We have been swinging for 8 years now. Ethel likes it because she feels that it frees her mind. I like it because I don't have to sleep with Ethel.

The newest erotic thrill for swingers is edible underwear. We like to cook our own. You really should try our BVDs l'orange, our brassiere with garlic sauce, our panties jubilee, and our Fruit of the Looms à la mode.

We don't like to do anything weird or freaky. Once in a while, we indulge in some "balloons over Europe," and now and then, some "scour the bailiwick," and occasionally, some "Tasmanian jump-ups," but nothing far out or kinky. Why don't we meet at a "hot sheet" motel and discuss this further?
MR. & MRS. ONE TRACK MIND
DALLAS

DEAR MR. AND MIZ MIND: Okay, but before we meet, please send a photo of the two of you in Buffalo Sandwich position.

DEAR JOE BOB: If you're going to run my "Vindictive Wimp Defense League" letter, please change the phrase "your continued verbal weeny-bashing" to "the continued verbal weeny-bashing." Please forgive my perfectionism as I forgive your imperfectionism.
Kiss Kiss.
JUSTIN REED
PHOENIX

DEAR WIMP: Are you suggesting I would fail to recognize a misplaced weeny-bashing modifier?

DEAR MR. BRIGGS: Have you heard that the Mormons & the Babtists are co-producing a porno movie? It's called *DEBBIE DOES NOTHING.*
Sincerely,
ETAOIN SHRDLU
BURLINGAME, CALIF.

DEAR RECENT IMMIGRANT: Yeah, it's on a double bill with Deep Breathing.

the jerkolas at New World Pictures wouldn't send me the video. Main reason I wanted to see it is cause ripaway bra queen Sybil Danning's agent kept callin up and tellin me how *awful* it was and "Don't even waste your time on it."

And, of course, soon as I hear that, I know what's going on:

Fight on the set! Fight on the set!

Sybil Danning and Wendy O. Williams in the same movie!

Two many Amazon push-up bras in one place!

Catfight! Catfight!

Here's the inside skinny on what happened. It was *supposed* to be this Big-Mama hair-pullin eye-scratchin Brawl-a-Rama between Sybil and Wendy, only what happens? One of em—and most people say it was Wendy—*refuses* to do the scene with the other one. Sits in her trailer chewin live rats. So they gotta rewrite the ending with Sybil, as the evil warden, just disappearin off the screen, and Wendy, as the bad girl prison-gang leader, ridin on top of a runaway school bus that crashes into a guard tower and blows up Edna, the fat chocolate-bon-bon-eating homosexual jailer. To which Joe Bob says:

Excellento! Four stars. Best women-behind-bars of the year, even though it's got the same exact plot of the last 37 bimbos-in-cages. Thirty-five breasts, thanks to mucho shower scenos. Elementary-school food fights, chocolate-milk mixing, redigesting, and face-in-beans slamming. Kerosene hurling. Bimbo branding. Three cat-fights. Two riots. Two dead bodies. Two hosedowns. One DDT-down. One motor vehicle chase, with crash-and-burn. Exploding Edna. Drive-In Academy Award nominations for Pat Ast, as Evil Matron Edna, for burning an emotionally disturbed girl's stuffed bunnyrabbit and saying "The name of the game is control, ladies! Complete control!"; Wendy O., for combin her hair like a prize rooster; Sybil D., for attempting to quote Saint Joan; and Linda Carol, as the innocent blondie, for making the sign of the quadruple-breasted lake lizard with a blue-collar worker.

VIDEO RELEASE OF THE WEEK:

The Toolbox Murders (1977): One of the most popular video rentals, even though there's really only one reason to watch it—Cameron Mitchell, in his greatest drive-in role, as a sadistic Bible-quoting sex killer who wears bad silk shirts and uses every appliance in his toolbox as a murder weapon, including a power drill, claw hammer, screwdriver, wire cutters, and, best of all, a nail gun. Features such immortal dialogue as "You need more than a spilled Pepsi to say she was kidnapped." Joe Bob recommends fast-forwarding to the scene where Cameron ties Laurie to the bedposts, forces her to imitate his dead daughter, feeds her milk and cookies, makes her deny doing any "unnatural acts" with her boyfriend, and starts blubberin when she describes what it was like to go to heaven. Based on a true story in El Lay. Recommended for Cameron's one big scene only. Two stars. JBB says check it out. ■

Whangdoodling the Meese Commission

Last week at the Joe Bob Briggs Texas-OU Weekend Blowout Party and premiere of the Dancing Bovina Sisters, the world's only one-ton chorus line, I read off all the dirty parts of the Meese Report to the audience. Most of em didn't believe it, how the President's Commission on Obscenity, Pornography, and Nasty Bedroom Equipment could have so much great writing in it.

A whole lot of it I still can't say in the newspaper, but I wanted everbody to know that we figured out what it was that bothered Ed Meese the most:

The misuse of whangdoodles.

Listen to the following facts:

1. There are more than 1,200 references to whangdoodles in this report, which only lasts 1,960 pages.

2. Members of the Meese Commission traveled to one of my favorite stores, Mr. Peepers in Houston, to personally view whangdoodles on three separate occasions.

3. The Meese Commission collected over 100 magazines, including seven copies of *Floppers and Whoppers,* to prove that whangdoodles are being improperly manipulated by portions of the general public.

4. It's not in the report, but Ed Meese himself is known to have asked privately for the complete elimination

of whangdoodles, or at least have a whangdoodle moratorium.

5. I quote from page 1,446 of the report: "It is clear to this Commission that most Americans are not mature enough to use whangdoodles in a responsible manner. We would recommend some form of whangdoodle licensing process as one solution."

6. Many people are still under the impression that they are protected from government intrusion by the 1903 Supreme Court ruling, Beavers vs. Saginaw County, South Dakota, which stated that "whangdoodles are regarded as private property, subject to any use the owner might desire, except when they are located on a railroad right-of-way." And, of course, we can all remember how many whangdoodles were lost to the greedy railroads right after the war.

7. In fact, the Beavers ruling does not apply to certain whangdoodles, especially when they are used for lawn and garden care.

8. Several members of the Commission confided to reporters that Mr. Meese does not himself own a whangdoodle and forbids his wife to purchase one.

Outdoors this week we got *Deadly Friend,* Wes Craven's first drive-in flick since *A Nightmare on Elm Street,* and I'm glad to say that Wes hasn't let all the piles of green stuff go to his head. This one's ever bit as disgusting as *Elm Street,* but not quite as scary. It's basically a *Breakfast Club* version of *Bride of Frankenstein,* with this kid who comes to town haulin an artificial-brain robot named Bee Bee. When the girl next door gets bashed down the stairs by her slimehead father, the kid sticks the robot brain in the girl, steals her body, and tries to get his new girlfriend-monster to stop killin all the neighbors and grabbin biker gangs between the legs.

No breasts. Six dead bodies. Seven gallons blood, some spurting, with three bloody noses. Exploding head. Head disguised as a basketball. Vase plunging. Exploding robot. Mother drugging. Shovel hurling. Body scalding. Neck breaking. Father charbroiling. Gratuitous brain surgery. Incest fu. Drive-In Academy Award nominations for Matthew Laborteaux, as Paul the genius, who likes to tinker around with brain surgery in his garage; Kristy Swanson, as Sam the dead girlfriend, for excellent spook robotics; and Wes, for delivering. Three and a half stars.

VIDEO OF THE WEEK

Truck Stop Women (1974): One of the goofiest Mafia movies ever made, starring Claudia Jennings, the only Playmate of the Year who could ever act and the woman who would of been the greatest drive-in actress in history if she hadn't been killed in a car accident. Soap opera star Lieux Dressler runs Anna's Truck Stop in New Mexico, which is a front for a whorehouse, truck-theft operation, and stolen-goods fencing outfit, but the eastern mob finds out that her daughter Rose (Claudia Jennings) is jealous of Mama and will do anything to get control of the business for herself. Rotten to the core, Claudia is a spoiled country girl who thinks of herself as royalty. "Jackie Onassis wouldn't eat a chicken-fried steak!" she screams, slammin her dinner plate on the counter. So she offers up her body to whatever sleazeballs might help her get what she wants. Filmed at the height of the CB craze, it features a couple of decent truck chases and eight or nine Bobby Hart country-western songs, includin "I'm a Truck" ("There'd be no truck drivers if it wasn't for us trucks") and "Big Bull Shippers." Exceptional breast count for this kind of movie: 23. Four stars. ■

JOE BOB'S
MAILBAG

Letter that didn't make it in *Rolling Stone*—
TO THE EDITOR: I enjoyed reading Joe Bob Briggs' article, "Working on the Chain Gang" until I got to the paragraph which begins, "The other bimbo in the scene with me is named Victoria Powells . . ." When a few paragraphs further down the page I read, ". . . the movie theater you're about to come out of with these two bimbos," I stopped for a moment to consider *how offensive* I found these two short passages. (I won't even mention any other passages that put women down, this is offensive enough).

Although this article was written about a movie and doesn't deal with sexism, I resent reading about women being referred to as "bimbos." One man mentioned in the article tries to "keep his matted blond hair from breeding"; while another explains why, according to his agents, he is "throwing his career away on this movie." Yet it is the women who are described as "bimbos."

Maybe Mr. Briggs had his brain rattled by all those chain saws. In any event, I just wanted to point out this slur and hope I don't read any similar ones in *Rolling Stone* again.
Sincerely,
DONNA M. VALLO
NORTH TARRYTOWN, N.Y.

DEAR BIMBO: I enjoyed your letter until I got to the sentence about my brain. Then I paused to think HOW OFFENSIVE I find it when a person who don't even know the difference between bimbos and REAL WOMEN starts talkin about MY brain.

Another letter that didn't make it in *Rolling Stone*—
DEAR ROLLING STONE: I understand R.S.'s side of writing about the Texas Chainsaw movies because it's a popular phenomenon lately. OK, fine. I'd just like to say that the people who make these kinds of movies don't have an understanding of right and wrong and don't care. Also, there's a sort of lackadasical tolerance of this kind of thing nowadays that makes me sick. Finally, the people who go to these movies are a bunch of sub-humans.

So all you people, stand up for what's right, don't tolerate this ———. When your friends want to go, tell them no, its sick. When they say whats a matter, chicken? no sense of humor? tell em to ——— off. All you movie moguls should tell the directors writers and producers to shove it up their ———, cause were a respectable company of clean cut people who want to produce quality material to uplift the hard working masses.
Thank You,
JOHN SIMONS
LONG BEACH, CALIF

DEAR HUMAN: You're either right or you're wrong.

DEAR JOE BOB: I hope you win your battle with the *Slimes Herald*, so you can keep your name.

But if you should lose, just remember: a Joe Bob by any other name would smell just as bad.
ONE OF YOUR FANS
DALLAS

DEAR ONE OF: The judge told the Slimes Herald *they couldn't steal my name, and so right after that the high sheriffs stopped hasslin my books in one of the great victories over Communism since they took Prague in 1968. Now the wimps at Dell Books are FORCED to publish.*

I'm still thinking of changin my name to Phil Donahue.

The Play-by-Play from Reykjavik

Here's all the reasons the Nuke Talks broke down:

1. Soviet Premier Mikhail Grabachek thought people actually READ *U.S. News and World Report.* President Ronnie corrected the record and told him that only people over the age of 87 read *U.S. News and World Report,* and so Nick Daniloff was not just a HOSTAGE. He was a RIDICULOUS HOSTAGE. The Geneva Convention on the taking of Ridiculous Hostages states very clearly that they must either be placed in a circus within seven days or released to the custody of a badly dressed CBS news crew.

Grabachek agreed, but fell short of promising not to take anymore ridiculous hostages.

2. Ronnie asked Grabachek if he saw *Gorky Park,* and then Grabachek tried to get it added on to the list of bombs in the U.S. nuclear arsenal.

3. Grabachek asked Ronnie if he was still buildin killer satellites that could wipe out Warsaw. Ronnie's answer: "Naw, just a few new cable channels. Maybe *Ted Turner* is doin somethin else out there. I don't know. Haven't seen him lately, but I'll ask him."

4. Grabachek refused to stop sendin acrobats in shiny pants over here.

5. Grabachek asked Reagan whether we're gonna let Moses "The Animal" Washington out of the Florida State Prison so he can go over to Russia. Washington, serving a 187-year sentence for a triple murder, seven armed robberies, and a hot check he tried to cash at a Stop-n-Go in Pensacola, has got several write-ups in *Pravda* as a political prisoner who wants to continue his work in a Communist country. Reagan used the weak excuse that "we can't do that cause he might come back."

6. Finally, Reagan said, "Mike, how many cities can you blow up?"

And Grabachek said, "Eighty-eight and a half."

"What's the half?"

"We took East St. Louis off the list. Somebody got there first. How about you?"

"Mike, I wouldn't lie to you. We can only blow up 72 measly Communist cities."

"I don't beliff it."

"No, it's true. Really. Okay, *maybe* 75, 76 if the boys out in Kansas at the missile shed got a good night's sleep."

"Kansas?"

"Whoops! Forget I said that."

"The missile shed's in Kansas?"

"No. It's *hundreds* of miles from Kansas. It's closer to, like Minnesota than Kansas. Or Idaho. But not Kansas."

"I must go back Russia now."

"All right, Mike, we'll be seein you. No surprises now, okay?"

"You kidding? We love Ted Turner. Weekly Bulldog Football is *okay with us.*"

"You're an animal, Mike. You're an animal."

Speaking of animals, one flick you can't see in Communist Russia is *Link,* the finest monkey movie since *Mad Monkey Kung Fu.* What we got here is Terence Stamp livin by hisself up in a house in Scotland, doing some disgusting monkey experiments. (They don't say exactly what Terence is doing, but Ed Meese should probably be told about it.) Then he hires a bimbo assistant from one of his college classes, thinkin that maybe he can go for the groceries once she gets up there, but by that time the monkeys are *takin over,* wearin all Terence's good clothes, smokin up the cigars, and killin the neighbors. There's a bunch of plot in here about how monkeys are really eight times stronger than us and how Jane Goodall went down to Africa and lived with the monkeys and found out they could be *just as mean* as we are. And then, one night, a monkey decides to do a circus trick and Terence disappears.

One breast. Four dead bodies. Two dead monkeys. Seven dead sheep. Dead cat. Two dead birds. Dead dog. One motor vehicle chase, two crashes. One monkey chase. One dog chase. Killer attack dogs. Killer attack monkeys. Monkey dog-bashing. Microwaved telephone. Culturally biased monkey-IQ test. Attempted monkey suicide. Exploding monkey. Mail slot fu. Shotgun fu. Monkey fu. Drive-In Academy Award nominations for Terence Stamp, whose dying words are "Go away, I'm busy"; and Elisabeth Shue, the bimbo assistant, for reading

Three Little Pigs to a monkey. Parts of this flick are in Monkey Vision. Three and a half stars.

VIDEO RELEASE OF THE WEEK

Rabid (1976): Back in his early drive-in days David Cronenberg, of *The Fly* fame, gave my favorite porno star Marilyn Chambers her big chance to make a real movie you can watch without wearin a raincoat. Basically what happens is Marilyn gets tossed off a motorcycle, burns up, and gets took to the nearest hospital, where the doctor is known as the Colonel Sanders of plastic surgery. So he takes her thigh skin and grafts it on her face and chest, and pretty soon she comes down with something that looks like rabies only it's about 10,000 times worse cause she has this little bloody Roto-Rooter that comes up out of her armpit and slices people up so she can feed on their blood ever six hours. She turns most of Montreal, Canada, into zombies before her boyfriend catches her munching on a mutual friend. Excellent green goo. On-camera body count: 17. Breast count: 8. On the 1976 Drive-In Top Ten List. Four stars.

Joe Bob says check em out. ∎

Playin' Without a Full Set

Last week I bought some *Encyclopaedia Britannicas.* I didn't mean to. I went to the State Fair of Texas, and I was just hangin around over by the "Mister Mutilator" commercial blender demonstration, which is right next to the strap-on hiney-vibrator cushions ($34 this year), and

the next thing I knew I wanted to have three billion years of wisdom inside my brain.

There was this guy named Wendell, and he didn't have a job so he was sellin encyclopedias at the State Fair, and he come up to me and convinced me I was stupid for not havin a map of

Swahililand in my trailer house and a picture of ever mammal that eats its young on Muslim holidays.

The way he does this is he says, "Is there ever anything you wanted to look up but you didn't have nothin to look it up in?"

And I said, "Just one thing. How many mammals are there that eat their young on Muslim holidays and what do they look like?"

And he jumped right on that, and said, "Looky here." And then he explained how you can't just look under "M" in the encyclopedia like in the second-grade *World Book,* cause that wouldn't work. You got to go to the 240-volume Orthopedia first and look under "I" for "Islamic," which is the same thing as Muslim, and then you got to go to the 38-volume "Great Ideas of the Northwestern World" and flip through it till you find a picture of a whale or a manatee, and then you double the numbers next to that and it tells you what page to go directly to in the *Encyclopaedia Britannica* for further reading.

After he explained it, I knew I had to have one, so I asked him how much it was.

He told me the particular one we were looking at cost $95,000 retail, but they had it on State Fair special for $92,000. But I couldn't afford that one, so he went down to the Mink-Tail bindings with complimentary Atlas of Antarctica, and that was just $48,000, and I told him I couldn't pay for that one, either. And so he said, "Well, we do have this one over here that costs $1,500."

And I don't know, it was just such a bargain I couldn't pass it up, and so I explained how I didn't really have any money on me, and he said, "No problema," and he put me on the 30-year payout for just $144 a month. And then after I signed all the papers, he said they'd have to send em out to me from Chicago, cause Encyclopaedia Britannica is this company up there of some of the wisest guys in the world, with Ph.D.s and L.L.D.s and V.D.s, and what they do is they sit up in Chicago all day long thinkin about nuclear energy and writin up new volumes of the encyclopedia and then they put out all the collected wisdom that the world has ever wised up to and they get a bunch of unemployed oilfield workers named Wendell to convince people like me that they don't need to eat next year cause they'll be payin out this money to be smart. And then at the end of the year they send you a Yearbook and charge you another $144. And after he explained it I knew I'd made a great deal, cause they *are* the smartest guys in the world I ever met.

Speaking of Phi Beta Kappa aerobic dance instructors, *The Toxic Avenger* is the latest masterpiece from the drunks at Troma Films in New York City, who spent *one hundred dollars* making this flick, up from their usual budget of 75. This movie's been makin so much money in New York City that Bob Berney, the maniac manager of the Inwood Theatre, jerked four Yugoslavian films about lesbians off his schedule and put it in for special midnight-movie screenings startin on Halloween night and continuing *ever single Friday and Saturday night at midnight* between now and next weekend. It's the story of a sensitive health spa mop-boy, the mutant offspring of Jerry Lewis, who gets tricked into dressing in a pink tutu by four yuppie hit-and-run drivers and then falls into a vat of lime-green nuclear waste, turns into a Mister Potato Head, and rampages through the New Jersey metropolis of Tromaville, ripping apart the street scum, until he falls in love with a blind girl with huge breasts and goes on a campout. Featuring some of the finest Jewish character actors in southern Ohio, directed by the man who brought you *When Nature Calls . . . You've Gotta Go,* this is the drive-in *China Syndrome.*

Eight breasts. Nineteen dead bodies. One motor vehicle chase, with three explosions. Automotive pinball (dead Puerto Ricans count 30 points, children under 12 extra credit). Monster sex. Hiney barbecue. Rear-wheel head crushing. Dope-smoking toxic waste haulers. Hula-hooping monster. Little-old-lady crowbar bashing. Nautilus head slicing. Gratuitous gay hairdressers. Tutu fu. Drive-In Academy Award nominations for Pat Ryan Jr., as

---

Communist Alert!

Of all the high sheriffs who butcher my column ever week, one of the most beloved is Russell Scott at the *Daily Texan* in Austin. Last year, at the annual *Daily Texan* awards banquet, Russ showed up dressed in a turban with an alarm clock and road flares strapped to his chest. The Travis County sheriff's department sent actual cops to the costume party; they arrested him while he was buttering a potato for impersonating an Arab terrorist, ripped the road flares off his chest, cuffed him, threatened to arrest two other people who intervened, took him to jail, charged him with "possession of a hoax bomb," left him in a cell with a guy charged with pushing heroin, and REFUSED TO DROP THE CHARGES. We're talking Reetards with Badges.

---

the beached-whale mayor, for literally losing his guts on camera; Andree Maranda, as the blind bimbo, for her two enormous talents; and Mitchell Cohen, in the title role, for sayin "I think I'm out of control; every day I go out and I mash people and I tear them apart."

Three stars.

VIDEO RELEASE OF THE WEEK

Poor White Trash (1957): There's a lot of *wrong* info being spread around about this drive-in classic, includin everthing that's on the video box. Here's what you need to know: It's the screen debut of Peter Graves as an architect from Poughkeepsie, New York, who goes down to the Louisiana swamp, falls in love with a dark-haired honey that just got raped the night before by a local crocodile named Ulysses, and ends up makin the sign of the triple-throated walrus during a tropical hurricane. It was originally released as *Bayou,* but the producer was so p.o.ed that he bought it back from United Artists, put it out again in '61 as *Poor White Trash,* and played it on double bills with Roger Corman's *Shame* (also called *The Intruder,* the film debut of William Shatner) up until the '70s. What made it so *hot* is the rape scene with Lita Milan, which isn't much of a rape scene but for 1957 it was a sizzler. Great brain-damaged Cajuns doing circus tricks between scenes. On the Drive-In "Best of the Fifties" list. Four stars.

Check em out. ■

Lament for a Square Square

A bunch of New York Mr.-Potato-Head teevee bosses gave me a hundred bucks to drive up there and be on The Movie Channel all next month, and so we spent the day standin around this grungy studio over by Madison Square Garden, poppin tall boys and watchin the New York union crews pick the moss out from between their teeth and waitin on the High Sheriffs of Showtime, Inc., to get finished sayin "Mr. Briggs, just what did you mean by this expression 'makin the sign of the double-humped sperm whale'? I believe we should reshoot the entire sequence." It was great.

Now for the depressin news.

Ed Koch is going crazy. The man is a maniac. He has somethin called a "Times Square Redevelopment Plan," and when I first heard about it, I thought, "Great! They're finally gonna clean the place up by *kickin the* New York Times *outta there*." But you know what they're doing instead?

Rippin down, closin out, shuttin up some of the greatest indoor moviehouses ever created, includin the one I'll always remember as ALWAYS THREE KUNG FU HITS, not to mention *LIVE SEX ACT. Live Sex Act* played for about *eight years straight.* The only movie I ever heard that played longer than that was *Dos Peliculas.*

Anyhoo, the only point is I want you to just *listen* to some of the garbahj they're puttin in these great drive-in palaces in the name of urban renewal.

Sweet Charity: Debbie Allen twinklin her tootsies and gettin handed around by people who think Bob Fosse is groovy.

42nd Street: They can't dance, don't make em.

A Chorus Line: Even after I named it the best horror film of 1985, they kept on hiring emotionally disturbed

---

JOE BOB'S MAILBAG

DEAR MR. BRIGGS: What a surprise to hear from you personally [about the horrors of chihuahua racing in Nuevo Laredo]. And how gratifying to learn that you've come around to defending the little "rat-faced weasel dogs" you so mercilessly mocked in your March, 1986 column.

My comment to you is heaven help any animal you champion. You may derive demented delirium from irreverently fictionalizing animal exploitation and abuse but be assured there are many who do not. I, for one, am not concerned with what you think of us. I'm only sorry to learn that your employers did not send you back to the rock from under which you undoubtedly once emerged.
Very Truly Yours,
CAROLYN L. KAYE
PENINSULA CHAPTER
IN DEFENSE OF ANIMALS
MONTARA, CALIF.

DEAR CAROLYN: When I make comments about putting schnauzer dogs in high-speed electric blenders, I don't really MEAN it.

You can permanently damage the blades that way.

New York actors and actresses, forcin em to spill their guts onstage and confess they're homosexuals and they hate their parents, and then dancin their little hearts out in *the show that refuses to go away.*

Big River. It is.

Cats. Needs a litter box.

You Never Can Tell: Yes you can.

Mummenschanz: There are only two kinds of people in the world—those that hate mime, and liars.

And finally—da da!—*Oh, Calcutta:* Yes, it's true, these people are still takin their clothes off after 20 years and doing jokes from *The Dean Martin Show.* Please exterminate them immediately, Ed, so we can get back to the serious business of watchin *Vampire Playgirls* on 42nd Street where it belongs.

Speaking of extermination, *Trick or Treat* is one of the finest dead-high-school-kid flicks of the year, even though the title smells. Basically what we got is a story about how a metal-head rock star dies and then comes back to life to jump out of kids' stereos, take over their minds, wreck their rooms when their mother's not lookin, kill all the jocks and their crudhead girlfriends, and return to the high school that *excluded him* so he can jump up onstage, laser the entire high school to death with his guitar, pop the heads off some rattlesnakes, and try to get some local airplay. Course, he turns out to be your typical self-destructive rock personality: *He lasers his own drummer! In the middle of the song!*

Here's one for the Babtists, provin that these Ozzy Osbourne perverts *do* take over the minds and bodies of our American young people. In fact, Ozzy is *in the movie,* as the Rev. Aaron Gilstrom, preachin about how rock music turns you into a pervert. Gene Simmons is in it, too, for about 15 sec-

onds, and if you have any doubts about it, just listen to this:

It's directed by Terry the Toad (remember? *American Graffiti*?), and the man is a head-bashin fool.

Four breasts, including two stunt breasts. Eight dead bodies. Three motor vehicle chases, with crashes, burns, explosions, river dive. A 64 on the Vomit Meter. Snake-head biting. Rock-star flushing. Cafeteria chocolate-milk fu. Pioneer fu. Sansui fu. Fisher fu. Guitar fu. Excellent tunes by Fastway, Only Child. See Jane Run, and Whodini. Drive-In Academy Award nominations for Tony Fields, as Sammi Curr the dead rocker, for puttin on mad-dog leper-face makeup and slimin the high school and screamin "No wimps! No false metal!"; Marc Price, as the kid who communicates with Sammi Curr by playin his records backward; Doug Savant, as the campus goon who almost gets a drill press through his eyeball, then gets exploded by the Metal King; Ozzy, as the TV preacher, for his critiques of the albums *Torture's Too Kind* and *Do It Like a Dog;* Elise Richards, for havin lakeside devil-dragon metalhead sex with a ghost and gettin her car turned to green goo by a Sony Walkman; and

---

Communist Alert!

The Waialae Drive-In in Honolulu, owned by former U.S. Senator Hiram L. Fong, just got converted into a driving range. The tees are set up 270 yards from the screen, and the golfers try to *hit the screen* for a buck fifty a bucket. We're talkin some sick High-wayans.

Charles Martin Smith, aka Terry the Toad. Four stars.

VIDEO RELEASE OF THE WEEK

Married Too Young (1953): This one is the *Reefer Madness* of teenage dating, starring the weenie Harold Lloyd Jr. as a teenager who falls in love with the whining Jana Lund, gets hot with her one night on Lovers Lane, and ends up gettin a quickie marriage license because they *just can't wait.* Pretty soon they got bills to pay, time-payment furniture, and parents that want em to know how sick they are for being married. It's a screamer, specially when Harold gets so desperate that he agrees to—oh my God! not that!—*file off some numbers on a stolen car.* Highlight is when the judge brings the parents into his courtroom, points at em, and says "You call yourself mothers! Fathers! A giraffe in a zoo takes better care of its young! Home is where the heart is!" Four star "wild-youth" flick.

Joe Bob says check em out. ∎

Why I Love Wayne Newton

Big Wayne.
    You know who I mean.
They call him "Mr. Huge."
Nobody does it better,.
Here he comes, Donka-Shanin across the stage called success.

It's time to talk about the only pure native American Indian musical art form—Wayne Newton. You know, a lot of people didn't think the Indians could sing. A lot of people thought they just made bronchial chest noises.

And then came Big Wayne. Ever since he reached puberty at the age of 35, there's been no stoppin the man. You know, Vegas smoke shows come and go, but there's only one guy who wears a pencil mustache in public. And that man is Wayne Newton.

Forget Elvis. Forget Sinatra. Forget the Beatles. Forget Springsteen. Forget Michael Jackson. Forget Conway Twitty.

I forgot what I was talkin about.

Oh, yeah, Wayne. It started on the *Ed Sullivan Show,* with "Bill Bailey." Remember? Remember the little crinkles in his cheeks when he grinned like an encyclopedia salesman? Well, from there it was all a long uphill climb to the '80s, when he did the Fourth of July show at the Washington Monument, reaffirmed his faith in James Watt's Interior, and denied that he was a member of the Mafia. In between there were private helicopters, a Nevada horse ranch, a director of personal security, a chain of casino and resort investments, and the world's largest belt buckle. But we all know that story. What I wanna talk about right here is what Wayne means to me.

It's the modesty that gets to me. It's the simple life he lives—just Wayne, his sales staff, his production coordinator, his sound man, his executive fan-club director, and seven guys named Enzio. That's it. They all relax together at Casa de Shenandoah, take an occasional drive in Wayne's 1932 Stutz Bearcat, and plan ways to cure cancer. Who else thinks of things like that? Sammy? Jerry? Dino? Perhaps. Except for Dino.

JOE BOB'S MAILBAG

DEAR JOE BOB: As producer of *Reform School Girls* I would like to thank you for your excellent (and perceptive) review of our picture. However, I need to correct the mis-informed (misguided?) "inside skinny" you apparently received regarding the ommited fight scene between Charlie (Wendy O. Wil-liams) and Warden Sutter (Sybil Danning).

The scene was *not* dropped due to lack of cooperation on the part of Wendy O. In fact, Wendy, always the beautiful trouper, was ea-ger to perform the scene to the director's specifications. No one was more disap-pointed than Ms. Williams at the loss of the scene due to creative reasons.

Furthermore, the ending of our film (bad girl Charlie's undoing of evil matron Edna) was designed from the beginning to feature the gifted abilities of our main stars, Wendy O. and Pat Ast. Both ladies delivered in spades. Wendy's window-smashing, roof-top-riding was an unnecessary fight scene that was dropped.

I would appreciate it if you would include this information in your next syndicated col-umn in order to set the record straight.
Yours truly,
JACK CUMMINS
HOLLYWOOD, CALIF.

DEAR JACK: No catfight? No trailer-pouting? No "you'll-never-work-in-this-town-again"-ing? What are you guys doing out there, becomin human beins?

DEAR JOE BOB: I had open-heart surgery last year and the doctors tell me that I have only 30 or 40 more years to live. Before I die I really need to know:
—What is the true meaning of human existence?
—What exactly is a "whangdoodle"?
—Whatever happened to Bebe Rebozo?
Thanks for your help & inspiration.
DEWEY CARTER
BOULDER, COLO.

DEAR DEWEY: He mistook his rebozo for his whangdoodle and learned the meaning of a slow, nasty death.

But Wayne don't just think about it, he *does something* about it.

Do you have Wayne's first hit al-bum, *The Best of Wayne Newton?* The one that came out *before* "Red Roses for a Blue Lady"? The one where Wayne is so *cute* on the cover, with his little apple-dumpling cheeks and his Frankie Avalon wave and the gold cuff links with his tux? Well, I do. And I wanna tell you something about it: Wayne does "You're Nobody Till Somebody Loves You" *better than Dino*. I'm sorry I have to say it. I know there's a lot of drunks out there who love Dino. But the man's monster. The man's genius. The man's . . . well, let me just put it this way:

The Indians didn't call him "Wayne" for nothing.

The *Best Of* album was Wayne's first Vegas act, the one he started when he was *fifteen* years old, the same one he did at the Copa in New York, where Ed saw him. But Ed didn't *discover* Wayne. The man who discovered Wayne was: Mahomina-homina-homina . . . J-J . . . homina . . . Jackie Gleason. The Great One found him on his great cross-country train ride. Maybe you don't remember just how Wayne sounded in '59, the year he broke in, but *here,* in its entirety, is his act:

"Swanee" (Jolson style)

"Rock-a-Bye" (down on one knee, Judy Garland–inspired Jolson style)

"Work Song" (Oscar Brown)

"Hava Negilla" (show stopper)

Roaring '20s medley (Wayne plays the banjo like crazy)

"When the Saints Go Marchin In" (bigger show stopper)

"Baby Face" (segue)

"Donka Shane" (Bobby Darin style, brings the house down)

"Bill Bailey" (earthquakes in the desert)

And later, after Bobby died:

"Mack the Knife" (like Bobby did it)

This is the act that made Wayne *the* King of Vegas. Darin couldn't do it and Elvis couldn't do it and Frank couldn't even do it.

Sure he paid for it—like in '65, when he went to the Hollywood Bowl and got booed cause everybody was into the Beatles that year and so they considered Wayne Squaresville. But where are the Beatles now? Huh? Answer me that? And where is Wayne now?

Wayne's still in Vegas, still in Reno, still in Tahoe.

Then there was the movie thing, when Wayne was gonna go on the Big Silver and have a big career as an actor. That was in '69, when he shot *80 Steps to Jonah* and played an orphaned migrant worker in trouble with the cops. It was the first in a series of one movie for Wayne. It was *almost* as big as Rowan and Martin starring in *The Maltese Bippy*.

And then, of course, there was the beautiful little Japaheeno girl who Wayne married and carried off to his beautiful Casa de Shenandoah ranch outside Vegas, where they raised Arabian horses and one daughter named Erin and they had this great 56-acre estate in town where his personal staff of 100 worked and everything was just great until the Big D in '85, which is the same year Wayne put the Wayne Newton Fan Club on inactive status and started hangin around with Ron and Nancy.

It was the worst thing that happened to Wayne since the Aladdin hotel thing in '80, when he bought the place for $85 million and then sold it the next year for $8.5 million.

That's why I want everybody to remember Big Wayne in their prayers this year. We're not gonna let anything happen to our boy. No Bobby Darin head trips. No Elvis walkin-drugstore routines. No visits to the Howard Hughes Suite. We want Wayne out there on tour, doin "Sweet Sixteen" again, reminiscin about what it was like to work with Vikki Carr and Bill Dana. We want Wayne installed as permanent Czar of the Desert—Mr. Vegas, Mr. America, the Main Man.

Just remember, the next time you land at Vegas Airport:

They don't call it Wayne Newton Boulevard for nothin. ∎

Editor's note: After reading the previous article, Big Wayne invited Joe Bob to Vegas so he could act like a big shot.

Getting It On with Donka Shane Wayne

Ever since I Donka-Shaned my way back from Vegas, where I went out last week to share a couple brews with Big Wayne, nobody *believes* me. I go around sayin "No, really, the whole deal, Wayne and me, sitting around in his *simple little dressing room,* just the girlfriend, the manager, the p.r. guy, the secretary, the director of personal security, a 280-pound bodyguard named Otto, and me."

Sammy wanted to be there, too—ka-ching, ka-ching-ching—but Wayne said, "No, not now, not when I'm tryin to win my $15 billion libel suit against NBC and gettin over the divorce and the Aladdin Hotel deal and, *most important of all,* talkin to Joe Bob. Tell Sammy it will *just* have to wait."

That's the kinda guy Wayne is. A big guy. The biggest guy in Vegas. But he can cover it up with a cumberbun.

Anyhow, once I got backstage with Wayne, what I wanted to know was "Hey, Big Guy, are you in the Mafia or not?"

Wayne understands that kind of question.

I figured, hey, if Wayne was in the Mafia, he would of given me a rack of free chips, right, and said, "Here, Joe Bob, enjoy. La pisa tutu!"

But all Wayne did was gimme that little grin and start singin "MacArthur Park," the long version. We had to hose him down to make him stop. Then he asked me if I liked the "Feelings"–Lionel Richie medley, and I told him yeah, how great it was, and he said, "You loved it, didn't you? Tell me you loved it, I *know* you loved it, please say you loved it," and so Otto had to slap him around a little bit and strap him into his American-eagle silver belt buckle for his own protection.

Anyhow, after we talked about how he's not in the Mafia and about the Big D and about the Carson deal where Johnny used to call Wayne a wimp on teevee but Wayne was *bigger* than Johnny and about Wayne's palomino, I decided it was time to get tough with Wayne. Told him I heard this rumor that he wasn't able to *go the distance* anymore. Told him I heard about how the last 14-hour show he did was in 1983, and that was only cause Frank was in the audience. Told him how he was craterin in to the new "Wayne Newton Clause" in the musicians union contract, which says they get an extra two bucks ever time the 280-piece Wayne Newton Orchestra has to play more than six hours at once. And do you know what Wayne said to me? Do you?

"Yo Mama." That's what he said. "Yo Mama."

I asked Wayne why he was speaking in Negro dialect, but by that time he was strappin hisself into the laser-equipped platinum-plated spacesuit he uses to open the show. Then he slid on his black patent-leather high-heeled Tom Jones-style attack boots, stuffed his groceries into black stretch-knit whoopee pants, whipped out the rooster comb, oiled up the thatch, and told six security guards he was ready to boogie.

Six hours later—after slingin sweat on pink ladies from Omaha and dry-icin the whole room and drop-kickin two backup singers into the eighth row as a special effect—he closed with "Dixie," "Battle Hymn of the Republic," and "America the Beautiful," the soul version, and gave me that little crinkledy-eye grin at the end and then collapsed backstage on his imitation anaconda-skin Lazy-Boy Recliner and ordered out for some possum sushi.

That's Wayne. The only Indian that ever sang a Mac Davis song and lived to tell about it. They don't call him Mr. Huge for nothin. ■

JOE BOB BITES THE DUST—AGAIN

Censored! How the Commies, or *Somebody,* Cut Joe Bob Out

Exactly 11 days before the national release of *The Texas Chainsaw Massacre Part 2,* the following scene was ripped out of the movie by Cannon Films, causing famous big-deal horror director Tobe Hooper to tell friends that he may *never be able to direct again.* We'll deal with the possible *reasons* for the Communist Censorship later, but first I want you to know what you will *not* be seeing in *Saw 2* and urge you to take copies of this scene to the theater. At the point where Stretch, the lady DJ, is knocked unconscious at the Saw Family Home, start chanting "We want Joe Bob! We want Joe Bob!" and demanding that the projectionist stop the movie. That's where this scene

was until just *11 days ago.* Eleven short days that represent the difference between me getting rich and famous, and me writing articles for the *Dallas Observer.* Don't take this lightly. It could happen to you someday, too.

The scene stars three of the finest minds working in show business today: Twinkle Bayoud, the Dallas socialite millionaire real estate party-throwing friend-of-Robin-Leach Lear-jetting blond "personal friend of Dennis Hopper" who showed up on the set and begged to be in the film; Victoria Powells, the Los Angeles actress who might be in a soap opera someday; and, of course, Joe Bob Briggs, with credits too numerous to mention.

Twinkle and Joe Bob play themselves. Victoria plays an unnamed Dallas Bimbo. The scene was directed by Tobe "Mr. Chainsaw" Hooper, with cinematography by Richard Kooris and special high-heel-throwing effects by Tom Stackpoole.

THE CENSORED SCENE

(Joe Bob and two yuppie bimbos are leaving a shopping-mall multiplex where they have just viewed *Exploding Heads Part 2*)

Twinkle: That was the most *disgusting thing I've ever seen.*

Joe Bob (*speaking with a mouth full of popcorn*): Nawwwww, Twink, it's *fake.* Did you think they really put that power drill through that girl's titty?

Bimbo: Yeccccccch.

Joe Bob: Naw, you see, what they do is they run this little rubber tube up under her titty (*Joe Bob grabs Twinkle's dress to illustrate*) and then they pump this stuff through there that's like Kaopectate all mixed up with cranberry Karo Syrup and then (*Joe Bob takes a handful of popcorn out of his box to illustrate*) they put these teeny tiny little cherry bombs on the bra and KABLOOEY! (*Joe Bob places the popcorn on Twinkle's breast and flings his hand open, simulating the nuclear destruction of her breast*) you got explodin titty all over the screen!

Twinkle: *Please!*

Bimbo: Yeah, but some little hurt puppy is going to see that and try to do it at home.

Joe Bob: Nawwwww. You just go home and *try* to put a power drill through your titty and see what happens. It ain't like real life.

(*At this point the trio has reached the doorway to a dark parking lot. They stop.*)

Twinkle: You want to jet to Austin? It's only 20 minutes.

(*Joe Bob shrugs. Twinkle and Bimbo walk out the door just as Leatherface springs out of the back of a catering van, revving his chain saw as he leaps. Joe Bob, frozen in his tracks, watches them butchered to death through a steady rain of bloody popcorn, fragments of designer dresses, mutilated high heels, and human body parts. He holds Leatherface's work in such admiration that he's unable to run.*)

Joe Bob (*closeup on his awestruck face*): Well, nail my dick to a tree.

(*His inaction has cost him. Leatherface notices his audience and turns on Joe Bob. As the chain saw plunges into his crotch, Joe Bob gives his final review.*)

Joe Bob: Four stars, man. (*His voice rises seven octaves and his face turns to Silly Putty.*) SAW FU!!!

A masterpiece, you say?

A scene so powerful that you no longer even want to see this movie, knowing that this scene is sequestered in a musty vault somewhere in Century City, California?

That's why I want you to take this scene into theaters tomorrow. Warn the projectionist ahead of time: It goes in Reel *Three.* When he stops the movie, stand as close to the front of the theater as you can and *read the scene in its entirety.* Then, and only then, will the audience be allowed to see the rest of the film.

If, that is, they still want to.

Now let's take a look at how such a thing can happen in the Newnited States of America in 1986 in a democracy. Let's try to answer the question "Who killed Joe Bob?" And let's start by reviewing possible motives.

Suspect Numero Uno: The Motion

Picture Association Ratings Board. As we all know, *Saw 2* is *unrated*. The reason it's unrated is that they showed it to the MPAA board twice, and the board said it was gonna get an X unless they cleaned it up. Many people *assumed* this was an X for violence and was probly the fault of Tom Savini, the makeup goremaster who constructed several body-hacking sequences for the flick. Is it possible that, in a flagrant effort to get an R rating, Cannon films took the Joe Bob scene out, assuming they were being given an X for acting?

Nope. Impossible.

Suspect Numero Two-o: Menahem Golan. Menahem, the co-owner of Cannon Films, director of *Delta Force,* the man that made Chuck Norris possible, producer of the last two *Death Wishes,* the man that put the capital *E* back in Exploitation. Menahem, the man who spent $4.6 million on *Saw 2* and basically told Tobe Hooper he could shut up when he was getting that kind of jack upfront. Menahem, my kind of guy. Could it be that Menahem wanted my part. Could it be that Menahem has waited all his life to touch Twinkle Bayoud's breast?

Nawwwwwwww. That brings us to . . .

Suspect Numero Three-o: Twinkle's husband, Bradley Bayoud. Could it be that Brad was upset at his main squeeze for demeaning the Highland Park family name by doing a scene with Joe Bob? Could it be that Brad thought his wife deserved "better material"?

Nope—cause Twinkle told me they're gettin the Big D.

Suspect Numero Four-o: L. M. "Kit" Carson, the screenwriter. Obviously we have to take into consideration the matter of professional jealousy. All Kit Carson ever wrote was the screenplay for *Paris, Texas,* which lucked into the grand prize at the Cannes Film Festival, which is in France. So Kit writes 130 pages of *Saw 2,* I write *two* pages, and well, what can I say? Just set em side by side, and *you* tell *me* who was gonna get the next six-figure contract from Paramount.

Unfortunately, Kit was passed out in his trailer while we were shootin the scene, despite gettin four full hours of sleep during the eight weeks of shooting.

Suspect Numero Five-o: Victoria Powells, the "Other Woman" in the scene. Maybe she fantasized for weeks about having me touch *her* breast, only what do I do? I give *all the breast-grabbing* to Twinkle. Or maybe she simply resents having her first line in a major motion picture be "Yeccccc-cch." But now that I think about it, it's more likely to be . . .

Suspect Numero Six-o: The mysterious "Ak Shun," the name used by a crew member who wrote an article for the Austin *Chronicle* after filming was completed. "Ak Shun" basically dumped all over the movie for requiring the crew to stay up till four in the morning to get shots of psychos drawing blood from a woman's ears and eyes with a coat hanger—stuff like that.

"If Hooper had his way," Ak Shun wrote, "the cameras would be rolling for another two months. He was beset by all manner of difficulties in this Cannon Films production, including Israeli editors who couldn't fathom his sense of humor (?); chain saws that wouldn't start on cue (37 were purchased for the film); makeup that melted in the heat of the *Austin American-Statesman* Building (which often peaked at 115 degrees); technicians who wanted to know why Hooper disappeared to his trailer every 45 minutes; Dennis Hopper ('I am the Lord of the Harvest'), who had all the patience of a rattlesnake in the West Texas heat; actors who couldn't remember their lines for more than 30 seconds, if that long ('It's a dog-eat-world-dog out there . . .'); a stunt coordinator who thought he was the director; special FX that wouldn't FX; and mysterious illnesses that periodically floored everyone in the production, caused by mold and mildew in the *Statesman* Building or the catering trucks from L.A., depending on whom you asked."

But here's the suspicious part:

"It wasn't a pretty sight, either, to watch the feature film debut of Dallas' drive-in movie critic Joe Bob Briggs." Then he describes the scene and goes on about it and says that when I get killed at the end, "Now, there's a climax for you. Wishful thinking, too."

I would just like to say right here and right now—Ak Shun, whoever he is, whatever he does on a crew, *will never work in Grapevine as long as he lives.* I'm gonna see to it.

Next suspect:

Suspect Numero Seven-o: Caroline Williams, the alleged "star" of this movie. She's the Dallas actress that plays Stretch, the lady DJ that Leatherface wants to cut up into itty bitty pieces until he falls in love with her and so he takes her home and chains her up and hides her from Daddy. Caroline may of been threatened by the performance. After all, I didn't touch her breast, either. She may of thought "Whoa! I'm from Dallas, he's from Dallas, the next casting director through here, lookin for the lead in a Louis Malle movie about Vietnamese fisherpeople—*this guy* could get *my* part." You could apply the same motives to Bill Johnson, who put on the old human-skin mask and did a brilliant sawing job as Leatherface; Bill

Moseley, as Chop-Top, in one of the most convincing cannibal roles in years; or Lou Perry, as L. G. McPeters. Lou, who also starred in *Last Night at the Alamo* and *Fast Money,* is the finest Texas good-ole-boy character actor in the binness. I think Lou's in prison right now, though, so it couldn't be him.

Unless of course, it was:

Suspect Numero Eight-o: Tobe Hooper, the Hoopman himself. Tobe claims he didn't do it. Tobe claims he *fought* for the scene, but Cannon made it a personal thing because, basically, Tobe and Cannon don't like each other's faces. Cause Tobe made *Lifeforce* and *Invaders from Mars,* two of the best drive-in movies of the last two years, and Cannon says they didn't do diddly at the box office and so, hey, they ain't listenin to him. I called up Tobe and demanded an explanation and he said, "The jerks didn't give me final cut. Honest, Joe Bob. It was in there till yesterday. They cut out a whole sequence of four or five scenes—we call it the Hunting Sequence, where the Saw Family is out hunting in their catering van—and yours was one of the scenes. Even after they cut the sequence, I put your scene back in as a 'stinger' at the end of the movie, a scene that plays while the credits are rolling. I thought it would work. You're coming out of the theater after *Saw 2* is over. It's like Leatherface getting one last victim. But they said, no, it didn't make sense, and they took it out even though I fought like hell for it. We feel awful about it. Please forgive me, Joe Bob."

I don't know. Whaddaya think? Are we gonna accept this explanation? Or are we gonna have to move on to the final suspect? I didn't wanna have to put it this directly, but I'm afraid it's time to name names.

Suspect Numero Nine-o: Mikhail Grabacheck.

What can I say? The man never sleeps.

Boycott *Saw 2*. Do it for your country. ■

Shameless Self-promotion

Joe Bob's column is syndicated nationwide through Creators Syndicate, 5777 W. Century Boulevard, Suite 700, Los Angeles, CA 90045. Joe Bob also appears on The Movie Channel, has a three-times-weekly radio show syndicated by Jameson Broadcast, and tours with his one-man show, "An Evening with Joe Bob Briggs."

To get Job Bob's world-famous newsletter, or maybe get some of his free junk that'll clutter up your dresser until you have to move and you throw it all out, write Joe Bob Briggs, P.O. Box 2002, Dallas, TX 75221.

Index

A

Abbott, Bruce, 64
Agnes of God, 106, 107
Airport, 125
Alexander, Terry, 77
Alien, 40
Allen, Debbie, 203
All My Children, 91
Ameche, Don, 106
American Graffiti, 204
American Ninja, 46, 96, 97
Amir, Gideon, 46
Amritraj, Ashok, 93
Amritraj, Vijay, 93, 94
Amsterdam, Morey, 189
Android, 142
Angel, 68
Ansara, Michael, 154
April Fool's Day, 136
Ariane, 53, 95
Aronson, Judie, 46
Attack of the Killer Shrews, 190
Attenborough, Richard, 86
Attias, Daniel, 70
Avenging Angel, 12, 68
Avery, Margaret, 106

B

Baker, Tim, 164
Balsam, Martin, 67, 125
Bancroft, Anne, 107
Bancroft, Bradford, 177
Band of the Hand, 144–45
Baran, Jack, 145
Barbarian Queen, 9–11, 80, 95, 96
Barry, Wendy, 154
Barrymore, Drew, 8
Bartel, Paul, 5, 156, 157
Basket Case, 39
Bava, Lamberto, 170, 171
Bava, Mario, 170
Bayou, 202
Bayoud, Bradley, 215
Bayoud, Twinkle, 111–13, 213,
    214, 215
Beach Girls, xviii
Beals, Jennifer, 44, 96, 106
Bear, The, 69
Bearse, Amanda, 37
Beast Within, The, xv, 37
Beck, Julian, 162
Belliveau, Cyd, 138
Benedict, Nick, 128–29

C

D

E

F

N

O

S

Z